THE UNIVERSITY OF CHICAGO

THE DODECANESE:
DIVERSITY AND UNITY
IN ISLAND POLITICS

DEPARTMENT OF GEOGRAPHY
RESEARCH PAPER NO. 108

By

ROGER E. KASPERSON

Michigan State University

CHICAGO · ILLINOIS

1966

In Rhodes the days drop as softly as fruit from trees. Some belong to the dazzling ages of Cleobulus and the tyrants, some to the gloomy Tiberius, some to the Crusaders. They follow each other in scales and modes too quickly almost to be captured in the nets of form. Only by a strict submission to the laws of inconsequence can one ever write about an island—as an islomane, that is. And then who could ever hope to pin down, to circumscribe, the charms of a resident Goddess?

(Lawrence Durrell)

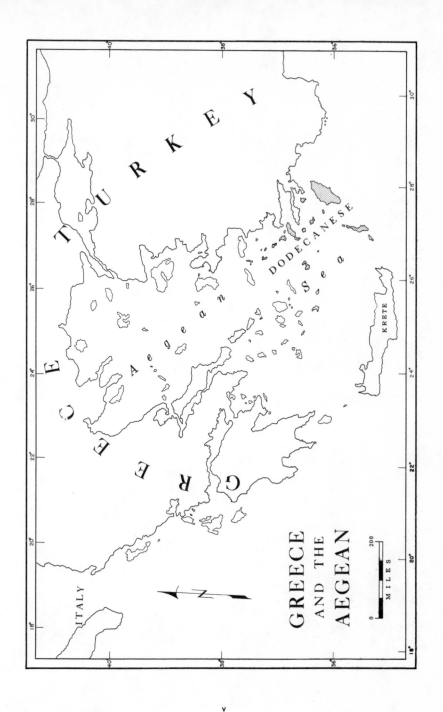

GREECE AND THE AEGEAN

v

PREFACE AND ACKNOWLEDGEMENTS

Field work for the present study was undertaken in Athens in September, 1963. After obtaining letters of introduction from the American Embassy and the Center of Social Research in Greece, the author prepared a comprehensive bibliography of studies on the Dodecanese, a difficult task given the general lack of bibliographic records of modern Greek literature. Moreover, the various libraries of Greece are often weak in their holdings of contemporary regional publications. More useful were the personal interviews with recognized scholars of the Dodecanese Islands.

The first month was spent in Athens not only in compiling the bibliography, but also in obtaining base maps, government documents, and publications on the Dodecanese. Preliminary encounters with government agencies and officials revealed the limitations of customary American research methods. Rather, informal introductions between colleagues in government service and between scholars turned out to be a more fruitful method of procedure. One successful interview initiated a chain of introductions which permitted successful progression through the maze of government agencies. In addition, the various research organizations of Greece (e.g., the Center of Economic Research, the Center of Social Research, Doxiades Associates, the School of Ekistics, and the Institute for Research in Communications) were especially helpful in this initial collection of information and data.

The following four months were devoted to field research in the islands themselves. During this time, all major islands were visited and local officials and inhabitants interviewed. Generally, between five days to one week were allocated to study on each island where the largest settlement underwent special study. If an island had several smaller villages as well, one of these would also be studied. Size, degree of isolation, economic specialization, and social characteristics determined selection of the sample. Inclusion of a maximum diversity of settlement types required a purposeful effort. Figure 2 shows the distribution of the sample.

To facilitate interviews the <u>nomarch</u> (governor) of the Dodecanese provided a letter of introduction to the mayor of each village. Personal letters
of introduction to local officials and inhabitants supplemented the formal introduction. In each village, local officials, agronomists, harbor authorities,
policemen, and priests were interviewed to obtain basic information and data on
both the village and island. The interviews of these officials were then cross-
checked with interviews of local inhabitants.

At the outset, Dr. Vasso Vassiliou of the Institute for Research in
Communications aided the creation of a formal interview for the local populace.
The wariness and suspicion of the local villagers, however, aroused hostility
and detracted from the results. It soon became clear that because of lack of
veracity in response and subterfuge in general, formal interviewing was yielding
unacceptable results. With greatly superior effectiveness, the researcher
shifted to informal discussion revolving about the same subjects. As a result,
one might best describe the field methodology employed as more akin to that of
the political anthropologist than that of the political scientist. This field
orientation will be apparent in the following study.

In Greece, the author is indebted to persons far too numerous to be all
included in acknowledgements. Special gratitude is due to Basil Coukis of the
Center for Planning and Economic Research; Mrs. Metridis of the Center of Social
Research; Vasilios Nikolopoulos and C. Bandaloukis of the National Statistical
Service of Greece; Mr. Logaras of the National Printing Office of Greece; Dr.
Vasso Vassiliou of the Institute for Research in Communications; John Papaïoannou
of Doxiadis Associates; Kosta Agapetides of the Greek Productivity Center; Dr.
N. G. Mavris, former Governor of the Dodecanese; Mr. K. Nikolopoulos, Govern-
ment agronomist at Kos; Konstantinos Livadiotis, Mayor of Pigadia, Karpathos;
Pandelis Karayiannis, Captain of the Tourist Police in Rhodes; Miltiadis
Logothetis, Director of the Commercial and Industrial Organization of the Dodec-
anese; Stavros Vaphidis, Director of Agriculture in Rhodes; Konstantinos D.
Yiannakopoulos, <u>Eparch</u> of Karpathos; and Denis Papamicail, sponge exporter of
Kalymnos.

Throughout the entire course of research and writing, the author benefited greatly from the supervision of Professors Norton S. Ginsberg and Marvin
W. Mikesell of The University of Chicago. Professor John Hawthorne, of the
Classics Department at The University of Chicago, first introduced the systematic study of Modern Greek to the author. Professor Janet Aitken, Chairman of
the Department of Geology and Geography at the University of Connecticut gener-
ously supported the research in map and photo reproduction and in numerous
other intangible ways. The Research Foundation of the University of Connecticut

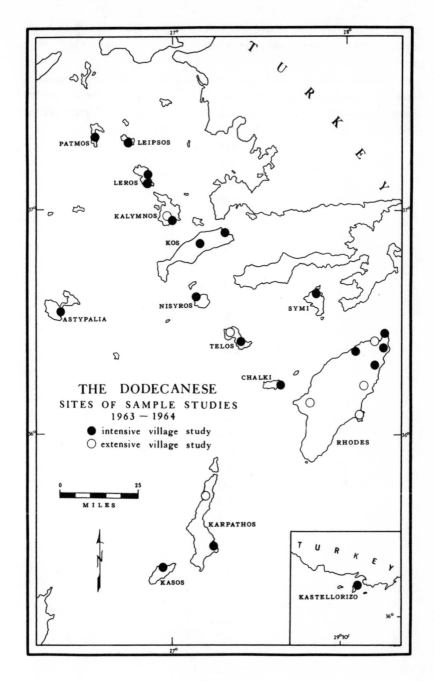

THE DODECANESE
SITES OF SAMPLE STUDIES
1963 — 1964

● intensive village study
○ extensive village study

0   25
MILES

N

TURKEY

PATMOS
LEIPSOS
LEROS
KALYMNOS
KOS
ASTYPALIA
NISYROS
SYMI
TELOS
CHALKI
RHODES
KARPATHOS
KASOS

TURKEY
KASTELLORIZO

provided typing services, as did Mrs. Anica Smith of Clark University. John Emerson, Walter J. Przybyloski, and Gerald Guerette furnished cartographic assistance.

Finally, to my wife who served as translator, interviewer, shipmate on winter Aegean seas, patient critic, and editorial advisor, I can only acknowledge her contribution to every page. For whatever errors, omissions and shortcomings still remain, I am, needless to say, solely responsible.

TABLE OF CONTENTS

Page

LIST OF TABLES

LIST OF ILLUSTRATIONS — <u>Continued</u>

LIST OF ILLUSTRATIONS

CHAPTER I

INTRODUCTION

. . . when we see how rashly some writers are always sketching a type of islander for whom the free wind is a perpetual call from the distant un-known . . ., whilst others (or sometimes the same) with the same boldness, embroider ingenious variations on the theme of isolation . . . it is not geography, but psychology, to which we are paying homage. For what finally matters is the idea adopted by the people—the political group—with regard to their geographical position . . . though this idea may be quite wrong or have no basis in reality.[1]

The fact that certain people live, for example, on an island has in itself no effect on their history; what has an effect is the way they conceive that insular position; whether for example they regard the sea as a barrier or as a highway to traffic.[2]

The people cannot conceive of their insular position in any way unless they live on an island. In any event, whether the sea is barrier or highway it enforces special adjustments.[3]

The fundamental problem of the present study is to explore the effects of selected economic, social, and political experiences upon political diversity and unity in the Dodecanese Islands. These particular islands form an admirable base for creating and testing hypotheses concerning the evolution of political differences among individual islands, and, in some cases, within islands themselves. The Dodecanese have only recently been liberated after centuries of foreign occupation and control. In addition, they reveal considerable variation in size, economic activities, and social characteristics. Finally, relatively little is known about the human geography of the islands.

Islands as a Special Problem in Political Geography

Islands constitute a somewhat special problem in the study of political geography. Certainly, they present to inhabitant and observer alike one of the most extraordinary of physical environments. By their very nature, islands con-stitute an unambiguous territorial delimitation, where different portions of the physical environment sharply intersect. The small island perhaps best approaches the notion of the "natural" region. Awareness of this highly personalized

---

[1]Lucien Febvre, A Geographical Introduction to History (New York: Alfred A. Knopf, 1925), p. 225.

[2]R. G. Collingwood, The Idea of History (New York: Oxford University Press, 1956), p. 200.

[3]O. H. K. Spate, "Toynbee and Huntington: A Study in Determinism," Geographical Journal, CXVIII (December, 1952), 423.

physical world by the resident inhabitants encourages a more encompassing sense of geographical distinctiveness.

A survey of the extensive literature on island groups adds surprisingly little theory to the effects of insularity upon political behavior and regional identity.[1] In addition, findings are contradictory as to the development of social, economic, and political differences among islands. While recognition is usually given to the fact that physical and social isolation breeds cultural divergence, the pattern of communications contributes to variable degrees of isolation among individual islands. Since the seas surrounding islands act both as barriers and highways, there is often greater divergence on large islands between the coasts and the interior than among island perimeters. Despite the oft-repeated contention that the peoples of every island show marked differences from each other,[2] whether evidence would confirm this on the basis of selected social, economic, or psychological characteristics is questionable.

This is not to deny insularity a role in the political geography of islands. The problem is that each island differs somewhat in size, situation, natural resources, and culture history. In such a multivariate situation, it is difficult to determine what role each of these factors has played. Noteworthy, however, is the fact that most discussion has dealt with this question in a peripheral fashion only, and consequently, means of testing hypotheses concerning the effects of insularity upon characteristics of political geography have not been forthcoming. A method of measurement may lie in the comparative analysis of modal distributions of selected aspects of personality and behavior.[3]

---

[1]This literature is far too extensive to be quoted here. For examples, see Douglas L. Oliver, The Pacific Islands (Cambridge: Harvard University Press, 1951); Bruce Grant, Indonesia (Parkville, Australia: Melbourne University Press, 1964); Kenneth B. Cumberland, Southwest Pacific (New York: McGraw-Hill, 1956); W. Cameron Forbes, The Philippine Islands (Cambridge: Harvard University Press, 1945); James W. Fox and Kenneth B. Cumberland, Western Samoa: Land, Life and Agriculture in Tropical Polynesia (Christchurch, New Zealand: Whitcombe and Tombs, 1962); John L. Fischer, The Eastern Carolines (New Haven: Pacific Science Board and the Human Relations Area File, 1957); M.B.R. Cawkell, D. H. Maling, and E. M. Cawkell, The Falkland Islands (London: Macmillan and Co., 1960); David Lowenthal, The West Indies Federation: Perspectives on a New Nation (New York: Columbia University Press, 1961).

[2]A representative view is contained in Karl J. Pelzer, "Physical and Human Resource Patterns," Indonesia, ed. Ruth T. McVey (New Haven: Human Relations Area File, 1963), p. 11.

[3]See A. Inkeles and D. J. Levinson, "National Character: The Study of Modal Personality and Sociocultural Systems," Handbook of Social Psychology, ed. G. Lindzey (Cambridge: Addison-Wesley Publishing Co., 1954), pp. 977-1020; A. F. C. Wallace, "The Modal Personality Structure of the Tuscarora Indians as Revealed by the Rorschach Test," Smithsonian Institution, Bureau of American Ethnology, Bulletin 150.

One recent study suggests that comparative content analysis may constitute a useful tool for studying differences in modal personalities at the national level.[1]

An approach directed at the behavior and personality of peoples in different places may get at the root of the problem more successfully. But since the most accurate measures of regional identity involve the goals, interests, and ideology of peoples, actual differences among islanders are less important than perceived differences. The literature of island studies suggests that although actual differences may be small, islanders nevertheless often think of themselves as markedly unlike surrounding islanders. David Lowenthal found, for example, that islanders in the West Indies emphasized and even distorted differences among island peoples.[2] It is not unreasonable to put forth a tentative hypothesis that islands tend to develop a "closed world" in terms of information, knowledge, perception, and goals. This is especially likely where communications are greater within islands than among islands. One might further hypothesize that this "closed-world" character reinforces itself in societies which have highly-developed loyalties to birthplace. In such areas, as the Dodecanese well exemplify, the tendency to emphasize differences among islands is especially marked.

Political Geography and Cognitive Behavior

From its inception, any study should clarify its research dimensions. Since the present analysis of the evolution of political unity and diversity in the Dodecanese Islands inevitably deals with such variables as ideals, attitudes, values, and behavior, some discussion of the role of cognitive behavior in political geography is appropriate.

Recent research in a number of disciplines has demonstrated important implications of the apperceptual world for the wide range of man's activities. In a pioneering article published nearly two decades ago, Alexander Spoehr emphasized the role of cultural differences in the utilization of natural resources.[3] The culturally conditioned human mind, acting as a filter for our knowledge of the external world, has affected our views towards other nations,[4]

---

[1]Hans Sebald, "Studying National Character through Comparative Content Analysis," Social Forces, XL (May, 1962), 318-322.

[2]David Lowenthal, "The West Indies Chooses a Capital," Geographical Review, XLVIII (July, 1958), 336-364.

[3]Alexander Spoehr, "Cultural Differences in the Interpretation of Natural Resources," Man's Role in Changing the Face of the Earth, ed. William L. Thomas (Chicago: The University of Chicago Press, 1956), pp. 93-102.

[4]William Buchanan and Hadley Cantril, How Nations See Each Other (Urbana: University of Illinois Press, 1953); H.C.J. Duijker and N. H. Frijda, National Character and National Sterotypes (Amsterdam: North-Holland Publishing Co., 1960).

the utilization of natural resources,[1] adjustments to environmental hazards,[2] the selection of capital cities,[3] the geographical bases of political parties,[4] patterns of voting behavior,[5] moral attitudes towards land use within the city,[6] the aesthetic appreciation of the landscape,[7] and the form of cities.[8] An essay on the theory of geographical knowledge has exhaustively analyzed the entire question.[9] Harold and Margaret Sprout summarize the cognitive approach to the study of human behavior:

> Instead of drawing conclusions regarding an individual's probable motivations and purposes, his environmental knowledge, and his intellectual processes linking purposes and knowledge, on the basis of assumptions as to the way people are likely on the average to behave in a given social context, the cognitive behavioralist—be he narrative historian or systematic social scientist—undertakes to find out as precisely as possible how specific persons actually did perceive and respond in particular contingencies.[10]

---

[1]See the symposium on perception and natural resources in National Resources Journal, III (January, 1964); Robert W. Kates, Hazard and Choice Perception in Flood Plain Management, Department of Geography Research Paper No. 78, University of Chicago (Chicago: By the author, 1962).

[2]Ian Burton and Robert W. Kates, "The Perception of Natural Hazards in Resource Management," Natural Resources Journal, III (January, 1964), 412-441.

[3]Lowenthal, "The West Indies Chooses a Capital."

[4]Roger E. Kasperson "The Know-Nothing Movement in Massachusetts, 1853-1857. A Study in Historical-Political Geography" (unpublished Master's dissertation, Department of Geography, The University of Chicago, 1961).

[5]Angus Campbell et al., The American Voter (New York: John Wiley and Sons, 1964), pp. 15-30.

[6]Walter Firey, Land Use in Central Boston (Cambridge: Harvard University Press, 1947), pp. 155-169. See also Walter Firey, Man, Mind and Land (Glencoe: Free Press, 1960).

[7]David Lowenthal and Hugh C. Prince "The English Landscape," Geographical Review, LIV (July, 1964), 309-346; David Lowenthal and Hugh C. Prince, "English Landscape Tastes," Geographical Review, LV(April, 1965), pp. 186-222; David Lowenthal, "Not Every Prospect Pleases—What is Our Criterion for Scenic Beauty?", Landscape, XII (Winter, 1962-1963), 19-23.

[8]Kevin Lynch, The Image of the City (Cambridge, Mass: The Massachusetts Institute of Technology Press, 1960). See also Kevin Lynch and Donald Appleyard, The View from the Road (Cambridge: Joint Center for Urban Studies, 1964).

[9]David Lowenthal, "Geography, Experience, and Imagination: Towards a Geographical Epistemology," Annals of the Association of American Geographers, LI (September, 1961), 241-260.

[10]Harold and Margaret Sprout, The Ecological Perspective on Human Affairs (Princeton: Princeton University Press, 1965), p. 118.

It is evident that the geographical diversity of men's minds, as reflected in their goals, interests, and accumulated experience, is instrumental not
only in defining the position of man _vis-a-vis_ nature, but also in shaping his
values, behavior, and institutions. Jean Gottmann observes that:

> In a space differentiated already by nature, this diversity of people's
> minds, of the spirit of nations, creates more differentiation. The differ-
> entiation of space accessible to men appears to be the _raison_ d'_être_ of both
> geography and international relations.[1]

The political partitioning of the world reflects a geographical diversity in
the experiences, ideology, and aspirations of men. The state, the foremost political institution, is predicated upon a large degree of consensus. Richard
Hartshorne contends that the major unifying force in the state is built about
consensus as to the state-idea, the idea shared by inhabitants of the primary
purpose for the existence of the state.[2] Gottmann has underlined the role of
iconography—the system of values, ideas, and symbols in which a people believe
—in distinguishing not only state from state, but also regions within the
state.[3] A wide-spread recognition of this point of view accounts for its general
incorporation into the conceptual basis of political geography.

Despite this general acceptance, however, the implications of this view-
point, on the whole, have not been fully realized in the study of political
geography. Such an approach involves the researcher not only in the spatial
characteristics of readily observable phenomena but also in the more elusive
world of perception, behavior, and ideology. Traditionally, such avenues of
investigation have been remote from the training and experience of political
geographers. Consequently, research directed to the relationship between geography and cognitive behavior has not been forthcoming. This concern will form
an essential dimension of the present study of unity and diversity in the Dodecanese Islands.

Geographical Diversity and Political Unity

The relative success and failure of political unification offers a valuable method for approaching the study of the political geography of the Dodecanese Islands. Jan Broek illustrated the potentialities of this approach in a

---

[1]Jean Gottmann, "Geography and International Relations," _World Politics_,
III (January, 1951), 162.

[2]Richard Hartshorne "The Functional Approach in Political Geography,"
Annals of the Association of American Geographers, XL (June, 1950), 95-103

[3]Gottmann, _op. cit._, p. 163.

thoughtful analysis of diversity and unity in Southeast Asia two decades ago.[1] The focus of the geographer has been, quite naturally, on the attributes which make areas and places different from or similar to one another. Within an area diverse in physical and human geography, various unifying forces are at work binding the separate portions together into social, economic, and political systems. A delimitation and understanding of the processes producing unification will do much to enhance our knowledge of the political partitioning of the world.

Valuable to such a study are the theories developed in political geography since World War II. The conceptual statements of Stephen B. Jones, Gottmann, and Hartshorne have focused attention on circulation or the movement factor in political geography.[2] Interruptions in circulation and movement can threaten unification and allow distinct regional interests and political behavior to develop. Physical barriers, uninhabited zones, and minority areas may generate forces leading to greater diversity in political attitudes and behavior. The development of concepts concerning movement and circulation have thus added another dimension to the interpretation of the causes of political diversity and offer rich possibilities for further analysis.

A recent review of research on political integration by Philip Jacob and James Toscano distinguishes ten variables which may exert integrative experience upon people.[3] These variables may well provide a starting point for an understanding of the evolution of political unity and diversity within any area. As defined by Jacob and Toscano, they include: (1) geographical proximity, (2) homogeneity, (3) transactions, or interactions among persons or groups, (4) knowledge of each other, (5) shared functional interests, (6) the "character" or "motive" pattern of a group, (7) the structural frame or system of power and decision-making, (8) the sovereignty-dependency status of the community, (9) governmental effectiveness, (10) previous integrative experience.

---

[1]Jan Broek, "Diversity and Unity in Southeast Asia," Geographical Review, XXXIV (April, 1944), 175-195.

[2]Hartshorne, op. cit., pp. 95-130; Stephen B. Jones, "A Unified Field Theory of Political Geography," Annals of the Association of American Geographers, XLIV (June, 1954), 113-123; Gottmann, op. cit., pp. 153-173; Jean Gottmann, "The Political Partitioning of Our World: An Attempt at Analysis," World Politics, IV (July, 1952), 512-519.

[3]The Integration of Political Communities, ed. Philip E. Jacob and James V. Tuscano (Philadelphia and New York: J. B. Lippincott Co., 1964), p. 10.

The concept of political integration and the delimitation and analysis of integrative factors have considerable usefulness to the political geographer. The overlap between these integrative factors and Hartshorne's "centripetal" forces is obvious. When placed beside the disintegrative or centrifugal factors creating political differentiation, such analysis can provide a meaningful base for the study of political geography.

Organization and Limitations of the Study

The organization of the study arises out of the methodology employed for analyzing the development of political diversity and unity among the Dodecanese Islands. The research attempts to determine the impact of selected experiences upon the geography of political attitudes and behavior. Put another way, the research is devoted specifically to an analysis of the last factor—previous integrative experiences—enumerated by Jacob and Toscano. The choice of experiences arises from the researcher's evaluation of their significance to the political geography of the islands. After a general historical and geographical orientation, agriculture, sponge-fishing, emigration and depopulation, tourism, and changing political sovereignty are all analyzed as experiences which have affected significantly present patterns of political attitudes and behavior.

A clear statement of the limitations of the research should serve to eliminate possible confusion as to intent and objectives. First, no attempt is made to define the many variables involved in the political differentiation of the islands. Rather, only those experiences most influential in the political geography of the islands are analyzed. Second, there is no intent to formulate the complete inventory of political differences and similarities among islands. The study seeks only to contribute to our understanding of the processes by which people in a particular area come to view themselves as distinctive and to develop certain characteristics of political attitudes and behavior.

Finally, although the objectives of the research are sharply limited, the scope of the study does include a constant analysis of the interaction of man, land, and the political order. Despite a long-recognized concern in geography, relatively little is known about the impress of political processes upon the landscape and upon the human use of the earth. At the same time, there is an equally-great concern about the effects of changes in the man-land system upon characteristics of political behavior.

CHAPTER II

GEOGRAPHICAL AND HISTORICAL BACKGROUND

Καὶ σὺ Ῥόδος, πουλὺν μὲν ἀδούλωτος χρόνον ἔσση,
Ἡελίου θυγάτηρ, πουλὺς δέ τοι ὄλβος ὄπισθεν
ἔσσεται, ἐν πόντω δ' ἕξεις κράτος ἔξοχον ἄλλων . . .[1]

(And you Rhodes, daughter of the sun, you will
remain free and have much fortune in the future,
and your strength in the sea will surpass all others . . .)

ἡμεῖς δέκα Ῥόδιοι δέκα νῆες[2]
(We ten Rhodians are ten ships.)

The Dodecanese are a group of islands lying along the northwestern
coast of Turkey, connecting the major islands of Samos and Rhodes (Figure 3).
The islands occupy a total area of 1,022 square miles, of which Rhodes has the
largest single portion—564 square miles. Historically, the islands have occupied an important location astride the major sea routes of the eastern Mediterranean, servicing ships trading between Egyptian ports and mainland Greece and
Anatolia. This location has also had strategic importance for military activity,
and the changing political fortunes of the islands have been closely related to
shifts of power within the Mediterranean.

Etymology and Delimitation

The term "Dodecanese" is of disputed origin, but was probably first
used under Leo III, the Isaurian Emperor of Byzantium, when one of his naval
commands was designated as the "Dodecanese or Aigaion Pelagos" (from which the
corruption "archipelago" is derived).[3] Several writers have claimed that
Theophanes, a Byzantine chronicler writing between 810 and 815 A. D., first
coined the term.[4] The name clearly refers to the Greek words "δώδεκα" (twelve)
and "νησιὰ" (islands). In Byzantine usage, the word "Dodecanese" was used as
a general name for virtually all the islands of the southern Aegean, including

---

[1] The prophecy of Sibyl.

[2] Ancient Rhodian proverb.

[3] Great Britain, Naval Intelligence Division, Dodecanese (2d ed.; London:
Her Majesty's Press, 1943), p. 3. For a general etymological discussion, see
Victor Guerin, Etude sur l'ile de Rhodes (Paris: August Durand Libraire, 1856),
pp. 47-53.

[4] Jack Nicholas Casavis, Italy and the Unredeemed Isles of Greece (New
York: Dodecanesian League of America, 1935), p. 3; Ernle Bradford, The Compan-
ion Guide to the Greek Islands (London: Collins, 1963), p. 219; Konstantinos A.
Doxiades, Δωδεκάνησος (Athens: 1947), Vol. I, p. 19.

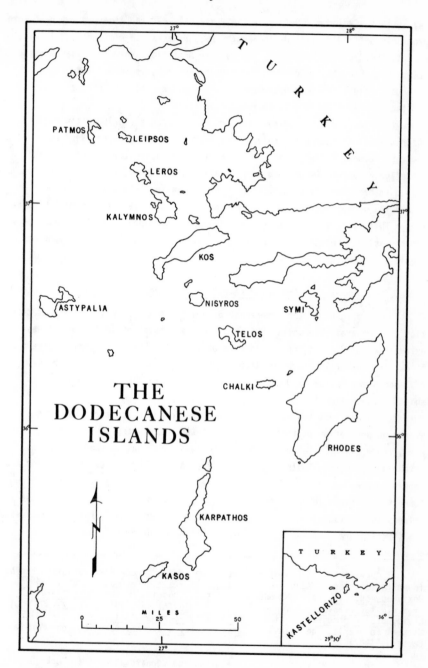

Figure 3

the southern Cyclades. Only relatively recently has the island group been more precisely defined to include the southern Sporades south of Samos and Ikaria, west to the Cyclades and Crete, and east to Anatolia. When the islands passed under Turkish control, Suleiman the Magnificent labelled them "Privileged Islands" because of their privileged civil and tax status. This designation continued until the Young Turks revoked it in 1909.

During the late Medieval period, the Dodecanese included the twelve major islands of Astypalia, Kalymnos, Karpathos, Chalki, Kasos, Kos, Leros, Nisyros, Patmos, Rhodes, Symi, and Telos (Figure 3). Later, as Leipsos and Kastellorizo gained importance in population and economy, they also were included to bring the list to fourteen. Other smaller islets are also found within the group, but most are either unoccupied or have only seasonal habitation. This study treats the fourteen islands cited above largely because they are the islands recognized by official Greek sources as the major components of the island group.

Ancient History and Settlement

The origins of the Dodecanese population are obscure; accurate statistics are not available until 1926 when the statistical office of Greece was established. This lack of accurate records is a problem throughout Greece and is due to a general lack of written evidence. It is possible, however, by means of legends and historical references, to reconstruct the major demographic shifts through time.[1]

The earliest traces of settlement are found in scattered evidence of a stone-age population at the western end of Kos. According to one legend, however, two races—the Telchines and the Heliadi—originally inhabited Rhodes. Strabo described the Telchines, a tribe from Asia Minor, as celebrated iron and bronze workers who "in fact fabricated the scythe for Cronus."[2] Another view connects the first inhabitants of Rhodes, Cyprus, and Krete and places these islands in the vanguard of Hellenic civilization during early historical times. The first literary reference, however, is found in Homer's Iliad where he

---

[1]Useful treatments of the evolution of the Dodecanese population can be found in Soterios I. Agapetides, Ὁ πλυθυσμὸς τῆς Δωδεκανήσου (Athens: 1948); Doxiades, op. cit., pp. 288-309; Nicholas I. Konsola, Ἡ στατικὴ καὶ δυναμικὴ ἐποπτεία τοῦ οἰκονομικοῦ χώρου τῆς Δωδεκανήσου (Athens: 1964), pp. 21-30; Livi Livio, Storia demografica di Rodi e delle isole dipendenti (Firenze: 1944); Michael Volonakis, The Island of Roses and her Eleven Sisters (London: Macmillan Company, 1922).

[2]The Geography of Strabo, trans. Horace Leonard Jones (New York: G. P. Putnam's Sons, 1929), Vol. VI, p. 275.

records that all the Dodecanese except Astypalia aided in the Achaian attack upon Troy.[1]

Following the Trojan War, piratical Karians from Asia Minor overran the Dodecanese, settling especially on the island of Rhodes. In the eleventh century B. C., however, the general unrest in Greece led to a migration of people from north to south. This movement was composed of three major groups, distinguishable by dialect and antecedents. From northern Greece, Aeolic Greeks occupied Lesbos and the adjacent coastal areas of the mainland. From central Greece, Attica, and the northeast Peloponnesos, a large movement of Ionians settled in Chios, Samos, and coastal areas from Smyrna (the present Ismir) to Miletus. In turn, colonists from Miletus populated the Dodecanese Islands of Patmos and Leros. These Ionian Greeks eventually united in a Pan-Ionian League of twelve cities with a common religious and political capital. The third group consisted of a large movement of Dorians from the Gulf of Argos who occupied the three ancient cities of Rhodes—Ialysos, Kamiros, and Lindos—and the cities of Kos, Knidos, and Halicarnassos. Dorians from the mainland coast also colonized Telos, Leipsos, and Kalymnos, while Chalki was populated from Rhodes and Kasos from Kos.[2]

After this repopulation of the Dodecanese, the renowned ancient cities of Rhodes emerged, each with its own territorial sphere of influence inside and outside the island. The city of Kos grew rapidly along with the mainland cities of Knidos and Halicarnassos. Eventually these cities joined in a religious and political league called the Doric Hexapolis (Figure 4). The League later dissolved when Halicarnassos passed over to Ionian connections prior to the fifth century B. C.

Disputes between Athens and Sparta occasioned more settlement changes. When a hostile force was sent into the Sporades in 412 B. C., the three cities of Rhodes united to build a new city at the northern end of the island. The city was designed by Hippodamus of Miletus, probably the first urban planner, who also built the city of Piraeus.[3] Except for Syracuse and Athens, Rhodes was unquestionably the most remarkable city of its time. The city itself covered the level ground near the harbors and rose gradually along the terraces of

---

[1]The Complete Works of Homer: The Iliad, trans. Andrew Long et al. (New York: Modern Library, 1950), Vol. II, pp. 57-58. A full discussion of the legends concerning the early settlement of Rhodes is available in Cecil Torr, Rhodes: In Ancient Times (Cambridge, England: University Press, 1885), pp. 139-151.

[2]Volonakis, op. cit., p. 100.

[3]Great Britain, Naval Intelligence Division, op. cit., p. 30.

the acropolis hill to the vast circle of walls with their lofty towers. The physical structure of the city, in fact, was often compared to the body of a Greek theater.[1] Boasting five artificial harbors, eight miles of landward walls, domination of a channel of extensive maritime commerce, and possession of mainland domains, Rhodes soon became a wealthy and powerful maritime power. In tribute to the city, Strabo noted: "The city of the Rhodians . . . is so far superior to all others in harbours and roads and walls and improvements in general that I am unable to speak of any city equal to it, or even as almost equal to it, much less superior to it."[2]

Inhabitants of Kos followed the lead of Rhodes by submerging their own factional quarrels to build a new city on a site facing the mainland and commanding the strait. Kos also prospered and produced renowned artists and the first scientific school of medicine.

While Rhodes and Kos built cities and consolidated their wealth, they became increasingly involved in Greek factional struggles. Consequently, Rhodes fell under the domination of Halicarnassos and in 340 B. C. the Persians occupied the city. Rhodes looked to Athens for support, but was ignored despite an eloquent plea by Demosthenes. When Alexander invaded Asia Minor in 335 B. C., however, the Rhodians reportedly sent ten ships to assist in the successful assault upon Tyre. For its part, Rhodes was rewarded with large mainland holdings on the adjacent coast.

After Alexander's death in 323 B. C., Rhodes rapidly became a powerful maritime state. She consolidated her foremost position among the other Dodecanese islands and over adjacent mainland areas (Figure 4). After the successful resistance to the mighty siege of Demetrios, Rhodes used the huge siege engines to construct the Colossus of Rhodes, one of the seven wonders of the ancient world. When both the city and her renowned colossus were shattered by an earthquake in 227 B. C., generous gifts from the rulers of Sicily, Syria, Asia Minor, and Egypt helped to rebuild the city.

By 200 B. C., Rhodes began to fall under the hegemony of Rome, which was aiding Greece in its defense against the kings of Macedonia and Syria. Rhodes was forced to join in an alliance with Rome which virtually destroyed its independence. In 155 A. D., it was incorporated into the Empire and in the same year suffered the first of three earthquakes which devastated the cities of Rhodes, Symi, and Kos.

---

[1]Torr, op. cit., p. 53.

[2]Jones, op. cit., Vol. VI, p. 269.

13

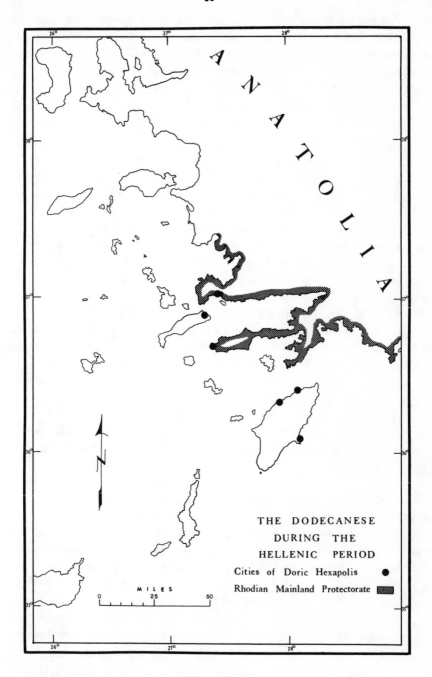

Figure 4

During and following the decline of Rome, the Dodecanese were subjected to predatory attacks by a succession of pirates and invaders. Wealthy, populous, and lying in an exposed position, the islands posed a lucrative target for the procession of Isaurians, Persians, Saracens, Venetians, Genoese, Crusaders, Knights of St. John, Turks, and Italians.

Middle Ages

In 470 A. D., the Isaurians attacked Rhodes and looted the city before being forced off by reorganized defenses. One hundred fifty years later, Persians under Chasroes again sacked the city. A still more serious threat arose with the development of powerful Saracen seapower. The Dodecanese, Cyprus, and Krete were all attacked during the Arab War against the Byzantine Empire. As the Saracens became masters of the Mediterranean, Kos was raided and captured, and both the city and island devastated. Karpathos and smaller islands met a similar fate. Rhodes fell in 654 A. D. and its celebrated colossus, prostrate since the earthquake, was broken up and sold to a Jewish merchant of Edessa who carted it off with 900 camels. Later Saracen pillages occurred in 658, 717, and 867 and finally culminated in the fall of Chania in Krete in 840.

Toward the close of the piratic period, an event occurred in 1088 on the small island of Patmos which was to be of religious and social importance to the Dodecanese. In that year Byzantine Emperor Alexius Comnenus gave the monk Christodoulos title to the entire island so that a monastery could be established to commemorate the site of imprisonment of St. John, who allegedly wrote the Apocalypse on Patmos.[1] The monastery became wealthy and served as a center of learning and Greek nationalism during long foreign occupations. It also served as a refuge for Greeks when the Turks captured Constantinople in 1453, and again in 1669 when Krete fell.

While Patmos was emerging as a religious center, the Venetians seized upon a serious crisis in the Byzantine Empire to occupy the Dodecanese Islands. In 1802, Alexius Comnenus granted Venetian nobles commercial privileges in the Dodecanese. After the fall of Constantinople to the Crusaders in 1204, the Byzantine Empire saw its Aegean island possessions divided among the city states of Italy—Venice, Genoa, and Pisa. After two centuries of political squabbling among these states, the islands were transferred to the control of the Knights of the Hospital of St. John of Jerusalem.

The Knights of St. John had originally been founded to care for pilgrims and had become wealthy through gifts and commercial profits. When the Order was

---

[1]For the early history of Patmos, see William Edgar Geil, The Isle That is Called Patmos (London: Marshall Bros., 1904), pp. 99-109.

forced out of its east Frankish fortress in Palestine, it took up temporary refuge in Cyprus. The Knights were unwelcome on Cyprus, however, and totally dependent upon the local potentate. After a complete reorganization in 1300, the Order was searching for a suitable location for its permanent headquarters. In addition, the growing military character of the Order demanded a base from which the Knights could contest the Turkish advance. A treaty with the ruling noble gave the Knights the islands of Rhodes, Kos, and Leros in exchange for certain revenues from the islands. The treaty was to go into effect only after the capture of the islands by the Knights. Pope Clement approved the expedition by giving it his official sanction.

Despite the successful capture of the islands, it became apparent that the Turks would not allow this threat to pass unchallenged. Accordingly, the Knights reconstructed and fortified the cities of Rhodes and Kos. The Knights reinforced their position by their occupation of the other adjacent Dodecanese islands—Chalki, Symi, Telos, Nisyros, Kastellorizo, Karpathos, and Kasos. The northern outlying islands of Patmos and Astypalia remained in Venetian and Byzantium hands (Figure 5).

The organization of the Knights reflected the diverse origins of its members.[1] Since they spoke a variety of languages, the Order was organized around language divisions or "tongues". Each "tongue" had a portion of the city's fortifications allocated to it for defense. While the dominant language of the Knights was French, Greek persisted as the spoken language of the inhabitants of Rhodes and the other Dodecanese islands.

The Knights were in possession of the islands for only a short time before their presence was felt. The Order virtually eliminated the heretofore widespread piracy, and maritime commerce flourished. Taxes collected from the Dodecanese islands and inherited properties contributed to the growing wealth of the Knights. That the distribution of this wealth was unequal is attested to by Baron de Belabre's portrait of the Order:

> After 1312 their character became transformed, and the members of the Order, who were supposed to look after the poor and to fight in defence of the Catholic faith, soon forgot their vows and lived in great luxury, dressing magnificently, eating rare foods from gold and silver plates, and giving nothing to the poor. They kept the finest horses, hawks and led a dissolute life, and many of the Knights had also large private means.[2]

---

[1] Cf. Lawrence Durrell, Reflections on a Marine Venus (London: Faber and Faber, Ltd., 1963), pp. 133-142; Volonakis, op. cit., pp. 235-291; Spyros Leotsakos, Ρόδος, τὸ σμαράγδενιο νησί (Athens: By the author, 1949), pp. 49-58; Doxiades, op. cit., pp. 52-53.

[2] Volonakis, op. cit., pp. 239-241.

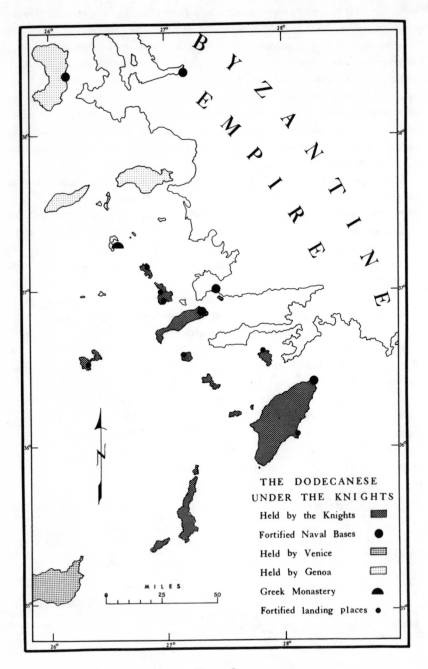

Figure 5

In 1320, the Knights underwent internal reorganization and the military forces and defenses of the Order were strengthened. Protected on the north, south, and rear by Venice and Genoa, the Knights became a powerful member of the Frankish hegemony over Greek seas. Allied with Venice, Genoa, and Cyprus, the Knights attacked Smyrna in 1344 and captured it in 1348. An assault upon Alexandria followed in 1365, and two years later an abortive attack upon Tarsus, Tripoli, and Latakia. With the loss of Smyrna in 1412, however, the tide of battle began to turn. In 1444, a large Egyptian force besieged Rhodes for forty days, but was finally driven off by a determined counterattack. In 1453, nevertheless, Constantinople was captured and ravaged, and Rhodes received an ultimatum. Upon its refusal, the Turks began preparations for a massive assault upon Rhodes.

A series of raids upon the Dodecanese islands culminated in an unsuccessful siege of Rhodes itself in 1480. The Turkish conquest of Egypt in 1517, however, outflanked the Rhodian position, and in 1520 Turkish attacks upon Mytilene, Chios, Kos, and Cyprus isolated Rhodes. A massive and prolonged six-month siege in 1523 finally forced the surrender of the Knights. The cemeteries which today ring the city walls are a grim reminder of the Turkish losses of 90,000 out of 200,000 men. Kos, Kalymnos, and Leros continued to fight on, but by 1537, all of the Dodecanese were absorbed into the Ottoman Empire.

Turkish Period

When the islanders surrendered to Suleiman, it was on the condition that their "ancient privileges" should be respected. Accordingly, the islanders were granted virtual autonomy under the suzerainty of Turkey. They were exempted from all taxation, except a small annual tribute, and guaranteed complete freedom of trade, especially for imports of timber from Anatolia. Further, Turkish administrators were not to interfere with Greek language, religion, and culture. Similarly, the monastery in Patmos was granted independence from outside interference. Also, Symi and Kalymnos maintained schools which were attended by students from all over Greece until the University of Athens was founded in 1837. The islanders were granted non-taxable sponge-fishing rights in all the seas of the Ottoman Empire. Finally, the Dodecanesians were permitted to retain armed fortresses which were needed for defensive purposes. Certainly, it is with justification that the Dodecanese acquired the title "privileged islands" for these liberal concessions (Figure 6).[1]

---

[1] Great Britain, Naval Intelligence Division, op. cit., pp. 35-36; Volonakis, op. cit., pp. 297-300.

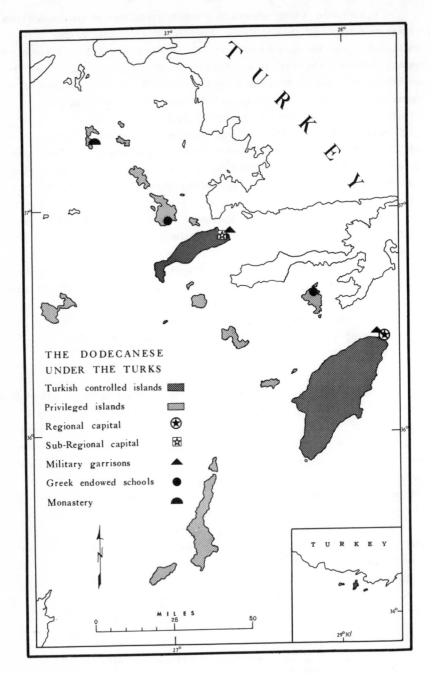

THE DODECANESE
UNDER THE TURKS

Turkish controlled islands
Privileged islands
Regional capital
Sub-Regional capital
Military garrisons
Greek endowed schools
Monastery

Figure 6

Despite these seemingly attractive guarantees, conditions on the islands suffered from Turkish rule. Visits by Turkish tax collectors often resulted in the fleecing of the islanders, as did periodic visits by the Turkish fleet. Secondly, Turkish authorities failed to take actions to stem the spread of disease which took a heavy toll among islanders. Even more harmful were the continuing corsair raids. Finally, the periodic wars between Turkey and the Christian states resulted in destruction and brutality by both sides.

When the Archbishop of Patras sounded the call for the War of Greek independence in 1821, the Dodecanese ardently joined the rebellion. The daring sea raids of the sailors of Kasos harassed Turkish naval actions, while Symi sacrificed the last of its forests, its chief source of wealth, to build ships for Greek patriots. The Dodecanese were initially included in the new Greek state, but in 1830 were exchanged for Turkish Euboea which was needed to safeguard Greek security. Astypalia became part of the Dodecanese when the Turkish half of Astypalia was exchanged for the Greek half of Amorgos.

The period following the War of Independence was one of prosperity for the Dodecanese islands. The Industrial Revolution in Europe touched off a great demand for sponges, and by 1840 Symi and Kalymnos simultaneously had discovered new sponge-fishing grounds off the coast of Libya. All islands profited from their entrepôt role by participating actively in the carrying trade between Turkey and ports in the Middle East and the Black Sea. Many Dodecanesians bettered their position by working in the cities of Smyrna and Constantinople or by investing in farms about the cities or along the adjacent coasts.[1] These new economic activities combined with the traditional exports of citrus fruits, wine, fresh vegetables, and olive oil to give the Dodecanese their soundest economic progress since ancient times. The population of the Dodecanese subsequently increased from 85,000 in 1828 to 149,530 in 1910.

Although a period of economic progress, this was also a time of constant struggles against the abuses by local Turkish officials. While the yearly tax on islanders was not oppressive, the collection methods were frequently unjust. Outright suppression began in 1866 when the Turks began a campaign for the forceful integration of the islands into the Empire. These actions undermined the pillars of Dodecanese autonomy.

The first Turkish attack occurred during the Kretan uprising of 1867 when a battleship with troops was sent to quell an attempted insurrection in Symi. In 1869 the Turkish fleet blockaded Symi, and troops seized the public buildings. Characteristic resistance in Kalymnos precipitated a month's siege

---

[1]See Paul Vouras, "The Development of the Resources of the Island of Rhodes under Turkish Rule, 1522-1911," _Balkan Studies_, Vol. IV (1963), pp. 45-46.

during which local inhabitants fled to the upper portions of the city. In 1871, Turkish tribunals replaced the local Greek courts. In 1874, Turkish controls of harbors and customs were established, and new taxes on salt, spirits, and sponge-fishing soon followed. In 1885 Turkish troops again besieged Symi, threatening to starve the local inhabitants into submission, and islanders were cut off from their mainland farms and local fishing grounds.

When the Young Turks assumed power in 1908, the Dodecanese hoped for more liberal concessions from a constitutional Turkey. Only one year passed, however, before the new regime cancelled all privileges in the Dodecanese—the Young Turks instituted new heavy taxes, decreed Turkish the official language, installed compulsory military conscription, and abrogated religious liberties. Riots and rapid emigration followed, but by 1910 the "ancient privileges" had been entirely destroyed. Events outside the islands, however, were soon to disrupt the growing Turkish tyranny.

Italian Period

In 1912, the Balkan War broke out and the Greek fleet quickly captured the northern Sporades. Italy meanwhile assembled a fleet at Astypalia and occupied the Dodecanese Islands. The Dodecanesians warmly welcomed this "liberation" and rendered valuable assistance in the capture of Turkish officials and military garrisons. Following the capture of Rhodes, the Italian military leaders issued a series of proclamations assuring the Dodecanese an autonomous government.

Encouraged by these declarations, island leaders gathered at the holy island of Patmos in 1912 to discuss their future. The representatives unanimously resolved to name the liberated islands "Aegean State," to adopt the laws of Greece, and to state their wish to be united with the "mother country, Greece."[1] By the First Treaty of Lausanne in 1912, the Italian Government agreed to withdraw its military and political officials from the islands, but confirmed its occupational rights until Turkey evacuated Libya. In 1915, however, the secret Treaty of London guaranteed Italy full possession of the islands.

Following the War, an Italo-Greek treaty promised to cede to Greece the Dodecanese Islands, with the exception of Rhodes which was to be given a broad

---

[1]The diplomatic machinations of this period are recorded in Dr. N. G. Mavris, "Certain Misconceptions in Relation to the Eastern Mediterranean and Greece," Social Science, XXI (January, 1946), pp. 22-30; Dr. Skinos Zervos and Pâris Roussas, The Dodecanese: Resolutions and Documents Concerning the Dodecanese, 1912-1919 (New York: A. Page & Co., n. d.); Délégation du Dodécanèse à la conférence de la paix, Le Dodécanèse ensanglanté demande sa liberté (Paris: F.A. Tourbier, 1919); Volonakis, op. cit., pp. 323-344; Great Britain, Naval Intelligence Division, op. cit., pp. 37-39.

degree of autonomy. Italy repudiated the treaty in 1920, however, and negotiations for a new agreement led to the Treaty of Sevres. This treaty stipulated that the islands, again with the exception of Rhodes whose fate was to be determined in fifteen years by plebiscite, would be returned to Greece. Ratification of the treaty did not follow, however, and Italy later denounced the agreement. Finally, by the Second Treaty of Lausanne in 1924, Italy acquired full possession of the occupied islands (Figure 7).

The early years of Italian administration in the Dodecanese were beneficial to the islanders. In 1923 the Italian Governor initiated a program of intensive commercial and touristic development of Rhodes. Accordingly, fine roads and hotels were built, antiquities restored, and attractive gardens and parks established. Meanwhile, the inhabitants enjoyed wide autonomy as to their language, education, and religion. In many respects, Rhodes, and to a lesser degree the other Dodecanese Islands, became the showpiece of the Italian Colonial Empire.

Despite this early progress, the advent of Fascism produced growing Italian interference with local liberties.[1] In 1926, Italian authorities assumed control over public education and began "assimilating" the schools to the Italian educational system. In 1930, the local Greek courts were suppressed and their functions usurped by Italian civil tribunals. In 1931, municipal school managers were deprived of all control over the employment of teachers. Any references to Greece in the classroom were prohibited. Growing attempts were made to assimilate the Greek Orthodox Church to the Uniate Church. These actions led to frequent rioting and to serious bloodshed in 1935 in Kalymnos.

The movement to integrate the Dodecanese into Italian culture and state culminated in the appointment of Senator del Vecchio as Governor in 1937. Upon his arrival in the Dodecanese, del Vecchio proclaimed that he had come "to bring Fascist life and the Fascist spirit to the islands."[2] Accordingly, the administration prohibited local inhabitants from speaking Greek and posted public notices requiring visitors to converse in Italian. Greek was taught in the schools only as an optional modern language. Italian teachers replaced their

---

[1] For the problems of the Dodecanese islander under Italian sovereignty, see The Dodecanesians Are Not Enemy Aliens, ed. Dr. N. G. Mavris (New York: Dodecanesian League of America, 1942); Dodecanesian National Council, The Dodecanese Islands: Two articles by American Experts (New York: Dodecanesian National Council, 1943); Dodecanesian Union of Alexandria, Memorandum on the Dodecanese Question and Especially on the Recent Decree Concerning Public Instruction (Alexandria, Egypt: Dodecanesian Union of Alexandria, n.d.); Clarence D. and Isabelle Booth, Italy's Aegean Possessions (London: Arrowsmith, 1928); Jack Nicholas Casavis, La tragedia del Dodecaneso, 1912-1943 (New York: 1953).

[2] Great Britain, Naval Intelligence Division, op. cit., p. 39.

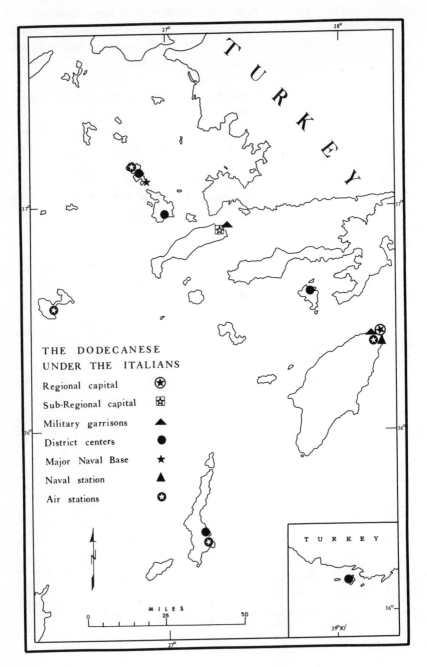

THE DODECANESE
UNDER THE ITALIANS

Regional capital ⊛

Sub-Regional capital ⊞

Military garrisons ▲

District centers ●

Major Naval Base ★

Naval station ▲

Air stations ⊙

Figure 7

former Greek counterparts. Termination of all intercourse with Greece and interference in maritime commerce resulted in widespread emigration. The situation did not improve until the islands were liberated during World War II, following which they were ultimately, in 1947, reunited with Greece.

Physical Geography

Physically, the Dodecanese are a continuation of the rugged topography of Anatolia. Nearly all the land still above sea level is mountainous and coastlines are precipitous. The islands reflect the complicated topography of the mainland—a maximum of diversity encompassed in the minimum of area. Crystalline schists and marbles are present, but only infrequently exposed. More important are the massive limestones which are well represented in all the islands, except volcanic Nisyros. The limestones produce little soil and most of the surface of the islands remains barren and denuded. Deposits of Tertiary rock, though less widespread, are of greater importance to agriculture, since, when weathered into deep and fertile soils, they form the chief areas of cultivation in Kos, Karpathos, and Rhodes. There are also some volcanic rocks and features, as in Nisyros and Patmos, the remains of volcanic vents. Sulphur and mineral springs are now important tourist assets on Rhodes, Kos, Kalymnos, and Nisyros.

The climate of the Dodecanese bears marked similarities to that of the rest of the Aegean but with modifications arising from proximity to Anatolia. Temperatures range from 32°F to 100°F with July and August the hottest months. The diurnal temperature range is greatest in spring and least in summer and always more marked in the interior of the larger islands. February is the coldest month, but frost is rare even then. Rainfall is strongly-concentrated in the winter season extending from October to late April and originates from cyclonic sources. Summer rain is almost unknown. Troublesome during the summer, however, are the strong "etesian" winds which are characteristically northerly and north-westerly.

The chief vegetation of the islands is the evergreen shrub. Formerly, the Dodecanese also boasted extensive forested tracts but, for a variety of reasons, they have disappeared. Fuel and timber, heavily imported in recent times from nearby Anatolia, are very scarce. Among wild animals, which have also largely disappeared and are rare, hares and badgers are perhaps most common. Reptiles, with the exception of the ubiquitous lizard and land tortoise, are also surprisingly uncommon. Domestic animals, especially the oxen, horses and pigs, are undersized and a source of much concern to government agronomists.

Population and Settlement

The first accurate statistics of population begin in 1926 with the founding of the Statistical Office of Greece. A long-term summary of population changes must therefore depend partially on estimates (see Table 1). During the period of Italian occupation, population figures show an increase in the Dodecanese population from an estimated 109,560 in 1922 to 129,235 in 1941.[1] It should be pointed out, however, that the 1941 population is not an accurate figure for the Greek population, since 13,025 Italians and "Levants" (i.e., Turks) are included. Rather, the Italian period is characterized by a constant flight of Greeks, particularly the younger men, to Egypt, the United States, Canada, South America, and Australia. This emigration and depopulation was especially marked in islands that suffered from Italian interference with shipping and sponge-fishing—Symi, Kastellorizo, Kasos, and Chalki.

From 1947 to 1961, the Dodecanese population increased from 115,345 to 123,021. The rate of increase, however, was very slow compared to that for the rest of Greece, largely because of the continuing emigration. While Greece registered a population increase of 9.9 per cent from 1951 to 1961, the comparable increase in the Dodecanese was only 1.27 per cent.[2] Moreover, among the islands only Rhodes (+5 per cent) and Kalymnos (+4 per cent) showed relative increases, while all the other islands declined in population. In 1961, Rhodes itself contained 68,873, or 56 per cent, of the entire Dodecanese population. It is noteworthy, also, that these population changes occurred during a period when the Dodecanese enjoyed political reunification with Greece and economic development programs.

The present population of the Dodecanese is overwhelmingly Greek. While the census does not enumerate numbers of minority groups, an estimated 2,500 to 3,000 Turks, concentrated chiefly on Rhodes and Kos, reside in the Dodecanese. In recent years, the Cyprus controversy has accelerated a steady drift of these Turks to Anatolia. The Turks who remain are primarily urban dwellers, concentrated in the cities of Rhodes and Kos and in outlying suburban communities. There are also a smaller number of Kretan Moslems who fled Krete at the time of its incorporation into Greece. In addition, descendants of Spanish Jews, who

---

[1]Treatments of recent demographic history are available in Doxiades, op. cit., pp. 290-309; Konsola, op. cit., pp. 21-30.

[2]Cf. Kingdom of Greece, National Statistical Office of Greece, Population de la Grèce au recensement du 7 April 1951 (Athens: National Printing Office, 1955), pp. 192-194; Kingdom of Greece, National Statistical Office of Greece, Population de la Grèce au recensement du 19 Mars 1961 (Athens: National Printing Office, 1963), pp. 56-58.

TABLE 1

POPULATION OF THE DODECANESE, 1420 - 1941[a]

Island	1420	1750	1821-1828	1850	1900	1910	1912	1917	1922	1931	1936	1937	1940	1941
Rhodes . . .	18,000	27,500	31,500	33,000	43,000	45,000	45,000	36,560	45,000	54,800	59,933	60,625	59,975	61,567
Karpathos. .			7,500	8,000	8,500	9,500	8,527	6,930	7,500	6,580	7,861	7,893	7,013	7,231
Kos. . . .			11,000	12,500	15,700	16,500	14,570	15,070	16,000	21,170	19,845	20,003	17,216	18,231
Kalymnos. .			5,000	7,600	19,400	20,800	23,200	14,950	15,500	16,500	15,439	15,538	15,544	14,872
Astypalia. .			3,000	3,000	2,500	2,000	1,780	1,380	1,370	1,610	1,754	1,767	1,745	1,771
Leros. . .			4,500	4,600	6,400	6,900	6,000	4,880	4,000	5,500	7,159	7,208	10,956	10,979
Kasos. . .			5,250	5,000	6,500	6,700	5,700	1,850	1,760	1,920	1,904	1,913	1,367	1,367
Telos. . .			2,000	1,950	1,900	1,850	1,300	2,100	1,160	1,230	1,226	1,227	1,129	1,131
Symi . . .			6,250	8,000	18,000	19,500	22,450	7,300	7,000	9,460	8,182	6,176	4,751	4,147
Patmos . .			4,500	4,000	4,000	3,700	2,720	2,660	2,550	2,990	3,208	3,214	2,695	2,665
Nisyros. .			3,300	3,500	4,700	5,000	5,000	4,300	3,160	3,430	3,404	3,422	2,586	2,592
Chalki . .			1,200	1,500	2,900	3,000	3,215	2,200	1,300	1,790	1,470	1,476	787	754
Leipsos. .									560	960	981	993	855	817
Kastellorizo .			2,500	3,500	8,500	9,000	4,020	2,000	2,700	2,230	2,269	2,262	1,386	1,111
Total	44,900	67,000	85,000	96,750	142,000	149,530	143,482	102,180	109,560	130,830	132,638	133,357	127,967	129,235

[a]Source: Konstantinos A. Doxiades Δωδεκάνησος (Athens: 1947), Vol. I, p. 289.

were expelled from Spain in the sixteenth century and who escaped the German purge, remain in the city of Rhodes. A single Jewish family resides in the city Kos. Finally, despite a large minority during the period of Italian occupation, only a few scattered Italian families remained in 1964.

Almost without exception, all population groups speak Greek. The Turks speak Turkish among themselves but usually understand Greek as well. The Kretan Moslems speak both a Greek dialect and Turkish. The Greek inhabitants speak dialects of modern Greek which vary somewhat from island to island but are particularly distinctive on the smaller and more isolated islands. Local inhabitants who have had only grammar school education speak and read only the popular language (δημοτική), while those who have attended gymnasium can read and write the more formal language (καθερεύονσα) of Athenian newspapers and government publications. A large segment of the population, however, experiences considerable difficulty in understanding newspapers from Athens.

The settlement of the Dodecanese population reveals several noteworthy characteristics. Perhaps most striking for the traveller to Rhodes and Kos are the walled cities, a legacy of the era of the Knights. Founded in ancient times both cities were fortified against pirates during the Byzantium era and refortified by the Knights. They occupy strategic positions, have important commercial harbors, and also boast population centers which dominate the larger islands on which they are found. Today their cityscapes show clearly the legacies of earlier invaders and different cultures (Figure 8).

The rural villages which account for the larger number of population nuclei contrast sharply with the walled cities. Characteristically, most Dodecanese islands have an older village located on or near the summit of an easily-defended hill or ridge. Often the village is built up about a Byzantine or Frankish castle which originally protected the settlement (Figures 9 and 10). A larger and younger port settlement, usually found below the village, is more accessible to the major harbor. Kalymnos, Symi, Patmos, and Karpathos all offer examples of this population shift which shows ports gaining at the expense of the older and more inaccessible settlements. Other villages are generally small farming hamlets—of several hundred in population—interconnected by poor road and sea transportation networks. Approximately one-half of the ninety Dodecanese settlements are found on Rhodes and Kos (Figure 11) alone.

Rhodes well illustrates the distribution of settlements on a large Dodecanesian island. Surrounding the city of Rhodes are a number of large, satellite villages which profit greatly from their excellent accessibility (Figure 12). These villages are strung out along the major highways which run along the perimeter of the island. Toward the interior and more remote sections of the island, villages are smaller and hamlets more common. The highways

Figure 8—The old city of Rhodes. This view from the wall corresponds closely with the area encompassed by the fortified limits of the ancient city. The Turkish population now occupies much of this older portion of Rhodes. The Frankish castle dominates the skyline while Turkish mosques are clearly evident in the lower and upper left of the photograph. Modern Rhodes has spread beyond the walls and most of the affluent citizens and more recent housing are found there.

Figure 9.—Chora, Patmos, vividly illustrates the strong need for security in the location of island villages during earlier periods of history. The monastery of Patmos, established in 1088 A. D., withstood piratical attacks and was never sacked. In recent time, maritime security has permitted an expansion of settlement adjacent to the harbor, and this hilltop village has declined in population. The growth of the village down the hillside can be seen in the right and left extremes of the photograph.

Figure 10.—Aghia Marina, Leros. Nestled under the protection of the Byzantine castle, this community shows a morphology common to many Dodecanesian villages. The large Greek church, located on a public square in the center of the community, is the religious capital and a fortress second only to the castle itself. Many of the houses embedded in the steep, terraced hillside have been abandoned as the village spreads to the lowland areas.

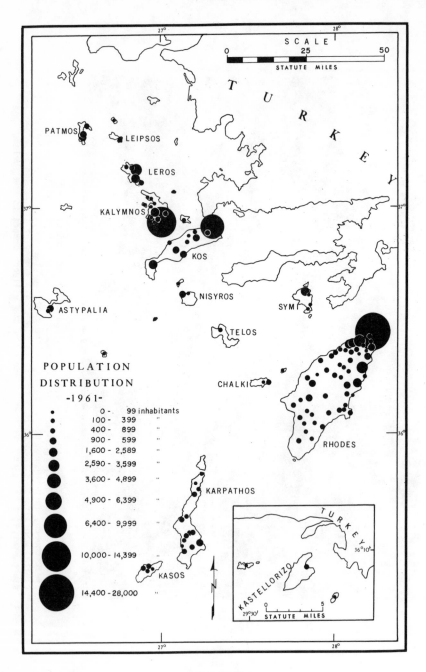

Figure 11

Figure 12

become poor, unsurfaced roads whose main users are the indispensible farmers' mules.

The morphology of the village itself presents some basic regularities, although no two villages would even approach complete uniformity. In many villages, a large community church sits in the central square. Very often the "δημαρχεῖον" (mayor's office) will also be found on or near this square. Located close by, often on the streets leading away from the square, are the coffeehouses which serve as the foci of social and political activity. Social life within the village revolves about this nucleus since Greeks fear and detest isolation from their fellow inhabitants. Even houses near the center of the village carry an implication of social status because of the higher frequency of coming and going outside their walls.

Economy

Resting traditionally upon agriculture and maritime activities, the Dodecanese economy has been undergoing changes in recent times. Foreign occupations have disrupted maritime commerce with the natural hinterland of the islands and closed adjacent fishing grounds. Extensive emigration and depopulation have caused serious labor shortages throughout the islands and contributed to a decline in the amount of land under cultivation. Greater facilities for transportation and lodging have added to the growth of tourism and tertiary activities at the expense of extractive sectors of the economy. Needless to say, these economic shifts have had a differing impact upon the economies of various islands of the Dodecanese.

Agriculture in the Dodecanese rests primarily upon crop cultivation and pastoral activities. With limited resources, inadequate capital and labor, and poor accessibility, the smaller islands are forced to rely chiefly upon subsistence crops to satisfy local needs. The larger islands, however, have developed specialized cash crops, closely linked to distant markets. Kos, formerly renowned for its lettuce, now produces chiefly tomatoes, meat, some melons, and wine. Rhodes specializes in olives, tomatoes, meat, citrus fruits, and almonds. Several other islands produce specialized crops—tangerines in Kalymnos and almonds in Telos. The more inaccessible areas of large islands and the small islands produce a diversity of crops, but they generally only help to satisfy local needs.

Fishing, formerly an important source of income throughout the Dodecanese, is now conducted on a large scale only on Rhodes, Kos, and the small island of Leipsos. In the other islands, fishing is a limited activity and the catch is used chiefly as a diet supplement. Sponge-fishing, once the important export of the Dodecanese, no longer occupies the attention of most islanders.

One hundred years ago, Chalki, Astypalia, Symi, and Kalymnos boasted a sponge-fishing fleet that formed the basis of their economy. Most sponge-fishers have emigrated, however, and the remnants of the industry are now concentrated on Kalymnos.

With the decline of these historical foundations of the Dodecanese economy, new activities are emerging to fill the gap. Initially developed by the Italians prior to World War II, a rapidly-growing tourist trade is becoming an important economic asset. Since the construction of the first hotels and publicity of the touristic attractions of the Dodecanese under the Italians, the flow of tourists to the islands has risen rapidly. In 1938, 28,500 tourists came to Rhodes; in 1955, 53,757 entered; and in 1963, a total of 233,604 visited the island.[1] While tourism has been a shot in the arm economically, its effects have been geographically variable. Inhabitants of smaller islands complain that Rhodes has been developed at their expense. For the most part, important tourist trade has evolved only in the islands of Rhodes, Kos, and Patmos. All the islands, however, see their salvation in becoming centers of tourism, and local tourist facilities are springing up - even in improbable spots such as Kastellorizo - throughout the Dodecanese.

A second source of financial strength results from the extensive emigration which has taken place during the last century. Remittances from Greeks living abroad have historically been an important source of income for the islanders. Greek emigrants retain a strong sense of family obligation and loyalty to their place of birth. Though statistics are unavailable, the flow of income into the Dodecanese from foreign countries is usually the islander's chief means of amassing capital for dowries or major purchases.

Circulation and Communication

The degree of movement by islanders and their participation in various forms of communication differ widely throughout the Dodecanese. Winter seas, political restrictions, and an underdeveloped economy have, in the past, posed formidable barriers to a greater awareness of and participation in the world outside the village or island. "When we emerged from Italian rule, from centuries of darkness, what did we know of Greece, of the world?"[2] Political independence and economic progress have burst the confines of tradition, however, and the former barriers to communication are crumbling.

Throughout the Dodecanese, radios are now a common, though much-prized,

---

[1] Figures were supplied by the Tourist Police of Rhodes.

[2] Personal interview, Rhodes, November 2, 1963.

possession. Poor farmers proudly point to their radios and boast that even their little island now has the most modern trappings of civilization. And well they might boast, for the radio is indeed a powerful agent of communication. When bad seas truncate islands from the rest of the world, even the most isolated islanders retain a basic knowledge of national and world events. Radio reports of the Kennedy assassination reached even storm-bound Leipsos when no ship had called for days.

Telephones, on the other hand, are still largely a public rather than a private convenience. Only relatively few merchants boast their own telephones. Exceptional are the more affluent Kalymnians and city-dwellers of Rhodes and Kos who have now begun to install telephones in their homes. The cinema is likewise restricted to these same areas and the inhabitants of smaller islands must rely upon the infrequent visits of the traveling theater. In fact, only the capital cities of Rhodes, Kalymnos, and Kos possess permanent cinemas.

Newspaper circulation is no less variable from island to island (Figure 13) or within an island (Figure 14). Since the circulation of both Athenian and local daily newspapers relies heavily upon sea transportation, it is not surprising that during summer most newspapers triple in sales. It is only fair to issue several cautions in the interpretation of Figure 13. First, the pattern of newspaper circulation is based upon subscriptions rather than total sales. Second, because of the fiercely partisan affiliation of both Athenian and local newspapers, each reader must read both pro-government and opposition newspapers to define the range, though seldom the mean, of interpretations of any issue. Also, it should be noted that the reader, by subscribing to newspapers of opposite affiliation, protects himself against political retribution or governmental changes. Third, per capita figures for newspaper circulation are perhaps more misleading than absolute figures since newspapers are faithfully passed from hand to hand, and are generally available to all in the coffeehouses.

For Dodecanesians, travel outside the village or island is usually restricted to occasions when medical treatment is mandatory or a rare visit to clo close relatives. There are two chief exceptions to this generalization: First, where smaller islands are located at very accessible points to Rhodes, Kos, Kalymnos, or Krete, islanders will travel frequently for specialized shopping and for amusements. Symians, for example, boasted of their frequent trips to Rhodes—"just for the cinema." Second, the more affluent inhabitants of Rhodes, Kos, and Kalymnos travel often for a wide variety of economic, social, and political services. In nearly all cases, there are strong sex differentials in favor of males, since men are the primary participants in these forms of social and political activity, and Greek women are as notoriously poor sailors as their husbands are renowned seafarers. In fact, the author has far too often observed

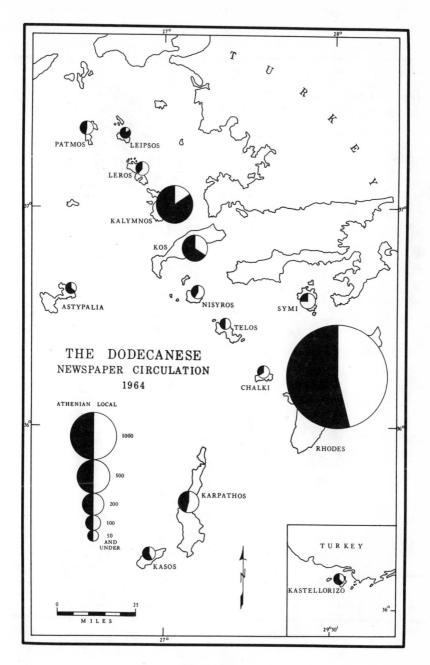

THE DODECANESE
NEWSPAPER CIRCULATION
1964

ATHENIAN LOCAL

Figure 13

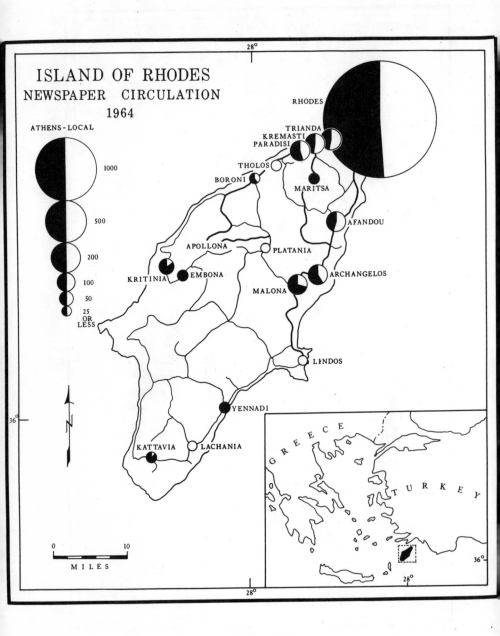

ISLAND OF RHODES
NEWSPAPER CIRCULATION
1964

ATHENS - LOCAL

1000

500

200

100

50

25
OR
LESS

RHODES

TRIANDA
KREMASTI
PARADISI

THOLOS
BORONI

MARITSA

AFANDOU

APOLLONA
PLATANIA

KRITINIA   EMBONA

ARCHANGELOS

MALONA

LINDOS

YENNADI

KATTAVIA   LACHANIA

GREECE
TURKEY

0   10

MILES

Figure 14

a Dodecanese woman become picturesquely "seasick" even before embarking, lemon-in-hand.

The pattern of trips reveals some interesting inter-island linkages. Rhodes is unquestionably the regional capital of the Dodecanese. Surprising, however, is the keen competition of Athens, primate city par excellence, for the greatest frequency of trip destination. In the northern half of the Dodecanese it also appears that islands have evolved specialized services so that individual trips generally are closely tied to specific services. Kalymnos with its numerous doctors and schools is a medical and educational center. Leros boasts several state-operated hospitals, while Kos has specialized shopping facilities and governmental services. Finally, as the links between Kasos and Karpathos with Krete, and Astypalia with Athens will illustrate, inhabitants of peripheral areas visit locales outside the Dodecanese.

An orientation to circulation and communication among the islands would be incomplete without some observations concerning communications within the Dodecanese village. An understanding of movement and communication within the social space of the village provides insight into the process of attitude formation and the characteristics of political behavior. Contrary to reasonable expectation, the church is not a key center for the exchange of information among men. The reason is simple—normally, only women attend church faithfully. For women, therefore, the church, along with local shops, is an important gossip center. The interchange of political ideas is limited, however, as women know little about politics and usually mimic their husbands' positions.

For men, nodes of interaction are the coffeehouses. These are open to all, with the exception that father and son do not frequent the same coffeehouse or sit at the same gaming table (be it for "ταβλι" - i. e., backgammon - or the Greek version of blackjack). Social class is not an obstacle to participation. Stratification by political persuasion, not social position, tends to limit communication among coffeehouses. The result is a highly-disjointed pattern of village interaction which often permits the formation of highly-divergent—and often widely-divorced from actual fact—levels of political knowledge and opinion.

Society and Polity

Almost without exception, the Greek inhabitants of the Dodecanese are members of the Greek Orthodox Church. During long centuries of foreign occupation, attempts were frequently made to convert the Dodecanesian, but to no avail. The Turkish Moslems of Kos and Rhodes are represented by the Mufti of Rhodes. The Moslem minority enjoys wide religious freedom with virtually no outside interference from the Greek majority—a remarkable fact in view of the intense emotions over the Cyprus situation.

Administratively, the Dodecanese constitute a _nomos_, roughly equivalent to an American state.[1] In Greece, the _nomarchs_ (governors) are generally competent and well-trained administrators appointed by the Minister of the Interior. Their appointment is often on grounds broader than party affiliation, and changes in the central government do not necessarily result in changes in _nomarchs_. In fact, this has been the case in the Dodecanese during the recent governmental changes in Greece. The _nomarch_ represents the central government in local areas and wields considerable power. The _nomos_ of the Dodecanese is divided into four subregions called _eparchies_. Finally, the smallest civil division is the _deme_, which is perhaps most analogous to the corporate area of a small American city in urban areas and to the township in rural areas. Under the 1912 law, _demes_ are units of approximately 10,000 population, but frequent amendments have allowed many exceptions.

Education is universal, compulsory, and free at the "δημοτικὸ" (grammar school) level, but children are commonly engaged in household or agricultural tasks during the school day. Only the more affluent islanders can send their children to gymnasium, although higher education is widely regarded as an important source of family pride as well as a sound future investment. Because of the high expenses of board, only a very small proportion of students from smaller islands are able to go on to gymnasium. A number of trade schools have emerged to fulfill the need for specialized training in manual occupations. Finally, althoughofficial sources claim that illiteracy has been eradicated, conversations with islanders reveal that a sizeable proportion (perhaps ten to twenty per cent) are "αγγράμματοι" (without letters). The illiterates are chiefly the aged, although a large number of younger people are also unable to read or write because of a general refusal to attend schools.

Family and kinship ties occupy the principal source of allegiance and constitute the basic economic unit. Nevertheless, most families try to send at least one son or daughter to the "ἐξωτερικο"[2] (outside world) to supplement the meagre family income with remittances. This method of amassing capital is particularly important because of the need to dower the daughters. The result has been the disruption of most Dodecanese families, with many villages showing an excess of females to males.

One final attribute of Dodecanese life merits mention as a backdrop to

---

[1]See the more comprehensive discussion of local government in Irwin T. Sanders, Rainbow in the Rock: The People of Rural Greece (Cambridge: Harvard University Press, 1962), pp. 218-240.

local society—the social relations between the sexes.[1] Perhaps partially a
result of centuries of Turkish occupation, women are relegated to a subservient
role in social and political life. This general relationship is exemplified by
classical attitudes toward male versus female children. If asked how many children he has, a Greek parent will frequently respond by citing the number of sons,
and he may or may not add daughters as an afterthought. Women are expected to
remain in the home passing their time in household and agricultural tasks, while
men spend most of their free time in the local "καφενεῖον" (coffeehouse).

The coffeehouse is a key social institution in Greece since it is a
meeting place where villagers discuss agricultural problems, community affairs,
and politics.[2] The coffeehouse is also frequently the place where people gather
to listen to Athenian radio broadcasts and to read newspapers brought in from
outside the village. Here is where public opinion is formed, and here is where
local and national politicians must win their battles. Indeed, during elections
the coffeehouses are the arenas where candidates for political office deliver
their speeches and vie for votes. In a large sense, the coffeehouses are the
Greek equivalent to the "tea house juries" of China.

---

[1]Ibid, pp. 127-175; Ernestine Friedl, Vasilika: A Village in Modern
Greece (New York: Holt, Rinehart and Winston, 1962), pp. 75-91.

[2]See the discussion of the social and institutional character of the
coffeehouse in Sanders, op. cit., pp. 205-217; John D. Photiadis, "The Coffee
House and its Role in Stavroupolis, Greece" (unpublished Master's dissertation,
Cornell University, 1956).

CHAPTER III

THE QUEST FOR AGRICULTURE

> When God finished building the world, he suddenly remembered that
> he had forgotten the country of Greece. Gathering together the
> remaining rubble of rock, he threw it into the sea and thus Greece
> was created.[1]

The topography of the Dodecanese islands attests to the spirit embodied in this folk legend if not to its accuracy. A continuation of the rugged Turkish highlands, the islands display precipitous coastlines where the steeply-sloping limits plunge into the sea. Large plains well-suited for agriculture are rare, and consequently most settlement is dispersed among the fragmentary pockets of alluvium scattered throughout the rugged island highlands. The massive limestone parental material precludes a fertile soil foundation. Since soil erosion is widespread, laborious attempts at terracing have vainly attempted to preserve the thin soil veneer that remains on the steep slopes. For most of the Dodecanese islands, the legend indeed accurately expresses the state of existing agricultural resources.

A sober appraisal, however, reveals a more balanced inventory of agricultural possibilities. Rhodes, Kos, and Karpathos have extensive fertile tracts which have served as the base for subsistence and export agricultural production since ancient times. On other islands, the more limited agricultural areas nevertheless have favorable possibilities for the development of tree cultivation and livestock raising. The land use of the islands in 1962 is shown in Table 2. The relatively small proportion of land under cultivation reflects the general limitations of the resource base. A further breakdown by island of the total cultivable land indicates the highly unequal distribution of agricultural activity throughout the Dodecanese (Figure 15).

Climatic difficulties in the Dodecanese contribute to the problems of the farmer. Uncertain winter rainfall (it rained only twice in the author's winter in the Dodecanese) and severe summer drought create chronic water shortages. The mild winters, on the other hand, do provide a favorable opportunity for agricultural production tailored to early season markets. On Rhodes and Kos early garden vegetables successfully invade the markets of mainland Greece, especially Athens, and more distant European cities. Moreover, mild winters are favorable to specialization in vines, olives, citrus fruits, and strawberries.

---

[1]Many versions of this legend exist in Greece. For a somewhat more colorful version, see Sanders, op. cit., p. 3.

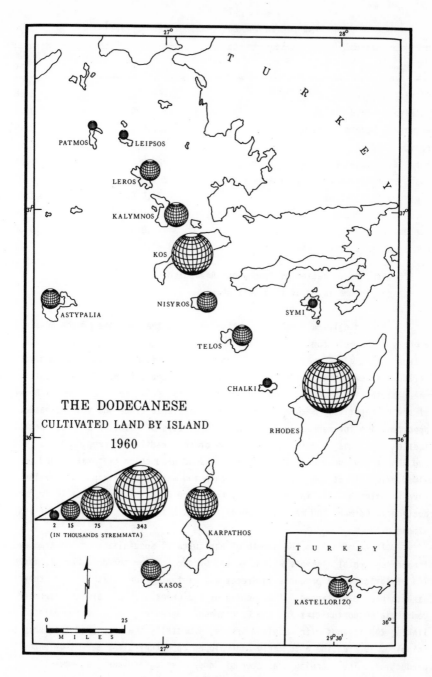

Figure 15. The Dodecanese Islands, cultivated land by island in 1960.

TABLE 2

LAND USE IN THE DODECANESE ISLANDS, 1962[a]

Land Use	Stremmata[b]	Per Cent of Total
Cultivated irrigation fields	66,700	2.58
Cultivated arid fields	220,700	8.53
Permanent vegetationaand trees	167,600	6.49
Fallow land	146,000	5.65
Forested mountainous grazing lands	822,000	31.84
Bushy mountainous grazing lands	257,600	9.97
Plains grazing areas	34,000	1.31
Forests and wooded areas	293,000	11.34
Barren areas	474,000	18.36
Roads and inhabited areas	84,900	3.28

[a]Source: Organization of Dodecanese Agriculture

[b]Each stremma is equal to 0.2471 acres

Accordingly, agricultural activities form the backbone of the Dodecanese economy. The main components of the agricultural sector are grains, olive and citrus trees, garden vegetables, and pastoral activities. This crop complex reflects a combination of subsistence and export production. Table 3 depicts the distribution of cultivated land by island for selected major crops. Because of the comparatively meagre returns from subsistence crops and the increased opportunities for marketing crops in urban centers of mainland Greece, specialization continues to gain at the expense of the traditional crop complex. Kos and Rhodes have developed strongly-specialized production of tomatoes and meat, aimed primarily at the local tourist trade and markets in Athens. Kalymnians have invested heavily in high-quality tangerine orchards and market their production in Germany and mainland Greece. Telos has long been renowned for its almond crop.

Instrumental in the growth of agricultural specialization are the newly-formed commercial linkages with mainland Greece. Prior to World War II, marketing of agricultural products in Greece was virtually non-existent, and other markets had to be tapped. The opening of the Greek markets permits increased commercial opportunities for the Dodecanese. Moreover, improved communications linking the islands with mainland Greece, especially the increased frequency of shipping, is creating a formerly-undeveloped opportunity for market-oriented production. The changing character of Dodecanese agriculture is, however, a

TABLE 3

DODECANESE AGRICULTURE: SELECTED CROPS BY AREA CULTIVATED, 1961-1962[a]

(In stremmata)

Island	Wheat	Barley	Oats	Grapes for wine & raisins	Grapes for eating	Lemons	Oranges	Tangerines
Kastellorizo	50	100	---	---	---	50	---	---
Symi	350	200	---	---	---	500	250	100
Chalki	100	200	---	---	---	50	---	---
Telos	800	1,000	150	---	---	900	550	110
Rhodes	54,420	6,220	9,410	14,046	2,147	54,850	127,200	61,390
Karpathos	1,650	3,950	440	1,650	127	2,915	2,480	820
Kasos	350	680	300	150	24	15	---	---
Kos	8,850	18,200	7,850	5,200	405	20,100	4,530	27,200
Nisyros	150	3,800	300	340	---	600	130	120
Kalymnos	300	1,500	250	530	93	2,200	5,000	27,600
Leros	200	1,050	150	2,060	49	2,000	2,300	5,700
Astypalia	150	1,150	70	330	42	1,000	850	5,400
Patmos	250	800	80	370	66	670	240	370
Leipsos	250	500	50	350	20	110	---	30

[a]Source: Organization of Dodecanese Agriculture

mixed blessing, as the more favorably endowed islands show gains at the expense
of the smaller and less productive islands. Agricultural progress thus contributes to the growing economic and social differences among islands.

Agricultural Production

Since reunification with Greece, a marked increase has taken place in
Dodecanese agricultural production. This progress involves gains both in the
area under cultivation and in the yields per acre (Figures 16 and 17). The
improvement in productivity reflects better fertilization and agricultural techniques, while increases in the area under cultivation are due much to the end of
foreign control and a return to a peace-time economy.

The decade between 1953 and 1962 has witnessed important readjustments
in agricultural production. Under the impact of programs for improving agricultural methods, production of wheat, edible legumes, and hay has declined while
production of tomatoes, melons, grapes, and olives has risen markedly. The
major changes in production are shown in Table 4.

Similar changes have occurred in livestock production (Figure 18). At
the end of World War II, the livestock population was devastated; in addition,
the Italians had levied a per-capita livestock tax and imposed strict regulations
limiting grazing on public domains. Following reunification, however, the Greek
Government implemented several schemes which have successfully raised livestock
productivity. The adoption of stock improvement methods, the extension of agricultural credit, and the institution of programs to combat animal diseases all
contributed to the agricultural progress. An important result of this activity
is the expansion of the commercial production of livestock at the expense of the
traditional rudimentary pastoral activities. Table 5 suggests the present composition of the Dodecanese livestock industry.

With the increase in agricultural production is a parallel growth of
agricultural revenue. Between 1947 and 1961, total agricultural revenue in the
Dodecanese islands increased 263 per cent. Table 6 reflects this progress. The
more-than-threefold growth of revenue from livestock production is particularly
significant because it illustrates the shift of the industry towards commercial
production.

Despite the increase in agricultural revenue, the present average per-
capita income for farmers is only 4,030 drachmas ($134.33). Compared with the
estimated 5,000 drachmas per-capita average for all Dodecanesians, the farmer
occupies a poor position. Moreover, the average per-capita figure conceals the
highly-unequal geographical distribution of agricultural income in the Dodecanese. On the smaller and more isolated islands, agricultural income nearly dis-
appears. Moreover, in all cases income is highly variable from year to year

45

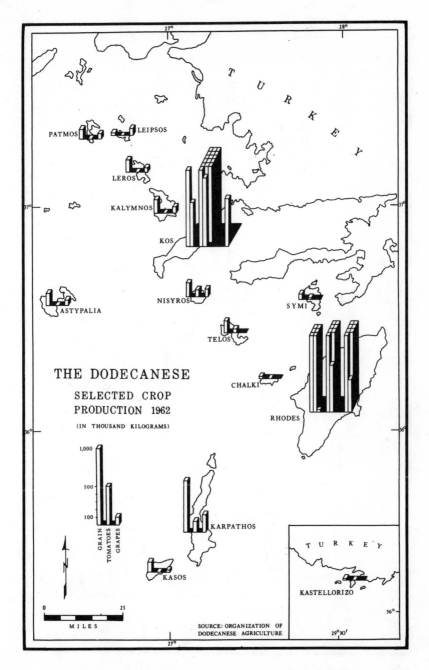

THE DODECANESE

SELECTED CROP
PRODUCTION 1962

(IN THOUSAND KILOGRAMS)

Figure 16.—The Dodecanese Islands, selected crop production in 1962.

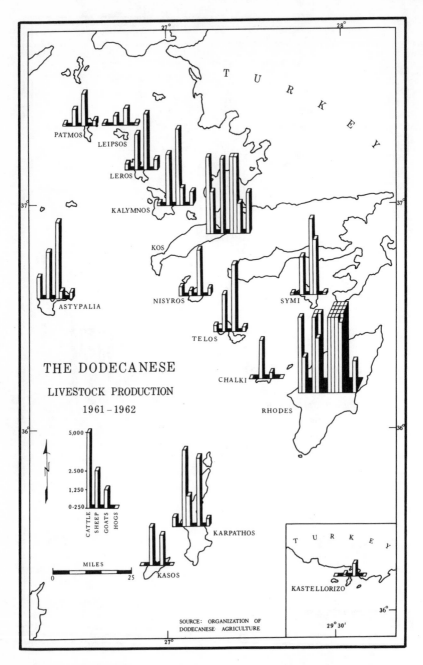

Figure 17.—The Dodecanese Islands, livestock production, 1961-1962.

TABLE 4

DODECANESE AGRICULTURAL PRODUCTION AND CULTIVATED AREA[a]

| Crop | Production in Tons | | | Areas in Stemmata |
	1955	1959	1962	1959
Cereals				
Wheat	7,340	4,443	5,334	78,650
Barley	3,812	1,938	3,378	52,500
Oats	1,556	846	972	21,800
Edible Legumes	858	477	598	12,000
Melons				
Cantaloupes	2,830	3,236	3,160	2,238
Watermelons	7,778	9,446	12,247	9,378
Vegetables				
Tomatoes	16,700	22,934	23,500	19,668
Onions	7,965	5,784	3,893	4,473
Fresh Beans	576	913	955	2,101
Squash	1,242	---[b]	1,410	---
Cucumbers	2,434	2,627	2,905	4,395
Eggplant	859	---	907	---
Cabbage	2,104	1,392	1,025	969
Green Onions	610	1,714	1,515	1,440
Industrial Plants				
Tobacco	342	188	132	6,244
Sesame	300	136	70	3,595
Arak	62	---	21	---
Vineyard Products				
Table grapes	3,476	14,000	21,000	2,408
Grapejuice (wine)	4,850	5,500	---	
Olive Products				
Olive oil	1,138	2,475	---	1,802,300[c]
Eating olives	397	539	---	
Citrus Fruits				
Lemons	325	500	500	77,560[c]
Oranges	759	2,100	1,500	120,635[c]
Tangerines	1,617	2,000	1,200	122,450[c]
Fresh Fruit				
Pears	227	211	140	42,980[c]
Apricots	150	899	---	39,880[c]
Peaches	33	362	305	20,785[c]
Pomegranates	205	264	200	28,410[c]
Fresh Figs	559	667	500	88,320[c]
Dried Fruits				
Almonds	186	413	150	28,470[c]
Dried Figs	869	---	945	---

[a] Source: Ministry of Agriculture   [c] Number of trees
[b] ---Lack of statistics

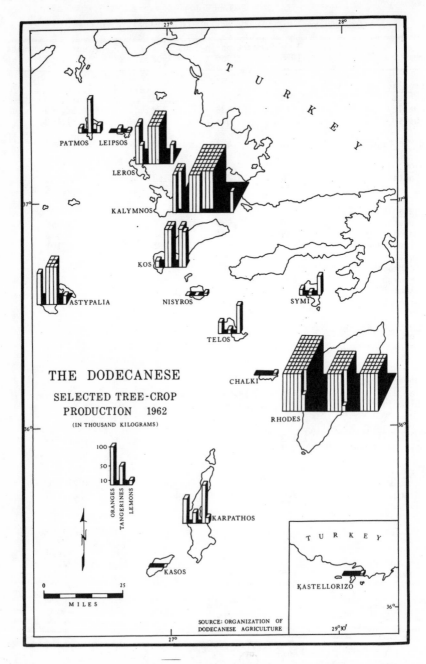

Figure 18.—The Dodecanese Islands, selected tree-crop production in 1962.

depending upon environmental and economic factors. The changes in agricultural income reflect the multitude of problems over which the farmer has little or no control.

TABLE 5

LIVESTOCK IN THE DODECANESE, 1960[a]

Type of Livestock	Numbers
Cattle	17,836
Sheep	71,336
Goats	103,784
Reproductive Hogs	2,505
Hogs for Fattening	10,791
Domestic Fowl	314,689
Rabbits	7,841
Horses	13,185

[a]Source: Kyriakou I. Phina, Ἡ γεωργία τῆς Δωδεκανήσου καὶ αιπροϋποθεσεις ἀναπτύξεως αὐτῆς (Rhodes: 1961), p. 21.

TABLE 6

CHANGES IN DODECANESE AGRICULTURAL REVENUE, 1947-1961[a]
(In drachmas)

Years	Revenue from Cultivated Crops	Livestock Revenue	Total Revenue
1947-1948	88,210,000	30,894,000	119,104,000
1957-1958	206,530,000	64,770,000	271,104,000
1958-1959	182,000,000	83,000,000	265,000,000
1959-1960	185,000,000	87,000,000	272,000,000
1960-1961	230,600,000	97,000,000	327,600,000

[a]Source: Organization of Dodecanese Agriculture

Agricultural Problems

The major environmental problems hampering agricultural development have already been discussed above. A number of economic and social problems, however, likewise thwart a fuller realization of agricultural potentialities in the Dodecanese. Among these are farm fragmentation, difficulties in marketing, rural labor shortages, a lack of capital for innovation, and the dangers of monoculture and semi-monoculture.

Farm fragmentation is a serious problem throughout the varied regions of Greece. In his systematic study of the problem in a sample of eleven Greek villages, Kenneth Thompson concluded that "Greece find itself with land tenure arrangements which can be said to be wholly incompatible with the full development of the sector of the economy that provides nearly one-third of the gross national income of Greece."[1] The Dodecanese are no exception to this widespread problem of land tenure. The largest single plot encountered during the research field investigation in the Dodecanese was a single tract of sixty stremmata (fifteen acres) on the island of Rhodes. Such a large plot is extremely rare, however, and in nearly all villages a single plot of ten stemmata (2.5 acres) is considered very large.

The implications of land fragmentation to the individual farmer are well-known. Valuable time and effort are lost in the constant travel from plot to plot. As a farmer in Kos put it, "We eat up our lives on the road."[2] In an area where productive agricultural lands are at a premium, valuable land is used for boundaries and paths. In addition, the difficulties of implementing more effective drainage, irrigation, mechanization, and conservation methods prevents a more rational use of land resources. Perhaps of greatest importance, however, is the despair which fragmentation generates in the individual farmer. A Rhodian farmer expressed this feeling in his sorrowful introspection: "A man doesn't love a small piece of land—one hour here, another there. He comes to hate his work. Soon he even wishes for his neighbor's death."[3]

Despite the deeply-felt need for "ἀναδασμός" (consolidation), little progress has taken place towards this end in the islands. Although regional agronomists proudly point to the success of land consolidation in "Κατταβιά", a small village on the remote southern tip of Rhodes, it cannot be ignored that the project was possible only because much land was still under public ownership. During field work, not one of the single villages included in the sample studies could claim even rudimentary progress toward consolidation. Differences in the quality of land plots or their trees and nostalgic values derived from a long history of family ownership prevent any attempt to redistribute land.

Beside land fragmentation, most Dodecanese farmers view marketing problems as their most serious concern. In 1961, for example, the market price for

---

[1] Kenneth Thompson, Farm Fragmentation in Greece, Center of Economic Research, Research Monograph No. 5 (Athens, Greece: Center of Economic Research, 1963), p. 2.

[2] Personal interview, Kos, November 24, 1963.

[3] Personal interview, Paradeision, Rhodes, November 6, 1963.

tomatoes was poor, and the ensuing collapse of marketing organization resulted in heavy losses for many Dodecanesian farmers. These losses are symptomatic of poorly-organized arrangements for the marketing of crops. On Kos, farmers complained bitterly that twice within the last five years they have seen their products rot on the docks. Because of the capricious nature of both the market and its accessibility, the position of the farmer is very uncertain.

While farm fragmentation and marketing difficulties present the gravest farm problems, several other secondary factors compound the woes of the Dodecanese agriculturalist. Extensive depopulation has created serious rural labor shortages in the islands. The maintenance and construction of terraces are increasingly difficult. At periods of peak labor requirements, such as pruning and harvesting, the absence of young men and women may lead to a loss of parts of a crop. A lack of capital and high interest rates have long discouraged agricultural innovation and the purchase of larger and more compact landholdings in the Dodecanese. The activities of the Agricultural Bank of Greece have helped to alleviate this problem, but the scope of its programs needs to be broadened. A tangerine-grower on Kos exemplifies the vulnerability of the farmer to creditors:

> I've taken a six-month loan to better my farm and my payment is due on November 30. If the wind is bad or we have frost, I must ask for a postponement. Then do you know what happens? the interest rate will jump to twelve per cent. Another bad year and it doubles again. All that's needed is several bad years and I could even go to jail.[1]

A final problem relates to the dangers of agricultural progress in the islands. The transition from a subsistence-oriented economy to a market-oriented economy has produced greater specialization at the individual-entrepreneur level. While this shift has produced a greater cash income and a general rise in the standard-of-living, the Dodecanese farmer is now increasingly vulnerable to crop failure or fluctuations in market prices. In addition, changes in transportation and accessibility have brought the Dodecanese into competition from other producing areas in the Aegean. The former subsistence crop complex, by contrast, carried some built-in insurance against the failure of any one crop.

Geographical Contrasts in Island Agriculture

The environmental and natural resource combinations of each island embody major differences in the agricultural capabilities of the Dodecanese islands. On the basis of capabilities for future agricultural development,

---

[1]Personal interview, Kos, November 26, 1963.

Kyriakou Phina recognizes three major groups of islands in the Dodecanese:[1]
Group 1—Rhodes, Kos, Leros, Telos, Patmos, and Kalymnos—has the best possibilities for agricultural development, especially for specialized production for
distant markets. Group 2—Karpathos, Astypalia, Kasos, and Nisyros—is better
suited for pastoral activities and tree-cultivation. Group 3—Chalki, Symi, and
Kastellorizo—is better suited for other economic activities (e.g., fishing,
handicrafts) because of the islands' more barren nature and restricted agricultural resources.

Due in large part to these major differences of agricultural potential,
the relative success of each island in agricultural activities differs markedly.
Some islands rely heavily upon agriculture as the dominant economic activity
while others have attempted, often unsuccessfully, to develop collateral sectors
of the economy. The relative success of each creates major repercussions in the
economic, social, and political geography of the islands. Several examples may
suggest the various effects of agriculture upon island life. Since our concern
is primarily with the impact of agriculture, three examples have been selected
from the Group 1 class of islands where agriculture is the dominant activity.

Rhodes

Among the Dodecanese, Rhodes is distinguished both by its sheer size
and its large lowland areas of relatively fertile soil, located principally in
the northwestern and northeastern coastal plains. It has, therefore, a comparatively large area of arable land upon which to develop agricultural industries.
Moreover, the location of these agricultural lands in close proximity to Rhodes
gives these areas fine accessibility which is of crucial importance in the marketing of agricultural products.

Both accessibility and the resource base, then, play an important role
in the spatial pattern of agriculture in Rhodes. Conforming to the basic tenets
of Von Thunen's land-use theory, a zonation of agricultural activity has evolved
(Figure 19). Adjacent to the city of Rhodes, villages specialize in fresh fruits
and vegetables, vineyards, and olive production. Agriculture in this area is
market-oriented and more progressive than in inland areas. Further in the interior, greater reliance is placed upon grains and pastoral activities. Agriculture is transitional between market and subsistence orientation. Finally, in
inaccessible areas in the southern portion of the island, the traditional pattern
of subsistence agriculture remains little disturbed. Analysis of agriculture in
two Rhodian villages illustrates both the spatial zonation of agriculture within
the island of Rhodes and also the relations of agricultural activity to other

---

[1]Kyriakou I. Phina, ʿΗ γεωργία τῆς Δωδεκανήσου καὶ αἱ προϋποθέσεις
ἀναπτύξεως αὐτῆς (Rhodes, Greece: 1961), p. 35.

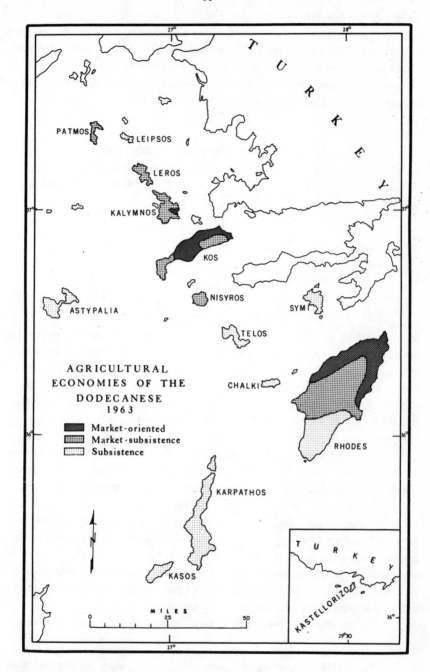

Figure 19.—Agricultural economies of the Dodecanese Islands in 1963.

aspects of village life.

   Paradeision.—Located less than one-half hour by bus from Rhodes, Paradeision exemplified the character of agricultural development within the most
accessible farmlands. In this village of 1,893 inhabitants, approximately sixty
per cent were engaged in agricultural occupations in 1963.[1] Estimated production
of chief crops in 1963 is contained in Table 7.

TABLE 7

VILLAGE OF PARADEISION
ESTIMATED PRODUCTION OF CHIEF CROPS, 1963[a]

Crop	Production (in tons)
Potatoes	1,000
Grain	100
Onions	600
Tomatoes	3,000
Cabbages and Cucumbers	100

[a]Source: Personal Interview with Village Secretary, November 15, 1963

In Paradeision, livestock serve only as a supplement to the more important cultivated crops. In most years, the Paradeision farmer receives a comparatively
high agricultural income of between 15,000 and 30,000 drachmas ($500-$1,000) per
year. The total income of the family in 1963, however, averaged closer to
100,000 drachmas ($3,333) when all male members of the family, receipts from
relatives outside the village (ἐξωτερικὸ), and part-time work in Rhodes are
considered.

   The chief source of agricultural wealth in Paradeision is tomatoes which
compete on the Athenian market with production from Krete and the Peloponessos.
Success depends primarily upon timing—whoever harvests the first good crop in
March and April skims the cream off the market. In 1962 and 1963, the market
price of tomatoes was good (three drachmas per kilogram) and Paradeision farmers
fared well. Even in poor years, however, the villagers have some protection
against market fluctuations because Paradeision has its own small factory for
manufacturing tomato paste. In 1961 when the market prices for tomatoes was
very low, Paradeision salvaged much of its crop through processing, while other
villages suffered complete losses due to spoilage.

   Unlike most Dodecanese agricultural communities, Paradeision boasts a

---

[1]The village secretary of Paradeision, Rhodes, supplied the following
data on November 15, 1963.

system of windmills which provides water for irrigation and household uses. The village secretary proudly informed us that each home had indoor plumbing and "toilets are the signs of civilization here." He further informed us that Paradeisians were "progressive people" who built irrigation canals and agricultural roads—activities not commonly undertaken by the local Dodecanesian community.

The relative success of agriculture in Paradeision has ramifications throughout the breadth of village life. Because of the possibility of self-improvement in agriculture and access to part-time employment in the nearby city of Rhodes, the rapid depopulation characteristic of rural areas in the Dodecanese has not affected Paradeision. Instead, between 1951 and 1961 the population of the village increased six per cent. In addition, there is a greater willingness to experiment with new crops and techniques. Although agriculture is by no means a lucrative occupation, the ability of farmers to realize a comparatively high standard of living is a boon to service functions in the community. The mayor of Paradeision summed up the achievements of the village by proudly pointing out that it was one of the few Dodecanese communities outside of the city of Rhodes to have a cinema. Perhaps the greatest benefit, however, has been a reaffirmation in the possibilities of successful tillage of the soil. The farming livelihood in Paradeision, however, is characteristic of only a small portion of the Dodecanese and more inaccessible villages are more representative of island agriculture.

Afantou.—Relatively inaccessible from the city of Rhodes, Afantou illustrates the characteristics of a transitional agricultural zone. Although one of the larger inland producing centers, it is substantially less prosperous and progressive than Paradeision. The major crops of the village for 1963 are shown in Table 8. Of the 2,800 inhabitants of the village, eighty per cent are engaged in farming although some are able to supplement their income by occasional work in Rhodes.[1] Despite encouragement in various forms by the central government and a relatively constant population, agricultural production is declining in Afantou.

The deterioration in agriculture stems from a number of sources. Foremost among these, according to village leaders, is emigration, which has led to the abandonment of fields and the loss of the younger and more vigorous segment of the population. In addition, the lack of factories to process crops leaves the local farmer exposed to the caprices of agricultural prices and shifts in the market. Farm fragmentation contributes to the difficulties in realizing maximum efficiency in production. Nevertheless, schemes for land consolidation

---

[1]The village secretary of Afantou, Rhodes, supplied the following data on November 6, 1963.

have aroused little popular support.

TABLE 8

ESTIMATED PRODUCTION OF MAJOR CROPS IN AFANTOU, 1963[a]

Crop	Estimated Production (tons)
Olive Oil	100
Apricots	450
Figs	50
Citrus Fruits	10
Tomatoes	150
Cucumbers	175
Peppers	2
Grain	50

[a]Source: Personal Interview with the Village Mayor, November 6, 1963.

Chiefly due to these hindrances, average farm income in Afantou is between 1,000-1,500 drachmas ($33-$50) per annum—"only enough to eat and perhaps
a little for a bit of clothing." The villager's major sources of income are remittances from Germany and the United States, supplemented by small sums earned
by occasional labor in the city of Rhodes. These sources raise family income to
an estimated 15,000-17,000 drachmas ($500-$567) per year. The contrast, however,
between agricultural receipts and these other sources is scarcely an encouragement for agricultural activity.

Paradeision and Afantou illustrate the diversity of agriculture within
the island of Rhodes. Greater contrasts would emerge if consideration included
the more remote and backward villages of southern Rhodes. With an island as
large as Rhodes, the great diversity among villages renders impossible any attempt to characterize universal features of island agriculture. The island of
Kos, the second most important agricultural island of the Dodecanese, displays
far greater uniformity.

Kos

"Kos is the spoiled child of the group. You know it at once without
going ashore. It is green, luxuriant and a little dishevelled. An island that
does not bother to comb its hair."[1] Thus does Durrell describe the abundant
verdure of Kos which contrasts so strikingly with the more formidable barrenness
of other islands of the Dodecanese. This ostentatious display of greenery provides clues to the source of agricultural wealth in the island.

_____

[1]Durrell, op. cit., p. 61.

The base for agricultural activity is the extensive plain lying along the northern coast. Each of the four villages and the city of Kos itself focus their farming efforts upon this fertile, lowland area, although the settlements themselves still lie on the central uplands which offered natural protection from pirate raids during earlier periods of the island's history.

Prior to World War II, Kos was renowned for its fresh garden produce, especially lettuce and radishes which were shipped, via special sailing vessels, to Egypt in all seasons.[1] At present, however, Koan farmers specialize heavily in tomato production (see Table 9). One cooperative and six private tomato factories, employing a total of 100 persons, have been established to process portions of the annual crop for shipment to mainland Greece. Livestock forms a strong secondary focus for specialization and Kos ships fresh meat to Nisyros, Kalymnos, Symi, Leros, and Rhodes. Because of the relatively advanced state of agriculture, the fertile land resources, good accessibility, and a related processing industry, Koans are generally relatively successful agriculturalists.

Nevertheless, important agricultural problems continue to thwart greater progress. Strong winds from the south are a major danger to olive and citrus fruit growers. Years of higher than normal humidity increase the numbers of caryatids, Mediterranean flies, which cannot yet be effectively controlled. Both of these environmental problems have caused major fluctuations in annual production.

Other problems arise from the cultural environment. One custom in Kos, and throughout Greece generally, caused by the chronic deficiency of meat in the diet, is "Χειροσφάγια" hog-slaughtering.[2] Every farmer slaughters a hog in the fall and fries the meat in little pieces. Beef, salt, and melted fat all are combined in a meat melange which lasts the year round. Since there are no butchers in most villages and consequently no meat available, this dietary innovation solves the problem of a meat need. The problem remains, however, that hogs are slaughtered prematurely before attaining full growth.

The tourist industry of Kos creates an added market difficulty for the Koan farmer. Whereas Rhodian tourism relies chiefly upon foreign sources, most tourists in Kos are Greek civil servants and laborers. Because of the resulting differences in tourist affluence, prices for food and agricultural commodities in Kos must be kept substantially lower than in Rhodes. Koan farmers, consequently, fare more poorly than their Rhodian counterparts. This agricultural contrast is apparent in the situation of one Koan farming village, Pyli.

---

[1]Great Britain, Naval Intelligence Division, op. cit., p. 109.

[2]Personal interview with K. Nikolopoulos, agronomist of the Agricultural Service of Kos, November 26, 1963.

TABLE 9

AREAS CULTIVATED AND PRODUCTION OF SELECTED CROPS IN KOS, 1962[a]

Crop	Area (in stremmata)	Trees	Production (in tons)
Tree Crops			
Peaches		3,000	8
Almonds		50,000	70
Figs		50,000	70
Lemons		20,000	450,000 pieces
Oranges		4,600	32,500 pieces
Tangerines		27,000	700,000 pieces
Olives		150,000	50 tons eating
			375 tons oil
Vegetables			
Tomatoes	17,500		22,500
Watermelons	7,000		7,500
Melons	1,200		1,200
Onions	600		600
Grains			
Wheat	9,000		495
Barley	22,000		924
Oats	8,000		344
Other Crops			
Tobacco	2,675		127
Sesame	700		17
Livestock			
Cattle	7,745 head		
Sheep	16,000 head		
Goats	17,500 head		
Pigs	5,200 head		
Poultry	20,000 head		
Hives	4,695 head		

[a]Source: Ministry of Agriculture, Kos.

Pyli.—A village of 1,884 inhabitants, Pyli is almost exclusively an agricultural community. During the redistribution of land following the expulsion of the Italians in World War II, each landless farmer in Pyli received ten to twenty stremmata to encourage his return to agricultural activity. Of 400 families, all except twenty families, who are pastoralists, rely chiefly upon crop cultivation.[1] No one travels to the city of Kos for supplementary work, nor is there any fishing.

---

[1]The mayor of Pyli, Kos, supplied the following data on November 28, 1963.

Each farmer has, on the average, twenty-five to thirty **stremmata**, usually divided into four or five parcels. The villagers specialize heavily in the production of tomatoes for canning. The village, as a whole, produces about 5,000 tons annually. In addition, a variety of other crops are grown—olives, watermelons, sesame, tobacco and grains. With fertile lands, good accessibility and nearby tomato-processing plants, the farmer of Pyli averages between 10,000-12,000 drachmas ($333-$400) annually for his family. Several families make as much as 30,000 drachmas ($1,000), a very large sum in the Dodecanese.

The chief problems of the Pyli farmers arise from fluctuations in market prices. Prices for tomatoes, for example fluctuate by as much as 100 per cent from one year to another. If a decline in prices coincides with a time when a farmer has indebted himself to build a well or irrigation ditch, he may even be put in prison. In Pyli, a lack of electricity hampers agricultural development through limitations on the expansion of irrigation. These problems, however, as serious as they may be, are minor compared to the misfortunes suffered on the island of Telos.

Telos

Despite the extensive fertile lowlands of Telos, agriculture remains underdeveloped on this island. Formerly, the island produced a diversity of crops such as almonds, figs, grapes, and tangerines. Within this crop combination, however, almonds were easily the most important money-earner. Prior to World War II, Telos reaped over 100 tons of almonds annually and shipped them to foreign markets.[1] Following the war, however, disease struck the almond trees and, in 1962, only forty tons of almonds were harvested, enough only for local use and for distant relatives. In addition, the market price for almonds has declined precipitously over the last decade.

Telos illustrates the precarious position of agriculture on most Dodecanese islands. Despite government assistance in combating the almond disease and in planting new trees, Telos farmers have been unable to adjust agriculturally. Telos suffers from poor accessibility since island steamers stop only irregularly—once a week in 1963. Islanders have turned to the old subsistence crop combination—grains, garden crops, and pastoralism. The most important effect, however, is that everyone is now trying to emigrate, as agriculture is no longer profitable.

The failure of agriculture reverberates in other sectors of island life. Because of a general lack of income and of commercial production, islanders are cut off from the outside world. Inhabitants now leave the island only for medical necessity or a visit to close relatives. One village is presently abandoned

---

[1]Personal interview with the village constable, December 31, 1963.

because of extensive emigration, while houses stand empty in the others. Islanders have lost all hope for self-improvement and now look entirely to the outside world for innovation.. A major disappointment for all islanders in 1963 was the failure of an anticipated group of foreign tourists to come to Telos. A stooped old woman expressed the prevalent sorrow by rhetorically asking, "Why shouldn't some foreigners fall here? It's a clean and beautiful place!"[1]

The contrasting examples of Rhodes, Kos, and Telos illustrate the geographical difference in Dodecanesian agriculture. Only the more accessible portions of Rhodes, Kos, and the tangerine-producing area of Kalymnos have specialized, market-oriented agricultural economies. Only in these areas does the farmer receive an income comparable with other sectors of the economy and an opportunity for market agricultural progress. On other islands, agriculture remains underdeveloped and, in many cases, production is declining.

Several attempts have been made to classify the islands according to their agricultural production or capabilities. J. L. Myres notes that Rhodes and Kos differ from all other Dodecanese islands in their high natural fertility and extensive agricultural resources.[2] Nisyros, Patmos, and Leros have fertile agricultural resources but are too small for large-scale production and have poorer commercial contacts. Finally, the other islands are characterized as less fertile and agriculturally more limited. Phina also recognizes three major groups of island according to their agricultural capabilities.[3] Both classifications are based on an intimate familiarity with agriculture in the Dodecanese, but neither makes explicit the criteria for classification.

The results of a classification of Dodecanese agriculture on the basis of present agricultural organization is contained in Figure 19. Market-oriented agricultural areas are those with predominantly specialized production for distant markets. In most cases, this is the most successful agriculture in the Dodecanese, and agricultural revenue per family averages over 10,000 drachmas ($333) per year. Market-subsistence agriculture is a transitional economy where specialized crops for sale supplement the traditional subsistence crops. Agricultural family income generally averages below 10,000 drachmas. Finally, the areas of subsistence agriculture focus upon production for domestic needs. Grains, olives, and fresh vegetables are the most important crops, but there is little or no surplus for sale. Generally, individuals in these areas rely heavily upon remittances for whatever income they can obtain.

---

[1]Personal interview, Livadia, Telos, December 30, 1963.

[2]Great Britain, Naval Intelligence Division, op. cit., pp. 73-76.

[3]Supra, pp. 52-53.

Political Geography and the Agricultural Experience

Agricultural activity in the Dodecanese has a number of implications for the political geography of the islands. The experience of each farmer in tilling the land inevitably influences the way he views his place in the local environment and in the world at large. This perceived role has resulted in a distinctive imprint on the Dodecanese landscape. Variations in agricultural production, organization, and income are, as emigration exemplifies, closely-related to a wide range of economic and social characteristics. The nature of the agricultural experience as a whole is an important element in shaping and influencing political attitudes and behavior. Finally, the role of government in altering existing agricultural patterns illustrates the reciprocity between local livelihood and the political order.

Man and Nature

Because of his low technological level, environmental problems exact a heavy toll on the wealth, indeed the very sustenance, of the Dodecanese farmer. His view of his relationship to the physical environment is one of constant con-flict. To a question concerning his prospects for the year, the Dodecanesian farmer invariably responds with a gesture of helplessness and, indicating his patch of land, will exclaim "ἔρημος" (desert), "βουνὰ" (mountains), "πέτρες" (rocks). Frequently, he will go on to explain that the farmer, like the sailor, must fight the natural elements. "Παλεύομαι" (we are wrestling) indicates the character of the relationship.[1] Farmers view their harvest as bounty wrested from the earth, and then only by prodigious efforts in the face of formidable odds.

Accompanying this cognitive dissonance between man and environment is a deep-rooted fatalism. Years of disastrously-poor harvests inevitably stand out more strongly in the islander's memory than the years of abundant harvests. Crop failures, droughts, severe winds—all are explained by allusions to God. A characteristic evaluation of farming prospects is: "Ἂν θέλει ὁ θεός, θὰ 'έχομε καλὸ χρόνο" (If God wills it, we will have a good year). Even showers are "Ὁ θεὸς βρέχει" (God raining). A general feeling of helplessness before environ-mental, and by extension all outside forces, gives rise to the most frequently heard of all Greek expressions "Τὶ νὰ κάνουμε" (What can we do?). This fatalism carries over into the social and political spheres and results in a widespread indifference or apathy and a marked lack of individual and community initative. Instead the Dodecanesian looks for help to the "ἐξωτερικὸ" (outside world),

---

[1] For a similar view towards nature on the Boeotian plain near Mt. Par-nassos, see Friedl, op. cit., p. 75. Friedl describes the nature of the villag-er's feelings with respect to each other and the world as "tension."

whether it be a government agronomist, a "βουλευτής" (representative) in Athens, or a wealthy (or supposedly so) relative in Australia, Germany, or the United States.

The lack of independent initiative and the fatalistic acceptance of prevailing situations and methods create major obstacles to economic and political progress in the islands. Phina considers the psychological problem of the Dodecanese farmer to be the greatest obstacle to agricultural development.[1] From his wide experience he concludes that "every agricultural innovation takes on the character of a clash with a hidden enemy, especially with the residents of mountainous territory."[2] In Nisyros, the island's seawalls and only road are eroding away in several places where a very small effort would correct the damage (Figure 20). Instead, the mayor sends a letter to Athens with the small hope that something may be done. When asked what she was doing to prevent coastal flood damage to her home, one woman replied she could only "write to Athens and tell them what God has done"[3] and hope that they would give her a small sum of money. In short, this apathy and fatalism have encouraged the drift of political functions and community activities from the local to the central government. In addition, these obstacles thwart attempts at economic planning or more direct assumption by the individual of political responsibilities.

The fundamental underlying hostility between man and nature also finds expression in attitudes toward land and agriculture. Contrary to popular notions of the peasant farmer, there is, on the whole, little love between the Dodecanese agriculturalist and the land he tills. Few islanders consider farming to be an attractive occupation. Like their classical ancestors, Dodecanesians share a general disdain for manual labor, and the dream of every farmer is that his son will be a professional man—a lawyer, doctor, civil servant—or even a respectable merchant. Greeks themselves view the essential social distinction as whether or not the work is clean (καθαρή δουλειά) and carried out in a white shirt and tie. Few desire to send their sons to agricultural training school, and those who do feel obliged to explain such an irregular choice. If the opportunity arises, the farmer himself will usually quickly abandon his land to open yet another in the myriad of small shops which trade in the low-value necessities of local village life. Or if periodic remittances permit a possible existence, however frugal, farm lands will be neglected while their owner assumes an idle position of leisure. Seldom are such remittances used for agricultural improvements.

---

[1]Phina, op. cit., pp. 36-37.

[2]Ibid.

[3]Personal interview, Nisyros, December 15, 1963.

Figure 20. A rapidly eroding seawall in Nisyros. The Turks originally constructed the seawall to protect the vital road running along the perimeter of the island. The Italians later rebuilt and strengthened it. Neglect by Greek authorities, however, has allowed the seawall to crumble and wave action is now undermining the nearby road. When asked what the local community intended to do, one local inhabitant responded, "What can we do? We have written to Athens."

In Karpathos, formerly an important agricultural island, inhabitants boast that their only production now is "dollars."[1] A Karpathian physician observed that people are no longer "very energetic" and seek more lucrative jobs abroad, while the former intensively-tilled lands are now largely abandoned.[2]

The effects of these attitudes toward the land are implicit in the Dodecanese landscape. Seldom does one encounter the soft, decorous, "garden" appearance of the Italian landscape. Durrell describes the difference between the Italian and Greek landscape as follows:

> Italy and Greece, if you like, the lovers: the Italy of the domestic arts, the passionate feeling for husbandry and family order, the feeling of a vineyard built with the fingers, pinch by pinch, into terraces of household wine: Italy that conquers as a wife or nurse, encroaching on nature with the arts of love. The Greece: the vertical, masculine, adventurous consciousness of the archipelago, with its mental anarchy and indiscipline, touched everywhere with the taste for agnosticism and spare living: Greece born into the sexual intoxication of the light, which seems to shine upward from inside the very earth, to illuminate these bare acres of squill and asphodel. It seems to me so clear that their arts of life are not divergent ones, but the complementaries of each other.[3]

Only the public gardens of Rhodes and Kos, themselves the legacy of the era of Italian occupation, constitute exceptions to the largely-barren, rugged, and untamed Greek landscape. That the islands remain largely an undomesticated landscape is the more surprising when one considers the extensive efforts of the Greek Government.

Government and Agriculture

A second important meeting ground of agriculture and political geography lies in the role of government as a vehicle for altering the Dodecanese landscape. This theme follows in the footsteps of Derwent Whittlesey's pioneering study of the impress of central authority upon the landscape.[4]

Following unification of the Dodecanese with Greece, the Greek Government undertook an active program of agricultural development, which accounts for much of the increase in Dodecanesian agricultural production and the improvement in farming methods and equipment. At the outset, the Government, taking into account the size and needs of each family, redistributed Italian agricultural areas to landless farmers. At the same time, maximum farm size was limited to

---

[1]Personal interview with the city mayor, January 7, 1964.

[2]Personal interview with Dr. Hadjimichali, November 6, 1963.

[3]Durrell, op. cit., p. 183.

[4]Derwent S. Whittlesey, "The Impress of Effective Central Authority upon the Landscape," Annals of the Association of American Geographers, XXV (June, 1935), 85-97.

250 _stremmata_. This redistribution of land was concentrated on the islands of Rhodes and Kos where Italian landholdings were extensive. Since redistributed landholdings are contiguous rather than fragmented, agriculture in these areas is usually more efficiently organized.

The Government also actively undertook a large number of land improvement works, such as the construction of agricultural roads, fences, drainage ditches, water cisterns, wells, and irrigation facilities. It also initiated activities to improve the productivity of land and to coordinate production with domestic demand. Another area of major effort was the creation of organizations for agricultural education. Committees were established in each community to handle local problems and to introduce improved farming methods. Demonstrations illustrated new techniques, and agronomists discussed schemes for more efficient land utilization and conservation practices. The Government also founded an agricultural school at Rhodes where local students receive advanced training.[1] In fact, Rhodes now even boasts an embryonic 4-H-type program, designed to stimulate interest in farming among the island youth.

A final governmental contribution is the Agricultural Bank of Greece which seeks to alleviate the lack of credit and exorbitant interest rates which have plagued Dodecanesian farmers for centuries. Although the Bank's interest rate is seven per cent, it finances projects of many types of local improvements for as low as two per cent. Chiefly as a result of its activities, credit has become readily available at low interest rates for the first time.

Various governmental activities have been instrumental in the surge of agricultural progress since World War II. Much of this effort has been concentrated on the larger and more important agricultural islands of Rhodes and Kos, and the gains registered are impressive. Nevertheless, one hears frequently-voiced complaints that the government is handling agriculture as it handles tourism, that the larger islands are being developed at the expense of the smaller islands which need the help more. Another political problem raised by government aid is that it tends to reinforce local attitudes towards the central government. The islander's view of his relation to Athens can best be illustrated by a turn-about of John F. Kennedy's maxim to read "Ask not what you can do for your country, but what it can do for you." No effort is spared in eking every penny from the government even if this requires fraud. Government is conceived as having a one-way relationship, and the Government's effectiveness is measured in terms of how well an individual eats now as compared with then.

---

[1]Phina, Ἡ αγροτικἡ ᾽εκπαίδευσκεις τἡν Δωδεκάνησον (Rhodes, Greece: 1963).

Political Attitudes and Behavior

The agricultural experiences in the Dodecanese have important ramifications for political attitudes and behavior. Interviews with farmers and public officials indicate a strong predilection to judge the quality and effectiveness of any government in terms of easily measurable improvements in the individual's economic and social position. Fierce ideological positions eloquently defended in coffeehouse debates are frequently betrayed at the polls in the interest of the individual's pocketbook. Fundamental in this view of national politics is the juxtaposition of the basic class structure with the political parties. A characteristic response to a question regarding an individual's party preference is the assumedly self-explanatory response "I'm a farmer" or "I'm a worker." Most Dodecanesians firmly believe that all farmers and workers in the United States are Democrats and that all merchants and industrialists are Republicans. In 1963, many Dodecanesians were, and probably still are, convinced that John F. Kennedy was killed by the rich Republicans. Given this perceived class basis to political parties, they tend to see all politics as a constant struggle between the forces of the right and left. In the Dodecanese, the prevailing view of Greek parties is that the E.R.E. (National Radical Union) represents the right, the E.K. (Center Union) the Center-left, the EDA (Agricultural Pandemocratic Front) the extreme left, including the Communists, and the K.P. (Socialist Progressives) a center splinter group under the personalized leadership of Spyros Markezinis.

A spokesman for a group of farmers at a political rally in Rhodes illustrated the close identification of political attitudes and behavior with economic position. He angrily remarked that

> Konstantinos Karamanlis (former Prime Minister and leader of the E.R.E.) has eaten all he's going to—it's time for us to eat. All we want is enough to live comfortably, to feed our children, to allow them an opportunity to become 'cultured.' This time we're voting for Georgios Papandreou (leader of the E.K. and Karamanlis' successor as Prime Minister). If we still don't eat, then we'll all become Communists in the next election."[1]

A farmer from Kalymnos put it more simply: "Look, I'm sixty-two. All my life I've had only this suit. If I die tomorrow, this is what I must wear."[2] To a Greek, this would be the final degradation.

In Kos, the mayor of Pyli explained a shift of voters from Karamanlis to Papandreou thus:

---

[1]Personal interview at a political rally for Georgios Papandreou in the city of Rhodes, October 23, 1963.

[2]Ibid.

> During the Karamanlis administration there were several years when there
> was an overproduction of tomatoes and poor agricultural prices. The
> farmers held the Government strictly responsible. Every year there was
> some agricultural problem that upset the farmers so they always hope to
> find better by a change.[1]

The fact that a government representative, a local agronomist, cautioned against
overproduction after a year of good prices did not matter.

Results of more formal interviewing on Rhodian villages substantiates
the importance of economic factors in local political attitudes.[2] Of twenty-
five farmers asked "What is the greatest problem facing Greece at the present
time?" fifteen noted the need for higher, stabler agricultural prices and more
export markets. Another six cited a general rise in the present low standard-
of-living levels. Furthermore, when asked "What is the biggest issue in this
election (November, 1963)?" fourteen of the same twenty-five stated a need to
improve the lot of the farmers. In an election marked by bitter ideological
issues, this concern with the farm issue is striking.

Analysis of voting behavior in the Dodecanese is extremely difficult for
several reasons. First, despite the traditional fierce individualism of Greece,
it is clear that there are severe restraints upon freedom of electoral choice.
Informal discussion with local inhabitants confirmed that many individuals vote
out of obligation, to merchants or to doctors. This is, for example, a key factor in the strong support of Leipsos, a poor and isolated island, for the E.R.E.
(see Table 10). Moreover, it is now reasonably well-established that there have
been extensive irregularities in past elections.[3] Interference and undue pressure in the 1961 election brought on the bitter Papandreou campaign against the
government of Karamanlis. Second, motivation is difficult to discern because of
the reticence and fear on the part of Dodecanesians to discuss such matters with
an outsider. For both of these reasons, interpretation of electoral geography
is hazardous.

Nevertheless, with some trepidation, several observations will be made.
First, on the negative side, there do not appear to be any significant rural-
urban differences in voting behavior. This may be due to the large numbers of
wage-earners and landowners residing in these urban areas rather than to lack of
importance in income and occupational contrasts. Nor are there significant differences in voting by island size or economic level (Table 10). On the positive

---

[1] Personal interview with the mayor of Pyli, Kos, November 28, 1963.

[2] Interviews were conducted in Koskinou, Paradeision, and Afantou.

[3] See Mario S. Modiano, "Greek Political Troubles," The World Today, XXI
(January, 1965), 33-42.

TABLE 10

ELECTION RESULTS IN THE DODECANESE, 1961-1964[a]

(by island)

ISLAND	1961				Election of 1963				1964		
	E.R.E.	K.P. AND E.D.	P.A.M.E.	INDEPENDENT	E.R.E.	E.K.	E.D.A.	K.P.	E.R.D. AND K.P.	E.D.	E.D.A.
Rhodes	47%	47	6	---	36	52	4.5	7.5	36	64	---
Kos	46	47	7	---	28	65	6	1	27	73	---
Kalymnos	33	62	5	---	25.5	70	3.5	1	19.5	80.5	---
Karpathos	54	45	1	---	30.5	62.5	1	6	29	71	---
Leros	47	52	1	---	31	39	3	27	31	69	---
Symi	51	44	5	---	33	60	4	3	30	70	---
Patmos	58	42	---	---	43	52	1	4	34	66	---
Astypalia	42	57	1	---	32.5	65	1	1.5	18	82	---
Nisyros	40	58	2	---	36.5	61	1	1.5	35	65	---
Kasos	75	25	---	---	60.5	38.8	---	.7	48	52	---
Leipsos	76	24	---	---	62	29	6	3	45	55	---
Chalki	39	61	---	---	37	54	---	9	28	72	---
Kastellorizo	52	45	3	---	23	75	---	2	13	87	---
Telos	69	31	---	---	34	64	---	2	19	81	---

[a] Source: Nomarch of the Dodecanese

side, however, interpretation of the electoral geography does cast light upon
changes in the bases of political support.

The election of November, 1963, resulting in the fall of the Karamanlis
regime after eight years and the success of the Papandreou-led center party, was
widely interpreted as being caused by a shift in the farm vote, especially in
northern Greece. Voting results in the Dodecanese substantiate the widespread
defections in predominantly agricultural areas. An important plank in
Papandreou's campaign platform was a promise to increase farmers' aid, loans,
and assistance; and, in fact, he intimated that arrangements to this end had
already been conducted with the Agricultural Bank of Greece.[1] The shift in
support to Papandreou and the E.K. was especially marked on poorer agricultural
islands such as Kastellorizo where the E.R.E. received 52 per cent in 1961, but
only 13 per cent in 1964. Telos, with severe agricultural problems, gave the
E.R.E. 69 per cent in 1961 but only 19 per cent in 1964.

In an attempt at further study of electoral shifts between 1961 and
1963, voting results in Rhodes were analyzed by major agricultural zones (Table
11).

TABLE 11

ELECTION RESULTS IN RHODES, 1961-1963[a]
(by agricultural zone)

Agricultural Zone	Election of										
	1961				1963				1964		
	E.R.E.	K.P. and E.K.	P.A.M.E.	INDEPENDENTS	E.R.E.	E.K.	E.D.A.	K.P.	E.R.E. and K.P.	E.K.	E.D.A.
City of Rhodes	45	45	10	---	35	54	5	6	38	62	---
Market-oriented Zone	45	48	6	1	35	49	5	11	35	65	---
Market-oriented and subsistence Zone	54	45	.5	.5	42	50	1	7	38	62	---
Subsistence Zone	62	37	1	---	43	46	1	10	43	57	---

[a]Source: Nomarch of the Dodecanese

[1]Speech delivered in the city of Rhodes by Georgios Papandreou, October
23, 19639

The results show a close correlation between poorer agricultural areas and major shifts in support from the E.R.E. to the E.K. Whereas support for the E.R.E. declined by ten per çent in the market-oriented agricultural zone, the decline in support in subsistence agricultural areas was fully nineteen percent. In this way, electoral results bear out the findings of both the formal and informal interviewing and attest to the important role of the agricultural experience in voting behavior.

CHAPTER IV

THE SPONGE-MEN

'Απὸ τὰ Δωδεκάνησα τρία 'ἔχουν τὴ χάρη   1
Σύμη, χάλκη καὶ Κάλυμνος ποὺ βγάζουν τὸ σφουγγάρι
(Of the Dodecanese, three have the favor
Symi, Chalki, and Kalymnos which extract the sponges)

Although agriculture has traditionally been the backbone of the Dodecanese economy, sponge-fishing has provided the islanders their most dramatic mo-
ments of economic prosperity and also has provided the setting for much of Dodecanesian folklore and literature. In addition, since the export of sponges has
long been a principal source of wealth, the sponge industry has played a fundamental role in creating economic, social and political differences among islands.
The struggle with the sea, as much as that with the land, has ramifications for
the political geography of the island group. The history of Dodecanese sponge-
fishing suggests ways in which these political differences evolved.

History of Dodecanesian Sponge-Fishing

Sponge-fishing has long been a source of wealth to Dodecanese islanders.[2]
Sponge impressions on painted pottery at Cnossus in Krete attest to the use of
sponges in the early Bronze Age. During the Kretan-Mycenean civilization (1900-
1750 B.C.), sponges were used for cleansing the body and for medicinal purposes.
Mothers also pacified babies by giving them pieces of sponge soaked in honey.
Even at this early time, Aristotle recognized that sponges fished from the deeper fields were lighter and more flexible than those taken from more shallow
waters. At a later date, according to Pliny, sponges were used as paint brushes
and mops, while Roman soldiers were known to carry pieces of sponge in place of
drinking containers. Because of this wide diversity of use, a widespread commerce in sponges developed the classical period.

During the Middle Ages, both churches and medical practitioners required

---

[1]I. M. Panagiotopoulou, "Λαὸς τῆς θάλασσας: Ἡ δωρικὴ ψυχὴ τῆς
Καλύμνου," 'Σλευθερία, June 14, 1963.

[2]The following discussion of the history of Dodecanesian sponge-fishing
is based upon the following: Demosthenos Chaviara Περὶ σπόγγων καὶ σπογγαλιεία
(Athens: 1916); Soterios I. Agapetides, Ἡ Δωδεκάνησος εἰς τὴν συνθήκην τῆς
εἰρήνης (Athens: 1947); Soterios I. Agapetides, Ἡ θέας τὸ μέλλον τῆς
Δωδεκάνησιακὴ σπογγαλίειας (Athens: 1946); Doxiades, op. cit., pp. 129-130;
Ernest J. Cresswell, Sponges: their Nature, History, Modes of Fishing, Varieties,
Cultivation (N. P.: 1930); Henry Moore, "The Commercial Sponges and the Sponge
Fisheries," Bulletin of the Bureau of Fisheries, XXVIII (1908), Part I.

the use of sponges. In the thirteenth century, Arnold of Villa Nova introduced the burnt sponge as a therapeutic aid for scrofula, a disease of the lymphatic glands. Because of their high iodine content, sponges were also used in the treatment of a number of other diseases. Finally, the use of sponges for bathing by the European nobility represented the last major consumption of this produce prior to the Industrial Revolution. Little wonder, then, that when Kalymnos surrendered to Suleiman II in 1521, it sent an homage of sponges and white bread, for "the sponge-diver does not grow corn, but buys flour, and buys of the best."[1]

The eighteenth and nineteenth centuries brought important changes to the Dodecanesian sponge industry. The Industrial Revolution produced a large-scale demand of sponges for industrial purposes and opened a great source of wealth for the islanders. Meanwhile, the nearly simultaneous discoveries by Kalymnos and Symi of new fishing grounds off the coast of North Africa replaced the depleted local sponge-grounds with a vast new supply. Until the Italian occupation of 1912, these rich new fields were worked almost exclusively by Dodecanesian sponge men from Kalymnos, Chalki, Symi, and Kastellorizo. Coinciding with an era of maritime commercial prosperity, this sponge-fishing activity contributed to a boon in the Dodecanesian economy and a rapid growth of population.[2]

Kalymnos illustrates the demographic effects of this short-lived period of sponge prosperity. Between 1794 and 1804, the inhabitants descended from their medieval rock castle into the new settlement of χώρα (Chora). By the Greek War of Independence in 1821, the population of the island had increased to an estimated 5,000 inhabitants.[3] By 1840, about sixty houses had been established immediately adjacent to the harbor at Ποθία (Pothia), the present city of Kalymnos, by the island's sponge men (Figure 21). Shortly before 1900, building plots in the new city were selling at prices comparable to thos prevailing in major European cities.[4] Similar economic and settlement changes occurred in Chalki, Symi, and Kastellorizo.[5]

The vicissitudes of the sponge industry illustrate the incontestable significance of political sovereignty to the demographic and economic history of the islands. Under the "privileged" status of the Dodecanese during the Turkish occupation, the laissez-faire policy of the government vis-a-vis the local

---

[1]Great Britain, Naval Intelligence Division, op. cit., p. 61.

[2]Table 1, Supra, p. 25.

[3]Ibid.

[4]Great Britain, Naval Intelligence Division, op. cit., p. 61.

[5]See especially Aristotelous D. Nestoridou, Ἡ σπογγαλιεία ἐν Χάλκη (Athens: 1930); Sot. I. Agapetides Ἡ Σύμη (Athens: 1930).

Figure 21.—The growth of settlement on the island of Kalymnos. An ancient village was located on the hillside where only a few houses now remain. Chora, situated at the head of the valley and protected by a medieval fortress, served as the major village until the nineteenth century. Maritime security and the rapid development of the sponge industry led to the creation of the present port city of Pothia. The city and the village are now coalescing to produce a pattern of continuous valley settlement.

maritime and sponge-fishing industries permitted an unprecedented period of prosperity. After the Italian occupation of 1912, however, the Italian monopoly established over the Libyan grounds forced Dodecanesian sponge-men into other areas. In 1915, all sponge-fishing was prohibited "for military reasons", while Italian sponge-boats continued their activities unmolested.[1] At the same time, the development of a competitive Turkish sponge industry and the poor local organization of sponge marketing added to the deteriorating situation. Large numbers of sponge-fishers migrated to Tarpon Springs, Florida, where they established a major sponge-fishing colony on the Gulf of Mexico. The extensive depopulation of the islands further disrupted the sponge industry and caused economic hardship throughout the islands. Since World War II, both the Dodecanese and the national Greek sponge industries have continued to decline despite governmental attempts to rejuvenate the industry (Table 12).

TABLE 12
GREEK SPONGE PRODUCTION, 1948-1962[a]

Year	Sponge Production (in kilograms)	Number of vessels	Number of divers and crew
1948	117,760	216	1,951
1949	161,280	229	2,706
1950	168,960	224	2,607
1951	143,360	194	1,970
1952	128,266	186	1,780
1953	68,836	120	1,108
1954	126,592	143	1,710
1955	135,484	159	1,614
1956	120,696	149	1,484
1957	120,184	169	1,634
1958	108,250	158	1,488
1959	100,000	105	1,186
1960	85,913	83	844
1961	70,645	87	739
1962	89,948	110	1,047

[a]Source: National Statistical Service of Greece, Statistical Yearbook of Greece, 1963 (Athens, Greece: 1964), p. 178.

---

[1]Great Britain, Naval Intelligence Division, op. cit., p. 61.

Island Contrasts in Historical Development

Prior to the Industrial Revolution, Dodecanesian sponge-fishers relied almost exclusively on local fishing grounds. The sponge industry was widely dispersed during this period, each island fishing the grounds in its immediate vicinity. In addition, the organizational and marketing arrangements of the industry were decentralized. Although a valuable source of additional income, sponges provided only a limited opportunity for large-scale development.

During the nineteenth century, however, important changes occurred in the spatial distribution of the industry. The depletion of local fishing grounds and the shift to the coastal waters of North Africa encouraged greater central-ization. Increasing needs for more mechanization, larger boats and crews, and more specialization led to a concentration of the industry upon the islands of Kalymnos, Symi, Chalki, Astypalia, and Kastellorizo. The large demand generated by industrial uses caused Kalymnos, for example, to open major depots in such European cities as London, Frankfurt, and Basel.[1] On the domestic scene, the grading, processing, and marketing of sponges employed women, girls, and old men in addition to the main working force. Moreover, as a basic industry, sponge production generated far-reaching economic reverberations through its multiplier effect.

Although actual statistics of output by island are not available, Doxiades notes that Chalki led Symi and Kalymnos at the turn of the present century.[2] Aristotelous Nestoridou records that between 1879 and 1899 people came from Symi, Kalymnos, Rhodes, and Astypalia to work in the Chalkian sponge industry.[3] The sponge-based prosperity of the islands was short-lived, however, as Italian restrictions and war destruction seriously damaged the industry. During those first years of Italian occupation, the population of the Dodecanese declined from 143,482 to 102,180 (Table 1). Depopulation in the Dodecanese was especially marked in the sponge-fishing islands. Symi, for example, declined from 22,450 in 1912 to 7,300 in 1917, while Kalymnos dropped from 23,200 to 14,950 over the same five-year period.

Nestoridou has left us a graphical portrait of Chalki during these dec-ades of decline.[4] Writing in the late 1920's, he observes that "Chalki is prac-tically deserted. Not a single μηχανικός (diver), not a single piece of work!"[5]

---

[1]Ibid.

[2]Doxiades, op. cit., p. 135.

[3]Nestoridou, op. cit., prologue.

[4]Ibid, pp. 1-105.   [5]Ibid, p. 106.

Of the population that remained, most were forced to find work in the nearby islands of Rhodes, Kalymnos, and Symi. By and large, however, remittances sent
from relations in the United States served to support the Chalkians. By 1930,
over $300,000 had been sent to this tiny island.[1] Ironically, instead of stabi-
lizing the declining population and economy of Chalki, the inflow of money only
encouraged others to leave in search of their fortune. Doxiades, for example,
observed in 1946 that because of equipment and funds sent from relatives in
America, Chalki could outfit four σκάφανορα, but only one actually worked.[2]

The other Dodecanesian sponge islands experienced a similar decline. In
1900, Symi had a population of 18,000 and a sponge-fishing fleet of between 100
and 150 vessels.[3] Under Italian occupation, this total shrank to forty ships
and gave rise to the frequently-voiced complaint that the Italians developed
Rhodes at the expense of the smaller islands. With characteristic island loyalty,
one Symian explained the decline of sponge-fishing as

> due to the relatively high literacy of Symians—they do not want such a
> dangerous and primitive occupation. Even in the past, Symians hired
> sponge-divers from other islands - Hydra, Aegina, etc. Today, sponge-
> fishing continues in Kalymnos, because the Kalymnians are not as pro-
> gressive as the Symians. Illiteracy has made sponge-fishing last there
> and die out elsewhere.[4]

Kalymnos was, in fact, the one Dodecanese island to emerge from the
Italian occupation with its sponge industry intact. During this period, the
industry became highly-concentrated on Kalymnos. Despite the difficulties of
Italian sovereignty, one prominent Kalymnian continued to build up his sponge
fleet and also established a hospital and old-age homes. Encouraged by this
local initiative, financial interests concentrated their activities upon Kalymnos
and even entered energetically into the sponge business themselves.[5] In addition, Kalymnians, both for sources of supply and for markets, ventured far more
into the non-Greek world than other Dodecanesians. Since reunification with
Greece, the other sponge islands have given up their local industries, and Dodecanesian sponge-fishing is now nearly exclusively the sole prerogative of Kalymnos.

---

[1]Ibid.

[2]Doxiades, op. cit., p. 135.

[3]Personal interview with the Mayor of Symi, December 30, 1963.

[4]Personal interview with Iannis Angelides, Symi, December 30, 1963.

[5]Personal interview with the Mayor of Leipsos, December 12, 1963.

Organization of the Sponge Industry

Systems of sponge-fishing

There are four major methods employed in Dodecanesian sponge-fishing.[1]
The γυμνοδύται (naked divers) represent the most ancient method. Clutching a
large rock with a rope attached (σκανδαλόπετρα), the diver descends to depths of
about six fathoms for periods of about three minutes. He collects the sponges
in a sack, ascends rapidly with the sponges, and another sailor in the boat
pulls the rock up by means of a rope. Under this system, sponge vessels are
only small boats manned by a captain, two rowers, and one or two divers. This
life is extremely difficult since the diver makes twenty to thirty descents in
a day, has little or no protection from the environment, and cannot eat or drink
during the day. Consumption of food and water is restricted to the one evening
meal. This system is the most difficult and least productive, but is still used
in the shallow local waters and in rocky grounds which cannot be fished by other
means.

A second method of sponge-fishing is by σκάφανδρο (diving-suit). Here
the diver is equipped with a rubber suit and headgear, and air is supplied by a
hose operated from the ship. In shallow waters of two to five fathoms, the
diver can operate up to two or three hours, while in deeper waters of thirty-
five to forty fathoms, especially off the coast of North Africa, the time is
limited to twenty minutes. Under this system, the ships are larger (five to ten
tons) and are equipped with a small propeller motor. Each ship contains ten to
twelve divers and usually an equivalent number of crew members. After the diver
brings the sponges to the surface, initial processing of the sponges is carried
out on board the ship.

The σκάφανδρο system was first used in the Aegean in 1860 and was instrumental in the great expansion of sponge production. It still is the most efficient system both in the quantity and quality of production. Nevertheless, it
remains highly unpopular with Greek sponge-fishers. Equipment is largely anti-
quated, and the method is dangerous to the divers. Ascent and descent must be
slow or death, paralysis, or illness can result from the "bends." Unfortunately,
many Dodecanesians descend slowly but are too impatient on the way upward. There
is also considerable danger from sharks, and several Kalymnians have recently
been killed or maimed by these "σκυλοψάρια." In 1946, Doxiades calculated that
for every 100,000 sponges fished, one diver was killed. In addition, mishaps

---

[1]The following discussion is based upon Doxiades, op. cit., pp. 129-149;
Konsola, op. cit., p. 62; Panagiotopoulou, op. cit.; William Manus, "Kalymnos
and its Sponge Divers," Greek Heritage, Vol. I, No. 3 (1964), p. 62; interviews
with George Lysikatos, gymnasium philologist of Kalymnos, on December 1 and 2,
1963.

occurred to eight per cent of all divers.[1] In 1961, twelve Kalymnian divers were crippled during the season's work (Table 13). As a result, one serious limitation to a further expansion of the Dodecanese sponge industry at the present time is the difficulty of diver recruitment.

The third system of Dodecanesian sponge-fishing is the _fernez_. As in skin diving, the diver has a light-weight suit, a helmet with a mask, and an oxygen tank mounted on his back. While the organization of the crew is similar to that of the σκάφανδρο, the _fernez_ is simpler and less expensive. The duration of the dive is shorter and depends upon the personal resistance of the diver to the colder waters of the deep. Generally, this system is less productive than the σκάφανδρο.

A final system employed by the islanders is the γαγάβα (dredge). In this method, a net or sack six to nine yards long is dragged along the bottom of the sea. Because of its highly destructive effects upon sponge fields, it is prohibited in all parts of the Western Hemisphere. Since all sponges, large and small, are taken up in the sacks, the grounds are rapidly depleted. In addition, dragging also reduces the over-all quality of the sponges, because many are damaged in this fishing process. Despite these harmful qualities, its use is still permitted in areas of the eastern Mediterranean, although the system is held in disrepute by most sponge-fishers.

Among these major sponge-fishing systems, the γυμνοιδύται (naked divers) have traditionally been the more important, especially when the major production of sponges was concentrated in the local shallow waters of the Aegean. With the shift of the industry to North Africa, however, the deeper waters have required increasing use of the σκάφανδρο. Moreover, as the fishing fleet has become more mechanized and centrally organized, greater efficiency and higher profits have resulted from the latter system. The extent of the shift to the σκάφανδρο method is illustrated by Table 14.

---

[1]Doxiades, _op. cit._, p. 138.

TABLE 13

SUMMARY OF GREEK SPONGE-FISHING (1961)[a]

Port of Departure	Vessels Employed					Sponge-Production in Kilograms						Crew			Accidents	
	Total	Diving Suits	Fermez	Gagave	Boats	Total	Diving Suits	Fermez	Gagave	Boats	Other Vessels	Total	Divers	Seamen	Deaths	Cripplings
Total Year	87	44	5	17	21	70,645	49,909	7,014	2,574	5,948	5,200	739	415	324	---	12
Summer Period	83	44	5	13	21	70,172	49,909	7,014	1,101	5,948	5,200	730	415	315	---	12
Kalymnos	39	21	5	--	13	45,877	33,412	7,014	---	5,451	---	464	299	165	---	12
Symi	8	--	-	8	--	1,695	---	---	1,695	---	---	33	---	33	---	---
Kos	5	--	-	5	--	406	---	---	406	---	---	13	---	13	---	---
Limnos	13	13	-	--	--	12,880	12,880	---	---	---	---	120	66	54	---	---
Trikiri Volos	10	10	-	--	--	3,617	3,617	---	---	---	---	82	32	50	---	---
Ermioni	8	--	-	--	8	497	---	---	---	497	---	18	18	---	---	---
Other Areas	--	--	-	--	--	5,200	---	---	---	---	5,200	---	---	---	---	---
Winter Period	4	--	-	4	--	473	---	---	473	---	---	9	---	9	---	---
Paros	4	--	-	4	--	473	---	---	473	---	---	9	---	9	---	---

[a]Source: National Statistical Service of Greece, Statistical Yearbook of Greece, 1962 (Athens, Greece: National Printing Office, 1963), p. 190.

TABLE 14

CHANGES IN THE DODECANESE SPONGE-FISHING FLEET, 1946-1962[a]

Type of Vessel	Numbers	
	1946	1962
σκάφανδρα	30	40
fernez	15	15
γαγάβα	29	15
boats	53	25
(a) with naked divers	b	5
(b) with harpoons	b	20
Total	127	95

[a]Source: For the 1946 data, Doxiades, op. cit., p. 135; for the 1962 data, Ministry of Industry.

[b]Data not available.

Sponge-Fishing Grounds

Dodecanese sponge-fishers carry on their activities over a wide area extending from the Aegean islands west to Corsica and south to the North African coast. While formerly concentrated in the Aegean Sea, the major fishing grounds now lie outside Greek waters (Figure 22). The largest and most productive grounds lie along the United Arab Republic, Libya, Tunisia, Syria, Cyprus, Turkey, and Krete. Prior to World War II, relatively few restrictions were placed upon Dodecanesian sponge-fishers throughout the Mediterranean. Since World War II, however, the governments involved have raised many obstacles. The postwar period has witnessed a constant struggle by the Greek Government to preserve fishing rights within the territorial waters of these states. Table 15 illustrates the crucial importance of these foreign sources to Dodecanesian sponge production. In the last several decades, native divers of these countries,

TABLE 15

DODECANESE SPONGE PRODUCTION BY FISHING GROUND, 1958-1962[a]
(in kilograms)

Fishing Ground	Year	
	1958	1962
Greek waters	32,640	15,239
Libya (Cyreniac Gulf)	31,046	----
Libya (Tripoli)	5,952	5,158
United Arab Republic	16,422	26,737
International Waters	7,424	----

[a]Source: Konsola, op. cit., p. 62.

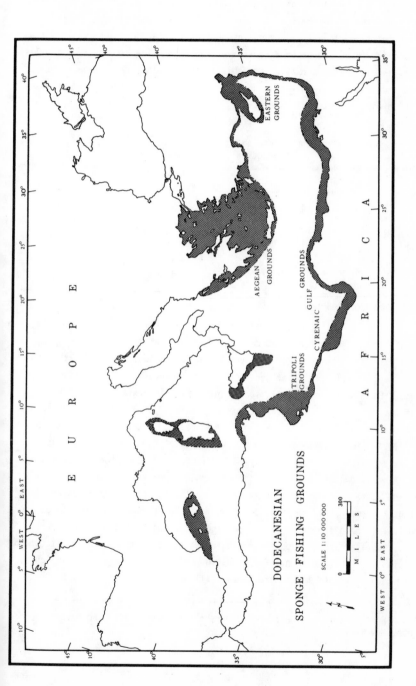

Figure 22.—Dodecanese sponge-fishing grounds in 1964.

trained by Greeks, have begun to exploit these areas for themselves. The major problem of the Dodecanese sponge industry at the present time is the procurement of fishing rights in these foreign areas.

Sponge Production and Marketing

Prior to World War II, sponge production in the Dodecanese was 120 tons; in 1962, this figure had dropped to forty-seven tons. The decline over the last six years is especially striking, as Table 16 shows. This decline is principally due to decreasing yields in the sponge-fishing grounds and increasing restrictions in foreign territorial waters.

TABLE 16

COMPARISON OF DODECANESE AND GREEK SPONGE-FISHING, 1956-62[a]
(Production in kilograms)

Year	Total Dodecanese Production	Total Production of Greece
1956	107,800	120,696
1958	93,484	108,250
1960	47,793	85,645
1961	47,055	70,645
1962	47,134	89,948

[a]Source: Nomarchy of the Dodecanese.

Despite the decline of sponge production, it remains the overwhelming source of export income for the Dodecanese islands (Table 17). Since approximately ninety-eight per cent of the sponge production is for export rather than domestic use, it eclipses other Dodecanese export products in value of foreign earnings. Between 1955 and 1961, sponge production accounted for ninety per cent of the value of all Dodecanese exports (Table 17). In 1961, sponge production accounted for $1,623,823, while in 1962 the annual take was approximately $2,000,000.[1] Since Kalymnos now is the sole sponge-producing island, this relatively vast wealth distinguishes her markedly from all other Dodecanese islands.

A breakdown of the destination of sponge exports shows that the United States and Western Europe are the major buyers (Table 18), although Japan has very recently emerged as an important consumer. Sales to the United States are presently falling off because of the resurgence of the Gulf of Mexico as a source of supply. In addition, technological innovation is causing substitution in uses, as in the replacement of sponges for coloring leather with spray guns. Japan in 1963 purchased the entire annual "silk sponge" production of 6,000

---

[1]The 1962 data was obtained by personal interview with the Mayor of Kalymnos, November 30, 1963.

TABLE 17

EXPORT TRADE OF THE DODECANESE 1955-1961[a]
(quantity in kilograms; value in dollars)

Category	1955 Quantity	1955 Value	1957 Quantity	1957 Value	1959 Quantity	1959 Value	1961 Quantity	1961 Value	Per Cent Average for Period
Sponges	95,616	$1,468,408	91,436	$1,714,118	82,260	$1,535,226	82,210	$1,623,823	89.9
Tangerines	400,000	40,000	468,000	46,800	609,000	60,900	900,000	90,000	3.2
Asbestos	791,000	1,316	34,637,400	53,689	21,133,000	38,733	13,065,000	37,733	2.1
Wines	-----	-----	323,949	24,139	143,060	12,273	65,689	5,739	1.7
Tobacco	-----	-----	84,231	56,044	27,557	24,665	476	412	0.8
Onions	-----	-----	317,500	15,540	-----	-----	-----	-----	0.4
Bricks & Tiles	1,803,000	15,764	458,000	7,456	-----	-----	-----	-----	0.4
Ceramics	2,500	2,237	3,000	6,527	2,026	3,953	2,053	3,230	0.2
Tomato Paste	100,000	23,240	-----	-----	-----	-----	-----	-----	0.2
Jewelry	-----	-----	8	655	10	1,675	32	5,719	0.2
Rugs	-----	-----	300	1,773	510	4,084	770	5,833	0.2
Tomatoes	-----	-----	-----	-----	-----	-----	-----	-----	0.1
Raisins	-----	-----	-----	-----	15,000	3,386	25,845	5,610	0.1
Woven Wool	-----	-----	-----	-----	481	5,933	-----	-----	0.1
Sable	32	3,892	16	1,190	-----	-----	-----	-----	0.1

[a]Source: Commercial and Industrial Organization of the Dodecanese

TABLE 18

DESTINATION OF SPONGE EXPORTS FROM THE DODECANESE, 1955-1961[a]
(Amount in kilograms; value in dollars)

Country	1955		1957		1959		1961		Average per cent 1955-1961
	Amount	Value	Amount	Value	Amount	Value	Amount	Value	
United States	36,671	596,527	36,781	707,785	31,556	680,292	16,636	402,959	39.0
France	14,153	173,650	17,915	285,565	14,967	230,837	20,132	403,806	16.4
West Germany	12,316	201,691	7,368	186,649	5,995	100,051	11,072	267,972	14.3
United Kingdom	8,621	196,300	3,902	73,536	8,214	88,660	5,509	77,893	7.8
Belgium	5,723	49,445	7,522	100,360	4,688	53,961	5,071	77,290	4.0
Czechoslovakia	1,174	28,173	2,570	72,078	3,379	107,025	4,369	77,300	3.9
Poland	2,927	35,270	1,085	40,407	1,142	39,662	500	13,950	2.1
East Germany	---	---	2,735	66,255	1,195	36,401	2,687	71,500	1.9
U.S.S.R.	---	---	---	---	1,000	22,000	4,759	81,205	1.8
Sweden	2,157	44,876	1,039	18,385	1,510	25,744	1,656	32,276	1.7
Italy	2,490	17,447	3,417	35,208	2,387	18,203	3,285	26,466	1.6
Spain	---	---	3,302	65,577	2,415	32,500	2,749	16,844	1.5
Canada	931	20,195	50	1,374	872	16,070	1,534	30,899	1.4
Norway	2,104	28,770	506	10,405	555	10,640	381	5,413	0.8
Switzerland	2,305	23,351	---	---	797	23,367	881	18,213	0.7
Denmark	970	19,504	822	10,360	162	1,858	---	---	0.4
Rumania	252	6,543	224	6,796	364	8,905	161	3,699	0.4
Austria	1,610	14,630	372	5,265	---	---	265	5,002	0.4
Portugal	160	2,639	145	3,545	185	4,032	350	8,120	0.3

[a]Source: Commercial and Industrial Organization of the Dodecanese

kilograms at a price of $200,000.[1] These sponges are increasingly being used in the Japanese cosmetic industry.

Problems of the Sponge Industry

Three major problems currently confront the sponge industry. First, as pointed out above, since the major sponge fields now lie in foreign waters, obtaining regular permits for fishing rights is crucial. Only vigorous governmental intervention kept the fields open during 1963. Since demand always exceeds the Dodecanese supply, obtaining a sufficient catch is the chief problem. Innovations are currently being made which may help to alleviate the problem of supply. In 1963, one firm in Kalymnos bought 10,000 tons of Turkish sponges for the first time and resold them on the world market.[2] Future increases in Dodecanese production depend on agreements which must be obtained from Syria, Lebanon and Cyprus to permit a shift to the potentially-productive fishing grounds further to the east.

A second problem arises from the extensive depopulation of the Dodecanese islands. The decline of sponge-fishing in Symi, Chalki, Astypalia, and Kastellorizo is intrinsically bound up with tremendous losses of population. Only Kalymnos among the sponge islands has been able to retain its inhabitants. Even in this case, however, despite the relatively high salaries for their labor ($2,000-$2,500 for the season), divers are increasingly difficult to find. The occupation of the diver not only requires courage and daring, but laborious work as well. As a result, many divers for Kalymnian ships are now obtained from other poorer islands. Nevertheless, labor recruitment remains a serious problem to the sponge ship owners.

The extensive financial requirements for entrance into the sponge industry constitute a third problem. The burdensome initial capital investment precludes a greater entrance of individual entrepreneurs. One ship costs approximately $35,000 for purchase and an annual operation. Despite the liberal terms offered by the Agricultural Bank of Greece for such an investment, few Dodecanesians are in a position to undertake such a venture. As a result, ships remain small and much of the fleet antiquated (Figure 23). Since interest rates increase at an increasing rate over time, a single poor year could be ruinous to the small investor.

---

[1] Ibid.

[2] Personal interview with sponge merchants on Kalymnos, December 2, 1963.

Figure 23.—The sponge-fishing fleet of Kalymnos in winter dry dock. These small ships ply sponge grounds extending from the local waters to the coastal areas of Africa. The ships provide few comforts, and divers and crew alike must brave constant exposure to danger and discomfort.

Impact of the Sponge Industry

Economic impact

The major economic ramifications of the sponge industry have been alluded to in the preceding paragraphs, but several noteworthy points may be reemphasized. Generally, the decline of sponge-fishing has brought disastrous results to the Dodecanese islander. The remaining population of Symi, Chalki, and Kastellorizo, chiefly old men and women, often are forced to migrate seasonally to Rhodes or Kalymnos for work or remain dependent upon remittances from abroad. These islands now no longer have an economic base to support their former large populations, since sponge-fishing and the maritime carrying trade have been destroyed. Although a Symian, for example, will desperately insist that his community is not a "χωριὸ" (village) and that he is strongly akin to the Kalymnian, only a skeleton remains of Symi's former thriving port and cultural center.

Other former prosperous sponge islands reveal a similar state of affairs. Little, isolated Kastellorizo, for example, maintains a scant population of less than 200 only by a heavy subsidy from the Greek Government. Allegations have been directed against this island for gun-running to Cyprus and in 1962 British investigators unsuccessfully combed the island for evidence of such smuggling. Kalymnos, by contrast, is now the sole direct beneficiary of the sponge industry. As a result, Kalymnos dwarfs all other Dodecanese islands in wealth. The Kalymnians are the victims of that unpopularity, admiration tainted by envy, that is the fate of the affluent in a poor society. These contrasts have themselves been instrumental in social and political differences among the islands.

Social and Political Impact

The social and political repercussions of the sponge-fishing experiences have been fully as striking as the economic ramifications. One can observe these repercussions in differences in emigration rates, vigor and initiative at the local level, intellectual characteristics, and inter-island perception. In addition, one can also perceive island contrasts in both political history and contemporary politics.

Although Greeks generally have a high respect for intellectual achievements, the sponge-fishing islanders appear to place greater emphasis upon education and the arts than other Dodecanesians. Characterizing Kalymnians, the noted journalist I. M. Panagiotopoulou observes that "μέσα στὶς βαθιὲς καρδίες τῶν σφουγγαράδων φωλιάζει ὁ ἔρωτας τῆς τέχνη. Καὶ ὁ πόθος τῶν γραμμάτων."[1] (Deep in their hearts, the sponge-fishers nestle a love of art and a yearning for letters.) Despite a lack of educational facilities and opportunities in rural

---

[1] Panagiotopoulou, op. cit.

Greece, Kalymnos boasts three gymnasiums, enrolling 800 students, fourteen elementary schools, and an advanced technical school. In addition, the Kalymnians are presently organizing night classes to eliminate the last vestiges of illiteracy resulting from the characteristic refusal of the islanders to attend Italian-run schools.

The result of this educational activity is an inordinate number of professional men, scholars, and artists in the sponge islands. Kalymnos, for example, is renowned for the sea stories of John Manglis, the poetry of John Zervo, the theological writings of Sakellarios Manglis, George Oikonomou, Michael Alachouzo, and the sculpture of Sakellarios Galouze, and Manoles Zaires. Symi is no less famous for professors such as Soterios Agapetides and numerous representatives in government service. The Mayor of Leipsos summed up the educational drive of Kalymnians by observing:[1]

> Every place, no matter where you go in the world, has a Kalymnian there who is a big businessman, doctor or lawyer. Since they have money, they send their sons to good local schools, and then universities. Local jealousy pushes on higher education—it is almost a status symbol there. Even a poor Kalymnian woman will take her child to Athens and scrub floors to send him to the University so that he will be a man.

In addition to these pronounced educational achievements, the sponge islanders have evolved one unusual social institution not found on other Dodecanese islands. The "Sophocles" society of Symi, founded in 1870 when Symi towered above Rhodes and Kalymnos as the cultural center of the Dodecanese, exemplifies this institution. Founded originally as a theatrical club, its function has changed to one of sponsoring a cinema on the island. This mutation occurred because of the depletion of the supply of actors through emigration and the objections of many Symians to girls appearing on the stage. The society obtains free films, and the proceeds go, for the short run, to a fund for the construction of a new modern theater. The original theater, we were pointedly informed, was bombed by the Germans. The long range goal, however, is to use the proceeds for educating poor but promising young students. A similar voluntary club in Kalymnos has a membership of largely professional men and sponsors speakers and panel discussions on a monthly basis.

The behavior of Dodecanesian emigrants illustrates another social contrast between sponge and other islanders. All Greeks have an intense loyalty to birthplace and the "πατριώτης" (an inhabitant of the same birthplace), but again this tie is especially emphasized by sponge islanders. Kalymnians and Astypalians, almost without exception, return to their island at some point in their lives. This devotion to their island is widely recognized throughout the

---

[1]Personal interview with the Mayor of Leipsos, December 12, 1963.

Dodecanese as a distinctive characteristic of these islanders. The diverse backgrounds which returning islanders bring with them also promote a greater worldliness in these islands.

Kalymnians and Symians especially emphasize their greater knowledge of the outer world, and most measures of movement and communication would seem to support this contention. During the summer, when ships are plentiful, Kalymnos receives 500-600 Athenian newspapers daily. Presently, she also boasts 300 telephones, and the number would probably double if the company could satisfy the local demand.[1] Measured either in absolute or per-capita terms, this rate far exceeds that of other Dodecanese islands. Symians and Kalymnians both travel more frequently to Rhodes and Athens than other Dodecanesians. Inhabitants of both of these islands will often go to these cities to see soccer matches, visit relatives, attend cultural events, or even to shop or attend the cinema, while most other Dodecanesian travel only for necessities. Symi and Kalymnos also have radios in nearly every home—a somewhat higher rate than normal in the Dodecanese. Finally, apart from the greater frequency of physical interaction, the author found inhabitants on these sponge islands to be better informed and more knowledgable of the outside world than their counterparts on other islands.

Another distinction of the sponge islanders is their cognitive individuality. To the resentment of other Dodecanesians, Kalymnians refer to their island as "little Paris" or "the navel of the earth." While most Dodecanesians stress their gentle and pacifist qualities, Symians and Kalymnians pride themselves on their more determined, vigorous, and active character. Children of other islands occasionally ask Kalymnians if they are "'άγριοι" (wild men).[2] On Kos, the author was several times warned that "if a Kalymnian doesn't like a 'ξένος' (foreigner), he will throw a tomato at him."

Sponge islanders tend to explain their distinctiveness by racial and environmental causes. Again and again the author was proudly informed that Kalymnians and Symians were Doric in ancestry, not like the Ionian inhabitants of Leros and Patmos. The Dorians, according to this view, are the adventuresome, the bold, and vigorous, while the Ionians are the gentle, the quiet, and the peace-loving. Kalymnians and Symians, in fact, see sponge-fishing and Doric ancestry as inextricable components of their "character."

The sponge islanders find another cause of their perceived uniqueness in the environment. "The mountains and climate make people here strong and dynamic —they are not interested in lying and kindnesses. Because we are obliged to

---

[1]Personal interview with the Mayor of Kalymnos, November 30, 1963.

[2]Personal interviews, Kalymnos, November 29-December 3, 1963.

live always from the sea, we are more lively, more energetic, more nervous."[1]
The nomarch in Rhodes will tell you that the Kalymnians seek their rights with
force, that they are lively. "In Kos and Rhodes, there is too much humidity—
the character of the people is not so dynamic."[2] Others contrast the life of
the sailor with that of the farmer:

> The sea and mountains, especially in combination, make for rugged,
> almost wild, energetic, independent men. The conquering of the sea
> and rough landscape makes the Kalymnian proud, unafraid to speak his
> mind. On Rhodes and Kos, people are all farmers—quiet people who
> want no trouble, who don't want to say anything out of turn, who want
> only to work in their fields, untroubled. The Kalymnians, however,
> are never afraid.[3]

While other islanders grudgingly concede a germ of truth to Kalymnian
and Symian boasts, they view especially the Kalymnians as braggarts and exagger-
ators. Asked his opinion of a Kalymnian, the typical Dodecanesian response is
"πολλὲς λέξεις" (many words) or "παππαγάλλοι" (parrots!). Most view the Kalymnians and Symians as vivid exceptions to the Dodecanesian gentleness.

Historically, this widely-accepted image of the sponge islanders finds
striking evidence. During the Turkish occupation, Symians and Kalymnians constituted the hard core of resistance. Throughout these centuries of subjugation,
Kalymnos, as Panagiotopoulou observes, "ἀπόμεινε καθὼς ἡ Μάνη, ὁλόρθη στὰ
μετερίζι τῆς."[4] (It remained, like Mani,[5] erect in its defiance.) During the
latter part of the nineteenth century, the Turkish fleet continually was forced
to combat local rebellions in Symi and Kalymnos. Despite the prosperity of
these islands during this period, they remained the hotbed of insurrection in
the Dodecanese islands.

The Italian occupation brought little change in this pattern of resistance. Despite harsh suppression, Symi and Kalymnos continued to serve as the
vanguard of Dodecanesian insurrection. The evidence of this estrangement remains
to the present day. Throughout the Dodecanese, the Italians built numerous,
characteristically ostentatious public buildings, roads, parks, and gardens. On
Symi and Kalymnos, however, the sole public projects were restricted to the construction of an administration center essential to the local governor.

---

[1] Personal interview with George Lysikatos, December 1, 1963.

[2] Personal interview, Kalymnos, December 3, 1963.

[3] Ibid.

[4] Panagiotopoulou, op. cit.

[5] Mani, renowned throughout Greece as the one place where "no Turkish
foot ever stepped," is located at the southern tip of the Peloponnesos.

As fascism became rigid occupational policy in the Dodecanese, the resistance of the islanders stiffened. In 1935 the famous "πετροπόλεμος" (rock war) erupted on Kalymnos when the Italians tried to declare the church of the Dodecanese autocephalous. The women of the island locked the men in houses, gathered on the mountainsides overlooking the harbor, and stoned the Italian troops. Later, when World War II broke out, Kalymnian and Symian doctors, lawyers, and teachers were prominent in an alliance of educated Dodecanesians who journeyed to the mountains of northern Greece to fight the Italians in Albania. Even today, many of the houses of Kalymnos still are painted blue and white, the national colors of Greece, a vivid testimony to the long years of spirited resistance to foreign rule. That the memory of these difficult years lives on was forcefully brought to the author's attention when he was mistaken for a German and stoned in the streets by the children of Kalymnos. In these islands of "φιλοξενία" (philoeny), such behavior would not likely be found on any other island.

This historical tradition of the irrepressible independence of the sponge-islander lives on also in contemporary politics. Perhaps because of this long struggle against alien rule, Dodecanesians, are highly sensitive to centralized power. Accordingly, they see themselves as strongly in the tradition of the renowned and liberal Greek statesman, Eleutherios Venizelos. This spirit of liberality is nowhere more marked than in the sponge islands. In 1961, when Konstantinos Karamanlis and the E.R.E. carried the Dodecanese by a scant 365 votes, Kalymnians voted nearly two to one for the Center-Progressive coalition. Table 19 illustrates the relationship of voting behavior between the sponge islands and the Dodecanese as a whole over the last three elections. As a group, the sponge islands voted consistently more toward the Center than the Dodecanese as a whole, and Kalymnos, the one presently-active sponge island, leads the group in opposition to the E.R.E. The political atmosphere of Kalymnos is well-illustrated by the fact that the Mayor of Kalymnos, a supporter of E.R.E., even refers to himself as "the Fascist." A noteworthy characteristic of political behavior in the sponge islands of Symi and Kalymnos is the far greater importance of ideological issues in electoral choice. In the elections of 1963 and 1964, the "triumph-of-democracy" call of Georgios Papandreou struck a very responsive chord in these islands. This greater concern with ideological issues is probably a result of higher educational levels, greater communication with the outside world, and the historical resistance to political suppression.

One final political characteristic of the sponge islanders should be noted. At the local level, inhabitants have developed more vigorous political institutions and display more faith in their ability to control their own destinies than is commonly found on other islands. In both Symi and Kalymnos,

TABLE 19

VOTING RESULTS OF DODECANESIAN SPONGE ISLANDS, 1961-1964[a]

(in percentages)

	1961				Election of 1963				1964			Per Cent change, 1961-1964[b]		
	E.R.E.	Center Prog.	P.A.M.E.	Ind.	E.R.E.	Center Union	E.D.A.	Prog.	E.R.E. Prog.	Center Union	E.D.A.	E.R.E.	Center Union	E.D.A.
Dodecanese Islands	48	47	5	--	34	56	4	6	32	68	--	-16	+21	-5
Sponge Islands (Kalymnos, Symi, Chalki, Astypalia, Kastellorizo)	38	58	4	--	28	67	3	2	22	78	--	-16	+20	-4
Kalymnos	33	62	5	--	25	70	4	1	19	81	--	-14	+19	-5

[a]Source: Nomarchy of the Dodecanese.

[b]Percentage changes are not strictly accurate because of the shifting coalitions of Greek parties. In 1964, for example, E.D.A. did not oppose the Center Union in constituencies where they had not offered effective opposition in the past. The Progressives, led by Spyros Markezinis, have contested elections as an independent party and in alliance with both the Center Union and E.R.E. Nevertheless, the figures do represent a reasonably accurate indication of party support over these years.

voluntary clubs provide members with a vehicle for intellectual activity and community projects. In both these islands, local inhabitants are busily constructing roads, public buildings, and improving other local functions. The Kalymnian government has even assumed responsibilities for the organization of the sponge industry and the search for distant markets. These activities assume a commitment to community and a confidence in local political institutions rare in the Dodecanese. Surely the historical experience of the sponge islander and the economic benefits have contributed greatly to this political individuality.

CHAPTER V

THE AFTERMATH OF EMIGRATION

Στὴν μακρινὴ τὴν Αὐστραλία καὶ πέρα στὴν ᾿Αμερικῆ,
᾿᾿Η στὸν Καναδᾶ, στῆ Βραζιλία, πόσα παιδιὰ πονοῦν κι᾿ ἐκεῖ!
Κακούργα, μετανάστευσις! Κακούργα, ξενιτειά!
Μᾶς πῆρες ἀπ᾿ τὸν τόπο μας τὰ πειὸ καλὰ παιδιὰ.
Κάμε κουράγιο, μετανάστη; κάμε, λεβέντη μου, ὑπομονή
Τοῦ γυρισμοῦ σου. Ἄχ! τὸ καράβη πάλι μιὰ μέρα, ἄχ! θὰ φάνει.[1]

(In distant Australia, and away in America
Or in Canada, in Brazil, how many youths suffer even there?
Criminal, emigration! Criminal, foreign land!
You've taken from our country our finest youths!
Have courage, emigrant; have patience for your return,
My brave youth. Ah! the ship one day will appear.)

᾿᾿Απ᾿ τὴν᾿ὄμορφη πατρίδα οι λεβέντες μας μ᾿ἐλπίδα
Φεύγουν στὴν ᾿Αμερικη
Νὰ δουλέψουν γιὰ νὰ ζήσουν καὶ μὲ πλούτη νὰ γυρίσουν
Στὴν Ελλάδα ᾿να πρωΐ
Φεύγουν τρένα και καράβια, φορτωμένα παλλικάρια
Καὶ γυρίζουν ἀδειανὰ
᾿᾿Απ της ξενιτειὰς τὰ μέροι, μετανάστη μου, ποιὸς ξέρει
᾿᾿Αν θὰ᾿λθῆς ἐδῶ ξανὰ;[2]

(From our beautiful fatherland, our brave, handsome men
go forth with hope to America
To work in order to live, and to return with riches
to Greece one morning
Trains and ships, loaded with brave youths, leave
and return empty from the places in foreign lands.
My emigrant, who knows if you'll return here ever?)

With Greeks emigrating at the rate of 80,000 per year from a population of only eight million,[3] the outflow of the nation's youth is a critical national problem. In the Dodecanese, as in Greece as a whole, few are the families which have escaped completely the dispersion of their members to distant countries. In a culture characterized by strong family ties, the disruption of the family is a source of great personal grief.

Although a problem of national proportions, emigration nevertheless entails substantial ameliorations. Andréas Papandréou notes, for example, that emigration, not industrial development, resolved the acute unemployment problem

---

[1]"Στὸν Καναδᾶ, στῆ Βραζιλία . . ." (To Canada, to Brazil . . .), a popular Greek ballad in 1964.

[2]"Φεύγουν οἱ μετανάστες"(The emigrants are leaving), a popular Greek ballad in 1964.

[3]National Statistical Service of Greece, Statistical Yearbook of Greece, 1963 (Athens: 1964), p. 286.

of the 1950's.[1] Remittances sent back by loyal nationals often maintain the family left behind and frequently even become the family's single most important source of income. This flow of capital from foreign countries may be the difference between a badly-needed piece of farm equipment, the construction of a larger and (most islanders would hope) more imposing house, the successful dowering of a daughter or sister, or the education of a younger brother. The emigration of one or more sons averts mounting pressure upon existing land resources in rural areas and militates against further land fragmentation by limiting property inheritance by fewer family members. When the opportunity for emigration arises, then, each family faces the unpleasant choice between needed capital and personal grief. This has been a difficult decision for some time as the history of population changes in the Dodecanese indicates.

The Evolution of the Dodecanese Population

Chapter II summarizes the development of the Dodecanese population prior to the twentieth century. Table 1 records population changes since the Greek War of Independence.[2] Between 1850 and 1910, largely due to the widespread development of maritime commerce and spongefishing, close relations with the adjacent Turkish mainland, and lenient taxation policies, the Dodecanese population increased rapidly. This economic and demographic rise continued unabated until the advent of Italian control in 1912.

The initial impact of Italian sovereignty, together with the economic disruption of World War I, resulted in a thirty per cent decline in the Dodecanese population by 1917. With the initiation of a large-scale Fascist developmental program for the Dodecanese, however, the population increased from 109,560 in 1922 to 133,357 in 1937. It should be borne in mind, nevertheless, that these figures do not reflect the growth of the Greek population, since most of the increase was due to the influx of large numbers of Italians, 2,906 of whom were concentrated at the new Italian military fortress at Leros, 9,528 at Rhodes, and another 1,851 of whom were distributed among other Dodecanese Islands.[3] The period of Italian rule was, in fact, a time of general economic depression, depopulation, and emigration for most of the islands.[4]

---

[1] Andreas Papandreou, "A New Economic Policy for Greece," Greek Heritage, Vol. II, No. 6 (1965), p. 76.

[2] Supra, p. 25.

[3] Doxiades, op. cit., p. 296.

[4] Supra, pp. 20-23.

The extensive Dodecanese emigration under Italian rule shows considerable spatial variation. Italian interference with spongefishing caused rapid
depopulation in Symi, Chalki, and Kastellorizo. Kasos, heavily dependent upon
maritime shipping, shared a similar fate. By contrast, Rhodes, Kos, and Leros,
the larger and, agriculturally, more favored islands, maintained and even increased their populations. The spatial characteristics of these demographic
changes are closely related to Italian policies and restrictions within the
Dodecanese islands.

Between 1947 and 1961, following reunification of the islands with
Greece, the over-all pattern of emigration and depopulation remained unchanged,
despite an intensive developmental effort by the central government. In the
decade between 1951 and 1961, the Dodecanese population grew only 1.27 per cent
as compared with the 9.90 per cent increase for Greece as a whole and a 5.32 per
cent increase in the Dodecanese during the previous decade.[1] Moreover, only
Rhodes, Kalymnos, and Kasos showed population gains, while all the other islands
revealed declines. In fact, Telos, Symi, and Chalki suffered losses over twenty
per cent in this brief ten-year period. The explanation for these population
declines lies both in physical demographic characteristics and in emigration
rates.

Physical Characteristics of the Dodecanese Population

In 1936 the Dodecanese birthrate stood at an unusually low rate of 13.3
per 1,000 inhabitants, chiefly because of the numerous Italian troops and the
absence of large numbers of Greek men. Although there was a slight increase
between 1942 and 1951, since 1951 there has been a steady decline in the birthrate (Table 20). Greece as a whole has experienced a similar marked decline

TABLE 20

THE DODECANESE BIRTHRATE[a]

(per 1,000 inhabitants)

Year	Population	Births	Birthrate
1936	132,638	1,764	13.3
1941	129,235	3,308	25.6
1951	121,480	3,261	26.7
1956	120,736	2,688	22.2
1961	123,021	2,378	18.4

[a]Source: The 1936 and 1941 data is from Doxiades, op. cit., p. 298;
the 1951-1961 data is from the National Statistical Service of Greece.

---

[1]National Statistical Service of Greece, Statistical Yearbook of Greece,
1963 (Athens: 1964), p. 24.

(24.53 in 1940 and 17.94 in 1961) since World War II.[1] Nevertheless, in the span of one decade, the Dodecanese birthrate has fallen a full 8.3 per cent. Indicative of the emigration of the Dodecanese youth and perhaps an increasing use of birth control methods, this decline is a source of grave concern to local officials and the inhabitants at large.

A similar pattern is also characteristic of the Dodecanese deathrate (Table 21). The 1941 figure, of course, represents an inflated rate caused by World War II. Presently, the rate parallels that of Greece as a whole, which was 7.61 for 1961.[2] Despite the fall of the birthrate, the surplus of births over deaths assures a constantly increasing population which encourages, and perhaps necessitates, emigration.

TABLE 21

THE DODECANESE DEATHRATE[a]
(per 1,000 inhabitants)

Year	Population	Deaths	Deathrate
1936	132,638	1,066	8.0
1941	129,235	2,024	15.7
1951	121,480	1,060	8.7
1956	120,736	999	8.2
1961	123,021	993	8.0

[a]Source: The 1936 and 1941 data are from Doxiades, op. cit., p.,298; the 1951-1961 data are from the National Statistical Service of Greece.

The historical effects of emigration are clearly evident in the present age-sex structure of the Dodecanese population. Since 1946, as Table 22 indicates, there has been a higher rate of men than women in the younger age groups,

TABLE 22

A COMPARISON OF THE DODECANESE POPULATION
BY SEX AND AGE GROUPS, 1946 AND 1961[a]

Age Group	1946				1961			
	Men		Women		Men		Women	
	Numbers	Per Cent	Numbers	Per Cent	Numbers	Per Cent	Numbers	Per Cent
0 - 14	14,928	16.2	14,002	15.1	21,700	17.6	20,300	16.5
15 - 44	20,632	22.4	22.270	24.3	22,400	18.2	25,200	20.5
45 - 64	6,032	6.5	8,609	9.3	10,400	8.5	13,200	10.7
Over 64	2,189	2.4	3,535	3.8	4,200	3.4	5,600	4.6
Total	43,785	47.5	48,416	52.5	58,700	47.7	64,300	52.3

[a]Source: For the 1946 data, Doxiades, op. cit., p. 294; for the 1961 data, National Statistical Service of Greece, Results of the Population and Housing Census of 19 March 1961 (Athens: 1962), Vol. I, Demographic Characteristics, p. 28.

[1]Ibid., p. 40.   [2]Ibid.

but between fifteen and forty-four an inverse relationship prevails. Wartime losses, combined with the large number of men emigrating to foreign countries account for this serious shortage of males. Perhaps the most noteworthy aspect of the comparison between 1946 and 1961 is the relative similarity between the two years. In the fifteen years since reunification, the out-drift of young men has not been prevented. A further breakdown of the age-sex structure would reveal that in 1961 there were still only seventy-seven men for every 100 women in the islands over the age of 25.[1]

While the age-sex structure has remained remarkably uniform over time, the ethnic and religious composition of the population has changed appreciably. While in 1947, only eighty-seven per cent of the islanders were Greek (Table 23), in 1951 this proportion had increased to ninety-nine per cent. Although the 1961 figures showed an increase in foreign immigration, these new "immigrants" were chiefly American citizens returning to their homelands, where they live "well" with their social security pensions, and Greeks fleeing the suppressions of Nasser in Egypt. In fact, the last fifteen years have witnessed a constant drift of the few remaining Italians and Turks to their homelands.

TABLE 23

THE ETHNIC STRUCTURE OF THE DODECANESE POPULATION,
1941 - 1961[a]

Year	Greeks	Italians	Total Foreign Citizens
1941	112,142 (86.8%)	14,285 (11.0%)	17,094 (13.2%)
1951	120,676 (99.3%)	37 (0.04%)	804 (0.67%)
1961	121,354 (98.7%)	b	1,667 (1.3%)

[a]Source: For 1941 data, Doxiadés, op. cit., p. 296; for 1951 and 1961 data, the National Statistical Service of Greece.

[b]Statistics unavailable.

Paralleling this ethnic readjustment are related changes in the religious affiliation of the Dodecanesians. In 1912, ninety-three per cent of the islanders were Greek Orthodox, whereas in 1941, due largely to the influx of Italians, this figure had dropped to 82.5 per cent. Cases of Greek conversion to Roman Catholicism were, nevertheless, extremely rare. Included in the 1941 remainder were Roman Catholics, 10.1 per cent; Moslems, 5.9 per cent; and Jews, 1.5 per cent.[2] By 1951, Orthodox Greeks accounted for 95.6 per cent and Turkish Moslems for four per cent.[3] The Italians had, for the most part, returned to

---

[1]Konsola, op. cit., p. 24.

[2]Soterios Agapetides, Ὁ Πλυθυσμὸς τῆς Δωδεκανήσου (Athens: 1948),p.13.

[3]Konsola, op. cit., p. 26.

Italy, and the Jews had been killed or forced to flee during the German occupation. These religious characteristics remained largely unchanged during the
fifteen years since reunification.

A final demographic characteristic of the Dodecanese islands in 1961 was
an average population density of 45.2 people per square kilometer.[1] Considerable
differences among islands are included in this figure, however, since the presently-active maritime and agricultural islands tend to be more densely populated
than the former sponge-fishing islands. Kalymnos, for example, has a density of
128.6 people per square kilometer, whereas Astypalia (15.6) and Chalki (17.2)
show far sparser populations.[2]

The Causes and Characteristics of Emigration

Causes of Emigration

The primary economic causes of emigration have been fully discussed in
the preceding chapters. The basic insecurity of the Dodecanesian before environmental changes, especially as manifested in fluctuations of agricultural production, forces him to operate under high levels of risk. The lack of an assured
price for agricultural commodities and the difficulty in programming production
for a given market compound this uncertainty. In addition, the annual agricultural cycle, with its long period of unemployment and the comparatively short
time of active farm work, creates a widely-felt need for a more stable form of
employment. This thirst for security in a physical and social environment characterized by uncertainty is the backdrop from which the motivation for emigration
must be assessed.

In the face of economic uncertainties and the inability of the economy
to provide attractive opportunities for the young, quite naturally the enterprising migrate to the cities and foreign countries where the probability of
success is much greater. Moreover, Dodecanesian families view the emigration of
at least one son as a necessary investment in economic security. One Symian
summarized this need succinctly: "In order to live, each family must send at
least one son to work on a ship or in a foreign land. The money he sends back
will support the family."[3] This need, though it conflicts with the desire to
keep the family together, overrules other considerations. Another small Rhodian
merchant greeted the researcher by exclaiming: "Can you take my boy to Rhodesia?

---

[1]National Statistical Service of Greece, Statistical Yearbook of Greece,
1963 (Athens: 1964), p. 24.

[2]Nomarchy of the Dodecanese.

[3]Personal interview, Symi, December 29, 1963.

Is there any way you can take him? We must send one from our family, too!"[1]
The remittances which these emigrants send back sustain the family in poor years
and usually constitute the sole means of acquiring wealth.

The social causes of emigration are less easily understood, though
equally important. The dowry system certainly assumes a vital role in creating
a strong motivation for emigration. Since an honorable young man cannot marry
until all his sisters have been successfully wed, Greek men feel a crushing obligation to accumulate wealth for their sisters' dowries. Because the value of
dowries is always vastly disproportionate to per-capita earning power, usually
including a house and furnishings, linens, utensils, and between $1,000 and
$3,000,[2] the only feasible method of acquiring such sums is to migrate for work
in more developed countries.

Historically, emigration has provided a means of escaping the inequities
of foreign occupations. Political and religious suppression under Turkish and
Italian rule initiated the outpouring of people during the twentieth century.
The Fascist policies of the Italian occupation were particularly instrumental in
driving large numbers of Dodecanesians to Egypt and the United States. Since
reunification, however, this motivation no longer is a dominant reason for emigration, and yet, the flight continues.

Finally, an elusive and poorly-understood cause of emigration is the
magnetic attraction of the Greek to the success and prestige of life in foreign
countries. Increased communications, the greater awareness of the affluence of
more economically developed countries, the triumphant pilgrimage of the boastful,
arrogant emigrants of earlier times—all unfold myriad attractions of the youth-
ful Dodecanese economic prisoners. Two melancholy Koan youths, reflecting on
their island fate, expressed this characteristic longing to leave as follows:
"No, we don't really like it here. We have had so much of this island that we
are bored. Each man does whatever come his way—what else? It is not good to
sit all day. Myself, I am waiting for my three weeks to end and then I must
return to the ship—another life of monotony, always the sea. If only I could
get to America—there you can work in a factory and wear nice clothes."[3] In all
cases, the cultural premium upon a better "station" in life plays an important
role in the desire to emigrate, whether it be to foreign countries or to Greek
cities.

---

[1]Personal interview, City of Rhodes, November 14, 1963.

[2]For more detailed discussions of the dowry institution and its economic
implications in other parts of Greece, see Friedl, op. cit., pp. 53-60; Ioanna
Lambiri, Social Change in a Greek Country Town, Center of Planning and Economic
Research, Research Monograph No. 13 (Athens: Center of Planning and Economic
Research, 1965), pp. 34-35.

[3]Personal interview, City of Kos, November 27, 1963.

Internal migration

Unfortunately, statistics of internal migration and urbanization have never been published for areas smaller than geographic regions (such as the Aegean Island region). Nevertheless, one might venture some general observations concerning the character of internal migrations within and from the Dodecanese by analysis of other less readily available data and the results of interviews.

There is an unmistakable rural-to-urban population movement both within the Dodecanese and in Greece as a whole. Although the Dodecanese population increased by only one per cent between 1951 and 1961, the city of Rhodes grew from 23,599 to 27,393, a gain of 16 per cent. In rural areas especially, there is a constant drift to Athens and Rhodes both because of the greater opportunity for work and also, for the Greek, the more attractive character of work in tertiary activities.

This rural to urban migration in the Dodecanese is consistent with the over-all pattern for both the Aegean islands and Greece generally. Between 1955 and 1961, the Aegean islands population registered a net increase of 5,400 in its urban areas, 1,400 in semi-urban areas, and a net decline of 6,900 in its rural areas.[1] Put another way, 5,300 of the 1961 urban population of Aegean islands and 3,100 of the semi-urban population were rural in 1955.[2] Greece as a whole showed a net population increase of 91,000 in urban areas, 12,600 in semi-urban areas, and a net decrease of 103,700 in rural areas.[3]

The characteristics of this rural-to-urban migration are also difficult to discern. Certainly, there is a strong concentration of emigrants in the fifteen to thirty-five age group. In addition, these areas of origin are closely-correlated with economically-depressed portions of the island group, especially the declining maritime islands and the subsistence zones of agricultural islands. The sex differentials of internal migration are difficult to determine, however, because of the lack of published statistics. Greater Athens, the chief destination of both Dodecanese and other Greek migrants, recorded a net inflow of 116,000 females and 102,000 males in 1961.[4] Moreover, the sex differential is most marked in the ages between fifteen and thirty-four where 62 per cent of all in-migrants were women.[5] The data include, however, the female change

---

[1]National Statistical Service of Greece, Results of the Population and Housing Census of 19 March 1961, (Athens: 1963), Vol. V: Internal Migration, p. 46.

[2]Ibid., p. 45.

[3]Ibid.

[4]Ibid., p. 51.

[5]Ibid.

of residence which accompanies marriage. Interview results in the Dodecanese indicate a larger outflow of men, especially in the fifteen to thirty-five age bracket, seeking work in cities and on ships. Almost without exception, unmarried women do not migrate for work in the tertiary industries of urban areas unless they can live with close relatives.

Characteristics of Emigration

The recent trend of migration, stratified both by sex and permanency, is shown in Table 24. The temporary emigration of Greeks for work in foreign countries, especially Germany, continued at a relatively constant rate between 1955 and 1962 except for a brief decline in 1958-1959. The chief characteristic of this migration was the virtual absence of females. Between 1955 and 1962, of a total of 6,677 temporary emigrants only twenty were of the female sex. Although a number of factors are involved, one stands out above the rest: Among

TABLE 24

EMIGRATION FROM THE DODECANESE ISLANDS,
1955 - 1962[a]

Year	Total	Males	Females	Total	Males	Females
1955	1126	842	284	888	888	---
1956	1303	1,020	283	790	790	---
1957	877	568	309	1,106	1,104	2
1958	556	275	281	432	432	---
1959	487	288	199	574	573	1
1960	1087	732	355	968	967	1
1961	1232	777	455	876	873	3
1962	2586	1,537	1,049	1,043	1,030	13

[a]Source: National Statistical Service of Greece.

Greeks, a woman, married or unmarried, is not allowed to live apart from her family, except with close relatives. Deviations from this norm cast serious doubts upon a woman's honor and jeopardize the family's social position among relatives and within the community. Lambiri's observation on the social position of an unmarried girl in the community of Megara applies equally well to the Dodecanese:

> ...their (the villagers') notions about the role a girl should play in public were very strict: her appearance and dress should be very modest and her behavior toward men should never denote familiarity. Only her fiance, brother, or first cousin could escort her. She was not even allowed to talk for long with other men. Any deviation from these traditional rules was considered as proof of immorality.[1]

[1]Lambiri, op. cit., p. 29.

The most satisfactory social arrangement and also the economically most efficient scheme, then, is for the woman to remain with the family and assume responsibility for farming while the man migrates in search of work.

Statistics of the reasons for, and destinations of, emigration from the Dodecanese are contained in Table 25. It should be noted that these data are not strictly comparable to those of Table 24 since the former are based upon the issue of passports, regardless of place of residence. Nevertheless, the overwhelming bulk of emigrants are from the Dodecanese, and the statistics provide some insights into the reasons for emigration.

In 1962, the major reason for absence abroad was family reasons. Although work was the largest single factor, tourism, commerce, and studies also played significant roles. The major destination of Dodecanese emigrants in 1962 was Europe, especially Germany, the goal of sixty-seven per cent of those emigrants. The United States and Australia are no longer the major destinations of emigrants. Germany has, in fact, launched a vigorous campaign to attract Greek workers into German factories. Industrialists often pay for transportation, provide housing, and even train German foremen in the Greek language. The result has been a major spatial reorientation of Dodecanese emigration.

The data also suggest that prior to the large-scale emigration for work in Germany beginning in 1961, the distribution of emigration by sex was close to parity. Since 1961, however, the preponderance of men over women has reached proportions of two to one. This increasing sex differential results from the growing migration of men, unaccompanied by their families, in search of temporary work.

If permanent emigrants alone are considered, several characteristics are outstanding. First, despite official attempts at discouragement, emigration is steadily increasing. The major sex differentials characteristic of temporary emigration disappear, although a small surplus of men over women remains. In either case, the migrants tend to be strongly concentrated in the twenty to thirty-nine age group. This age-sex structure of Dodecanese emigrants compounds the problems of depopulation occasioned by the increasing rate of emigration.

Depopulation

The extent of Dodecanese depopulation since 1821 is shown graphically, by island, in Figure 24. The map reveals a marked depopulation of the smaller maritime islands, especially those formerly active in sponge-fishing, and in the secondary, more isolated, agricultural islands. The most precipitous population declines have been recorded, particularly since 1912, on islands such as Symi, Kastellorizo, and Kasos which have suffered disproportionately in the concomitant economic disruptions of changes in political sovereignty.

The demographic results of depopulation have been a decline in population

TABLE 25

REASONS FOR AND DESTINATIONS OF DODECANESE EMIGRATION, 1958 - 1962[a]

(based upon passports issued by the Dodecanese Nomarchy)[b]

Year and Month	General Total	Men	Women	Destination Total	U.S.A.	Canada	S. America	Australia	Europe	Asia	Africa	Reason Total	Tourism	Business	Family Reasons	Studies	Health	Maritime	Miscellaneous
1958	1,678	834	844	616	270	74	3	105	42	10	112	1,062	85	100	727	108	18	23	1
1959	1,744	975	769	469	102	76	–	158	52	8	73	1,275	138	213	721	156	26	12	9
1960	2,436	1,492	974	958	251	138	5	360	87	23	94	1,478	246	290	726	169	28	18	1
1961	3,022	2,002	1,020	1,664	161	97	16	144	1,010	15	221	1,358	279	190	547	252	37	53	8
1962	4,460	3,025	1,435	2,932	291	96	6	235	1,964	30	310	1,528	415	190	607	185	39	82	10
1962: January	279	200	79	206	34	3	1	25	132	–	12	73	12	10	35	7	2	7	–
February	281	200	81	219	31	4	1	36	133	1	13	62	10	10	26	2	2	12	–
March	255	194	61	194	31	12	1	25	109	–	16	61	17	13	18	4	6	3	1
April	225	138	87	139	19	3	2	25	61	5	29	86	23	8	38	7	5	4	–
May	456	348	108	315	22	8	–	11	247	4	22	141	68	19	38	3	3	10	1
June	332	203	129	200	15	5	1	26	123	–	26	132	43	16	59	6	–	6	–
July	465	282	183	262	19	11	–	19	182	3	31	203	75	14	67	37	2	6	2
August	599	399	200	373	20	8	–	17	290	6	35	226	40	24	94	46	6	4	2
September	676	468	208	459	15	15	–	15	354	8	54	217	50	19	95	10	2	6	3
October	415	295	120	290	24	2	–	10	215	1	31	125	27	30	50	6	2	15	1
November	257	169	88	131	14	11	–	13	61	1	31	126	27	20	49	4	8	3	–
December	220	129	91	144	47	41	1	13	57	2	10	76	23	7	38	3	1	3	1

[a]Source: Nomarchy of the Dodecanese.

[b]Does not comprise the total of Dodecanesian emigrants and absentees, since passports are also issued directly by the Ministry of the Interior.

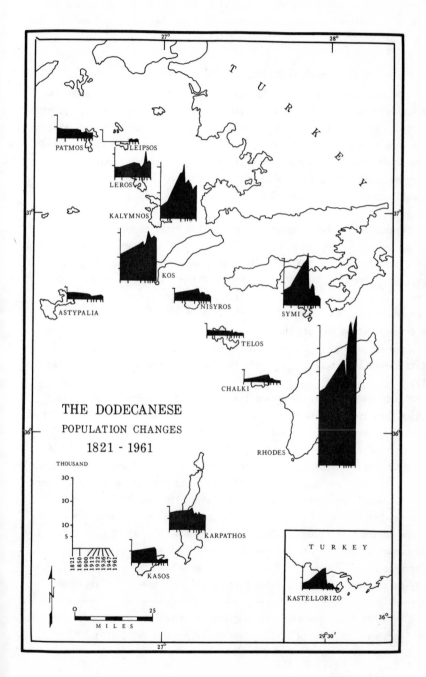

Figure 24.—Population changes in the Dodecanese Islands, 1821-1961.

densities, a relatively older population, and a major sex differential in the surplus of women over men. The spatial pattern of depopulation has particular significance in the latter two cases because of their economic and social repercussions. The ultimate effect of depopulation, then, has been to diversify further the human geography of the Dodecanese islands.

Emigration as a Factor in Island Contrasts

Since emigration and depopulation are unequally distributed among the Dodecanese islands, they alter the spatial characteristics of economy, society, and polity. Two case studies drawn from the two major types of islands experiencing severe depopulation illustrate the process of spatial diversification. Karpathos illustrates the population decline and accompanying problems of the secondary agricultural islands, while Kastellorizo exemplifies the difficulties of the maritime island truncated from its economic hinterland.

Karpathos, A Case Study

Lying midway between Rhodes and Krete, Karpathos is the third largest of the Dodecanese islands. Renowned for its mountains and forests, it boasted in 1910 a population of 9,500. At this time, Karpathos was a major agricultural producer, exporting chiefly raisins to Egypt in large caiques. In fact, during the early decades of this century, Karpathians recalled several occasions when grain production was so bountiful that the local fleet of caiques was inadequate to the transportation demand, and the surplus grain, piled on the shore, eventually rotted and had to be thrown into the sea. During this period, island agricultural production sufficed not only for local consumption needs but also for exports.

Since 1910, Karpathian emigration has caused a decline in the island's population. By 1961, the number of inhabitants had fallen to 6,707. The largest settlements of Karpathian emigrants are in the United States (an estimated 5,000), Athens-Piraeus (an estimated 3,000), and more recently Germany.[1] The system of emigration is similar throughout Greece. Each villager who emigrates attempts to bring other "πατριότοι" (villagers or islanders) to the place where he settled. Among Karpathians, source-destination linkages are Aperiani-New York, Olympo-Germany, and Pigadia-United States. Even marriages become a tool within the system. In December, 1963, three American sisters of Greek descent came to Karpathos and, within fifteen days, were married to young men who would not otherwise get to America.[2] Some cases are even recorded of marriages, followed by quick divorces, during which husband and wife never live together.

---

[1]Personal interview with the Eparchos of Karpathos, January 8, 1964.

[2]Personal interview with the Mayor of Karpathos, January 6, 1964.

The economic effects of emigration are considerable on this island.
Foremost among these is the varied impact of remittances sent back by those who
emigrate abroad. In an interview with the mayor of Karpathos, he boasted that
"Our chief product is dollars—over 40,000 dollars per month."[1] Certainly, this
inflow of wealth has contributed greatly to increased economic well-being. The
effect on the indigenous industries, however, might well be described as disastrous. One prominent Karpathian on Rhodes summarized the impact of remittances
by observing:

> Karpathos could produce many things—potentially, it could—but the
> people are not very energetic; that is, they are not great workers.
> They prefer to emigrate to America where they work well. They've
> organized into committees and send large sums of money to their
> fatherland for buildings and for other works.[2]

In fact, remaining Karpathians have largely abandoned their traditional occupations and now rely chiefly upon money and pensions from abroad.

The agricultural effects of remittances are clear. There is no longer
any significant agricultural surplus on the island, and consequently no agricultural exports. Karpathos does not even keep itself in grain now. Production in
1963 was limited to small amounts of wheat, olive oil, citrus fruits, and livestock.[3] Since foodstuffs are not produced in appreciable amounts, much meat and
vegetables have to be imported. Although emigration has produced a shortage of
manpower in many rural areas of Greece, agricultural declines in Karpathos cannot be explained because of labor limitations. Land resources are plentiful and
potential labor available. The primary cause of the fall in agricultural production, rather, is the choice of local inhabitants not to work. While fields
now everywhere lie fallow, the coffeehouses are full of Karpathians passing the
time with "American dollars"—card games are literally played with American bills.
Ironically, a source of outside wealth which could be used to stimulate the
local economy has resulted in quite the reverse.

The social effects of remittances are equally striking. Despite the
numerous empty houses, a legacy of emigration, several new houses are built in
Karpathian villages every year. Constructed at great expense, usually by returning successful emigrants, these large three- and four-story dwellings include
all the comforts of modern civilization, including all-electric kitchens and indoor plumbing. Despite their elegance and luxurious comfort, however, they remain closed, unoccupied. In Aperi, "Μικρή Νέα Ιōρκη" (little New York), local

---

[1]Ibid.

[2]Personal interview with Dr. Hadjimichali, City of Rhodes, November 6,
1963.

[3]Personal interview with the Mayor of Karpathos, January 6, 1964.

teachers, unable to find living quarters, are forced to live in Pigadia and to commute by bus every day. Meanwhile, the owners of these pretentious houses live in more humble quarters elsewhere. The writer met with profuse apologies when he chanced upon people in their "humble" homes—they had a "good" house up in Aperi. When asked why they built these houses that they do not live in, they reply, "Νὰ φαίνεται!" (So it will show!). Nowhere else in the Dodecanese did the repercussions of emigration appear in such displeasing form on so large a scale, not even in Kastellorizo, which has suffered a severer loss of population.

Kastellorizo, A Case Study

With the present tensions over the unresolved Cyprus situation, the tiny island of Kastellorizo is a lonely Greek possession. Containing an official population in 1961 of 481, although in reality closer to one-half that figure, the island lies a distant seventy miles from Rhodes, the nearest Greek island, but only one and one-half miles from the Turkish mainland. Despite the drawbacks of small size (four square miles), the island attained a population of 9,000 in 1910.

Supported by an active maritime fleet which capitalized on the carrying trade between Egypt and Turkey, the Kastellorizian population lived in relative affluence in the pre-World War I period. Kastellorizo also served as the winter quarters (November to March) and a repair depot for these ships. This activity became so prosperous that by 1911 the Kastellorizian fleet totalled 40,000 tons.[1] Fishing and sponge-fishing added diversity to the maritime economic base. Finally, local inhabitants benefited from the employment opportunities on the adjacent mainland and, in fact, most Kastellorizians had originally come from Greek settlements in Turkey.

Italian control over the Dodecanese and the concomitant amputation of the island from Anatolia destroyed the spatial linkages responsible for this economic prosperity. Large numbers of Kastellorizians emigrated in 1922 during the Greek-Turkish population exchange. Since that time, a steady depopulation of the island has resulted in a 1961 residual population of only 481 (Figure 25). Moreover, they remain only at the urgings of the Greek government, which, for political and strategic reasons, provides subsidies and work on "public projects" —a road leading nowhere for an island without automobiles, a hotel for nonexistent tourists. Remittances also help to support this skeleton population. Large-scale fishing is impossible because of the island's proximity to the Turkish coast. Moreover, the perceived migration of fish, all to the Turkish side of the political boundary where they became so plentiful that they could be

---

[1]Personal interview with the Mayor of Kastellorizo, November 19, 1963.

Figure 25—The nearly deserted island of Kastellorizo. A comparable photograph in 1911 would show numerous ships at anchor and the harbor ringed with houses. Much of the former housing was destroyed during World War I. The coast of Turkey, only one and one-half miles away, is clearly visible. Kastellorizo has been amputated from its natural hinterland, however, and the formerly extensive trade has now trickled to sporadic smuggling.

"scooped up with the hands,"[1] was undoubtedly a rationalization for the lack of greater enterprise. In addition, this view symbolizes the profound longing for the imagined fecundity, so lavishly described by Kastellorizians, of Anatolia. The Greek Government sent the island ten motor boats, but the Turks captured them. As a result only ten to fifteen tons of fish are now exported each year.[2]

These ecohomic disruptions have produced large-scale emigration from Kastellorizo over the last five decades. The Mayor Of Kastellorizo estimated the destinations of these emigrants since 1922 as follows: North and South America—1500, Greece—1500, Egypt—750, Australia—900, and Africa—50.[3] Since 1950 alone, over 300 emigrants have left the island.[4] What remains on the island resembles a ghost town. Fully eighty per cent of the dwellings now stand abandoned, with only approximately 100 houses still occupied.[5] All young people accept their departure from the island as a matter of course. In the last five years, there has not been a single wedding on the island—all young girls now go to Australia to find husbands. It is not surprising, then, that in 1963 the Mayor could introspectively observe, "We know the geography of Australia better than that of Greece."[6] And, indeed, he could better describe Perth than Thessaloniki.

This lack of knowledge of the rest of the Greek nation arises chiefly from the low level of communication with other Greek areas. Although the islanders are constantly in communication with the rest of Greece via radio and the island telephone, the small island steamer comes only twice a week in summer and often not for weeks at a time during the winter. Athenian newspapers, consequently, although available, are read only sporadically. In addition, the Kastellorizian community in Piraeus publishes a local island newspaper and sends it gratis to the island. Nevertheless, the islanders are unquestionably more poorly informed and disinterested in national politics than other Dodecanesians. The islanders are, for the most part, Australian-oriented and only island issues, usually economic matters, will bring forth any kind of discussion.

This economic and social context provides useful insights into Kastellorizian politics. In 1961, the islanders gave Konstantinos Karamanlis and the

---

[1]Throughout the islands, Dodecanesians shared this consternation at the remarkable political allegiance of aquatic life to the Government of Turkey.

[2]Ibid.

[3]Ibid.

[4]Ibid.

[5]Ibid.

[6]Ibid.

E.R.E. a slight majority, but in 1963 and 1964 voted solidly for the Center Union. Although Kastellorizians express their current political preference in ideological terms (e.g., "We of the Dodecanese are tied to Eleftherios Venezelos, the great man who helped to free us"; "Under years of foreign rule we learned to distrust strong power in Government"), the chief reason for the shift to the Center Union lies in the local loyalty to the island's sole minister, Mavros, a supporter of Georgios Papandreou. In the election of 1963, representatives of the Center Union sent telegrams to the islanders promising them an improvement in the island's electricity, provision of work opportunities, subsidies, etc.[1] Support was quickly forthcoming, for, as one islander confided to the researcher "We vote for whoever will do things. If you came and promised to help, we would vote for you!"[2] In a situation of demographic and economic atrophy, the inclina- tion to jump to something new, hopefully a ready-made solution at high politi- cal levels, increases rapidly, especially among people with volatile political temperaments.

Emigration and Geographical Diversity

The examples of Karpathos and Kastellorizo are illustrative of the pro- cess by which emigration has affected the social, economic, and political geog- raphy of the Dodecanese islands. Although these islands embody the repercussions of extensive emigration and severe depopulation, the process of spatial differ- entiation applies to other islands, albeit at a variable scale.

As the case studies exemplify, emigration fundamentally alters the exist- ing economic, social, and political structure of the islands. It is the uneven distribution, then, of Dodecanese emigration and depopulation which contributes to the evolution of island differences within the island group. The spatial pattern of depopulation by island since 1821 is shown in Figure 24. The general trend is marked fluctuations, largely due to both political and economic vicis- situdes.

Based upon analysis of historical changes, the Dodecanese islands may be divided into three major groups with appropriate nomenclature: Group one, the "diminutive maritime island," characterized by the case study of Kastellorizo, includes Symi, Chalki, Kasos and Leipsos. Emigration and depopulation attain their most precipitous rates in this class since economic dislocation here reached its greatest magnitudes. Concentrated in this group are the former sponge-fishing islands which represent the unsuccessful adjustment of the Dodec- anese to the changing characteristics, linkages, and markets of this industry.

---

[1]Personal interview, Kastellorizo, November 16, 1963.

[2]Ibid.

Group two, the "undiversified agricultural island," characterized by Karpathos, includes also Telos, Nisyros, and Patmos. This group has not successfully adapted to the changing economic bases of the Dodecanese since World War II and population losses are characteristic, although at more gradual rates than the diminutive maritime island. The inability to benefit from new sources of potential wealth keeps these islands in severe economic straits.

Group three, the "modified, multi-resource island," characterized by earlier case studies of Kos and Kalymnos, also includes Rhodes and Leros. All these islands have successfully diversified their economies in response to the changing sources of economic development. As a result, population changes approach stability or even fluctuating general increases. In most cases, these islands also represent a two-frontier orientation to both land and sea resources, and, in the case of both Kos and Rhodes, recent exploitation of amenities resources. Astypalia, the one exception to the classification, has a slower rate of population decline due to its agricultural possibilities and to a higher rate of emigrant returns.

While Figure 24 illustrates the changes by island since 1921, more intensive analysis of population changes by villages between 1951 and 1961 (Figure 25) affords additional insight. Contrasts both among and within islands reveal a general pattern of concentrated depopulation in the rural and more isolated areas. In Rhodes, for example, population increases are concentrated in the city and suburbs of Rhodes and in the adjacent market-oriented agricultural zone. Population losses, by contrast, are in the subsistence and transitional agricultural areas. Throughout the islands, a general rural-to-urban migration is visible. The legacy of emigration and depopulation, then, is most marked in these areas.

The Legacy of Emigration and Depopulation

Economic Effects.

The economic effects of depopulation are both beneficial and harmful. On the deficit side, the emigration of Dodecanesian youth, especially the young men, has created severe labor shortages in the more productive agricultural and maritime islands. At harvest time in Rhodes and Kos, farmers experience greater difficulties each year in obtaining needed help. Kalymnos now relies chiefly upon outsiders for sponge-fishing divers, and even as mandarine-pickers. In agricultural activities, the insufficient labor supply is compounded by a growing refusal of young women to work in the fields. As a farmer in Afantou, Rhodes, grumbled, "Women also do farming here—not the young ones, though! They're too proud to work in the fields. But the old ones aren't ashamed. They go."[1]

---

[1]Ibid.

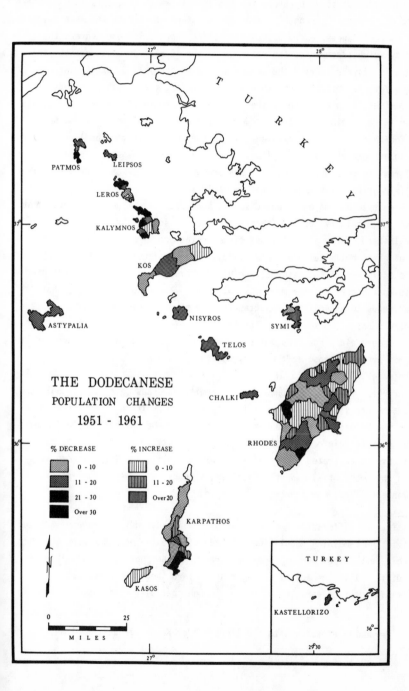

Figure 25.—Population changes in the Dodecanese Islands, 1951-1961.

Because of a general absence of the younger portion of the population, a variety of economic activities are restricted in their expansion.

On the plus side, however, the remittances which emigrants send back are a source of financial strength. Although Karpathos represents the more extreme effects of remittances, every Dodecanese island shares, in some degree, the prosperity which accompanies the mail. When the "Christmas boat" arrived three days late in Nisyros, during the writer's stay on the island, excitement had reached a feverish pitch. More than any one factor, these cash gifts have contributed mightily to the rise in the Dodecanese standard-of-living. The consistency of these receipts is also noteworthy and arises from the profound sense of obligation that every Greek emigrant has to the πατρίδα (fatherland) and especially to his own village and island. The librarian of Kasos, contemplating the role of remittances, mused, "Our islands are Greek, but our employer and benefactor is America. Take America and we would starve."[1]

Remittances are a two-edged sword, however. Seldom do land improvements, purchases of machinery, or investments in needed resources arise from these funds. Instead, these gifts are perceived by the Dodecanesian as a stark reminder of his own limitations. How vividly appears his own poverty as contrasted with the affluence of the external world! Whatever small gains have been eked from his work become all the more insignificant. The result is, then, that the islander tends to exploit the remittances. He gives up his small patch of land, abandons his βάρκα (boat), and begins to deluge his emigrant relatives with requests for more aid. How many emigrants who, deeply saddened and distressed by the sudden greed of those left behind, dutifully continue to send their checks just the same?

Perhaps the most profound role of remittances has been its psychological impact. The parasitic quality of a life based upon remittances is a new ingredient in the Dodecanese experiences. Increasing dependency has seemingly cultivated or perhaps reinforced attitudes toward the outside world. Again, convincing evidence demonstrates to the villager his inability to alter his own existence in any substantial manner. Fatalism, already so widely prevalent among the islanders, finds new sources of strength.

Social Effects

The sex differentials of emigration have resulted in a preponderance of females in the remaining population. In addition to the economic problems which inevitably result from such an age-sex structure, the shortage of eligible men causes difficulties in marital arrangements. Throughout the Dodecanese, the presence of unmarried girls is a common, though spatially variable, problem.

---

[1] Personal interview with the librarian of Kasos, January 3, 1964.

In a culture which places a premium on family and children, such an "unnatural" state is tantamount to personal tragedy. In some cases, as Karpathos illustrates, the problem is surmounted only by bringing in outsiders as participants in marriage contracts. Other areas, however, are unable to resolve the difficulties and contribute to the problem by creating additional unmarried, though honorable, brothers.

A second social effect is the break-up of Dodecanesian families. Because of the importance of emigration to economic security, few families escape the experience of familial disruption. To a people long exposed to the exigencies of the economic and political order, this constitutes an additional element in the traditional Greek melancholia.

Political Effects

A somewhat intangible political problem created by emigration—one constantly and repetitively decried by all major political parties—arises from the loss of the nation's youth. The flight of the young is widely equated with an inevitable loss of national vigor and vitality. "Only we old sticks remain—we who are too old to even make our lands bear fruit. Will Greece find greatness in us?"[1] Those who remain view themselves as the inmates of a vast home for the aged, prisoners of a climate of atrophy. Almost without exception, Dodecanesians feel that their islands have little hope for the future unless the outflow of the young is halted. Given this general deeply-felt conviction, it is not surprising that emigration has emerged as a controversial national issue.

In the election campaigns of 1963 and 1964, a reduction of emigration formed a major plank in the Papandreou platform. During his campaign visit to the Dodecanese, Georgios Papandreou promised that his administration would undertake whatever measures were needed to stem the tide of emigration. Undoubtedly, the failure of the Karamanlis regime to solve this question contributed to its downfall. The salient consideration that emigration involves forces beyond immediate practical control matters not in a land where all issues are politically accountable.

A final effect of emigration and depopulation, alluded to above, involves their imprint upon basic conceptions of social and political change. In addition to their fatalism, Dodecanesians have, exfept for the more precocious inhabitants of the affluent maritime cities, been largely inward-oriented through the centuries of foreign occupation and isolation from the rest of Greece. The roots of sustenance and ingredients of social change have been anchored in the soils of local resources.

---

[1] Ibid.

Remittances from emigrants have reversed both the outlook and the reality of available inputs for social change. The opportunities for acquiring wealth from the outside world have caused a spatial reorientation in the methodology of innovation. Whether it be a road for a village, a school (or school-bus as in neighboring Chios) for the community, or a hotel to attract tourists, villagers inevitably seek satisfaction of the demand through contribution among their compatriots abroad. While such an orientation is unquestionably a productive and efficient source for inducing change, undue reliance upon this orientation for innovation has led to the malaise of dependency upon the charity of others. This parisitic experience seems to have retarded more responsible local government and community organization.

CHAPTER VI

THE TOURIST AND THE ISLANDER

Μόνον ο τουρίστας μπορεῖ νὰ σώσει τὸ νησάκη μας. Ὡραῖο δὲν εἶναι;
Καθαρὸς ἀέρας γαληνή θάλασσα θαυμάσιες παραλίες—ἡσυχία. Πῶς δέν
τύχουν νὰ σταματήσουν ἐδῶ τουρίστες; Γιατί μᾶς ξεχνάνε οἱ κρουαξιέρες—
'ας σταματήσουν μόνον μία, δύο ὥρες... Ἔχωμε τόσο πολὺ νὰ προσφέρομε...[1]

(Only the tourist can save our little island. Is it not lovely?
Clean air, tranquil sea, wonderful beaches—peace. Why don't tourists
chance to stop here? Why do the cruisers forget us - let them stop
only an hour or two... We have so much to offer...)

The decline of maritime industries and the dislocation of agriculture
would have caused severe damage to the Dodecanese economy had it not been for
the development of new sources of economic strength. Other than the burgeoning
inflow of remittances, the rapid growth of the tourist industry has formed the
principal new ingredient in the Dodecanesian economic resurgence since World
War II.

First actively developed during the Italian occupation, tourism rests
upon a strong base in the Dodecanese islands. The sun-saturated, mild climate,
scenic beauty, archeological and historical sites, cultural distinctiveness, and
the low cost of living—all are major inducements for tourism. Although all Dodecanesian islands possess these endowments in varying degrees, only Rhodes, Kos
and Patmos have, thus far, benefited greatly from their exploitation. As a result, tourism has contributed to further economic and social differentiation
among the islands. The overall regional impact, however, has nonetheless been
extensive, as the larger framework of Greek national tourism indicates.

The Framework of Greek National Tourism

At present, Greece is launching a major drive to develop tourism as a
means of combating its chronic balance of payments deficit.[2] Shortly after its
accession to power in 1955, the Karamanlis regime created the National Tourist
Organization which soon initiated a vigorous program of hotel construction and
archeological development. The results of this activity are notable. Between
1960 and 1963 alone, the number of hotels in Greece increased from 1,567 to
1,698.[3] Over the same period, the number of visitors to archeological sites

---

[1]Personal interview, Telos, November 18, 1963.

[2]Commercial Bank of Greece, Report of the Chairman of the Board of
Directors for 1962 (Athens: Commercial Bank of Greece, 1963), pp. 38-39.

[3]National Tourist Organization.

increased from 156,975 to 1,682,997, with an increase in revenue from 1,018,965 to 12,692,104 drachmas.[1]

The increase in the number of tourists entering Greece between 1955 and 1963 is shown in Table 26.

TABLE 26

TOURISTS ENTERING GREECE,
1955 - 1963[a]

Year	Foreign Tourists[b]	Cruise Passengers	Greek Citizens from abroad	Total
1955	171,474	12,533	24,379	208,386
1956	181,051	12,286	25,064	218,401
1957	221,984	9,650	28,646	260,280
1958	227,336	22,284	26,973	276,593
1959	278,147	38,140	23,683	339,970
1960	315,805	55,525	28,108	399,438
1961	408,909	53,948	31,334	494,191
1962	508,821	56,454	32,649	597,924
1963	644,032	68,273	28,888	741,193

[a]Source: National Statistical Service of Greece
[b]Excluding cruise passengers

In the span of these nine years, the number of tourists increased over threefold, and cruise passengers increased almost sixfold. The United States (147,561) still constituted the largest source of tourism in 1963, with Germany (86,756), England (73,352), France (65,695), and Italy (32,872) following behind.[2]

A marked specialization, both spatially and organizationally, has accompanied the growth of tourism in Greece. National tourist schools now provide highly-trained personnel and better standards of service. A national tourist police, frequently composed of multi-lingual members, protects, regulates and helps tourists during their stay in Greece. Throughout the country, local demes are cooperating with the national government in programs aimed at enhancing existing resources for attracting tourists.

Corresponding to this organization development, greater spatial specialization is emerging in the various regions of Greece. Athens, for example, boasts the unmatchable beauties of the Acropolis and numerous other archeological sites, Byzantine churches, museums, and modern comforts. The surrounding areas of Attica and the Peloponnesos are likewise rich in archeological remains. The islands, however, provide the additional advantages of environmental amenities and scenic beauty which have helped to make them fashionable with the "jet

[1]Ibid.

[2]Ibid.

set," with artists, with islomaniacs. Such is the case of the Dodecanese which, led by Rhodes, the island of Aphrodite, beckons to both Greek and foreign tourist alike with diverse charms.

The Tourist Base of the Dodecanese

Environmental and Scenic Attractions

Both the physical and cultural environments contribute to the islands' potentialities for touristic development (Figure 27). The mild, sunny climate of the Southern Aegean, together with the rugged, bare topography of the archipelago, creates a natural setting priased by travelers for centuries. The omnipresent sun and the warm, clear waters of the Mediterranean create an idyllic haven for the prisoners of winter in more northern European countries. The mineral baths of the islands are an additional health attraction for the sick and the aged.

The islands also contain a variety of scenic beauties. Both Rhodes and Karpathos have forested rugged mountains where a splendid view and seclusion are readily and simultaneously available. The Italian occupation has left fine gardens and parks in the cities of Rhodes and Kos. The same cities still have numerous mosques from the years of Turkish sovereignty. On some of the more remote and poorer islands, villagers can still be seen wearing their native costumes, without affectation, as their daily dress. Finally, throughout the islands, the dazzling white, cubic architecture of houses distinguishes the islands from both mainland Greece and other European areas.

Historical and Archeological Attractions

The turbulent culture history of the Dodecanese has also bequeathed a legacy valuable for touristic development. The islands abound with artifacts from the high technical and artistic state of earlier epochs. Vaulted tombs and beautifully decorated vessels remain, for example, from the Mycenean Age. From the Archaic Age, the renowned "Rodiaka" plates, illustrated by colored likenesses of the Rhodian deer, were once exported to the limits of the then-known world from the ancient cities of Ialysos, Kamiros, and Lindos. The present city of Rhodes itself, with its spacious avenues and regular city blocks, reflects the creativity and ingenuity of Hippodamos. Finally, the Hellenistic period witnessed a further artistic development, especially in the plastic arts. The Colossos of Rhodes was built during this age in honor of the sun-god, Helios.

The more important archeological sites and museums containing these artifacts are very unevenly distributed within the Dodecanese (Figure 27). On Rhodes, the acropolises of Rhodes, Ialysos, and Lindos, the ancient city of Kamiros, and the medieval walls, castle, and fortifications of the Knights and the museum are especially noteworthy. On Kos, the Asklepion, the plane-tree of

120

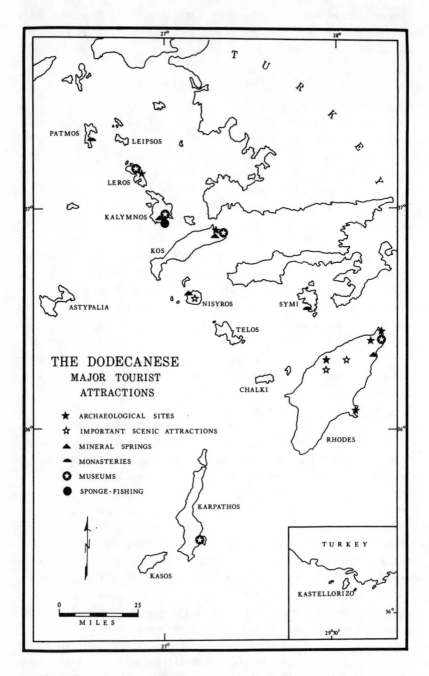

Figure 27.—The major tourist attractions of the Dodecanese Islands.

Hippocrates, a museum, and medieval ruins are the major attractions. Patmos contains sites of special religious significance in its cave of the Apocalypse and medieval monastery. The other islands also have both ancient and medieval ruins which are, for the most part, unrestored and of minor interest to non-archeologists.

Cultural Contrast

Several other assets of the islands for tourism are significant. Greece generally, and the Dodecanese in particular, provide a cultural contrast for the bulk of the tourists who come from areas of western civilization. The Dodecanese, for centuries under Turkish rule, have formed a cultural frontier between western and oriental civilization. Both the contemporary material and non-material culture reflect the accommodations that have transpired. For the European and American tourist, the contrast in dress, diet, and architecture lends added charm to other historical and scenic attractions.

Financial and Purchasing Advantages

A final set of tourist enticements arises from the low cost of living in the Dodecanese, compared either to the source countries of the tourists or to other areas in Greece. Hotels are approximately fourteen per cent cheaper than the national Greek average, gasoline eighty per cent cheaper, and food and clothing twenty-five per cent cheaper.[1] In 1964, luxury accommodations were still available for ten dollars a day, while an expensive meal seldom cost more than two dollars.

Since Rhodes and the other Dodecanese still enjoy a lower tariff schedule than the rest of Greece, textiles and luxury goods are available at very low prices. A tailor-made suit or topcoat out of imported English wool, for example, costs only forty-five dollars. A fine selection of hand-made Rhodian pottery and gold jewelry is available at favorable prices. Relics and antiques from the Byzantine period (mixed in with numerous more-recently created replicas) are also available. For Greek tourists, the islands of Kos and Rhodes have an anomalous function—the provision of umbrellas, status symbols in Greece, at substantially lower costs than elsewhere. The result is a plethora of specialized Dodecanese "umbrella shops" and the characteristic sight of the Greek awaiting the return ship to Athens, a number of umbrellas tucked under his arm—or, quite often, the angry customs officers berating the Athenian who has tried to "smuggle" more than one umbrella.

Characteristics of Tourism

Initially, it was the Italians who developed the Dodecanese, especially

---

[1] Konsola, op. cit., P. 85.

Rhodes, as a tourist center. Tourists, at the beginning of the Italian occupation, numbered only about 700, while in 1934 this figure had risen to 60,000
tourists, chiefly from Italy and Egypt.[1] The foundation established during this
interwar period served as the base for the rapid expansion of tourism which has
occurred since reunification. Over the last decade, for example, the number of
tourists has increased tremendously. Although statistics are unavailable for
each island, accurate detailed figures are available for Rhodes, which, in any
case, accounts for the overwhelming portion of the Dodecanese tourist industry.
Much more limited data is available for Kos and Patmos. Estimated figures for
the other Dodecanese were obtained by interviews with local officials. Figure
28 shows the overall pattern of tourism for 1963.

Rate of Increase

Figure 29 indicates graphically the increase in Rhodian tourism since
1952. During this period, the total number of tourists entering Rhodes has increased nearly sixfold. Only merchant ship crews have declined since the mid-
1950's, while all other categories, beginning in 1959, revealed a rapid acceler-
ation of the rate of increase. A similar rapid expansion has occurred on Kos
where tourism increased from 20,000 in 1959 to 34,500 in 1962.[2]

Composition

Analysis of the composition of tourism casts additional light upon the
significance of the increasing tourist rate. Foremost in the changing structure
of tourism is the increasing preponderance of foreign tourists. Native Greek
tourism only doubled in the decade between 1952 and 1962, but foreign tourism
rose by 1,778 per cent.[3] This tremendous increase in foreign tourism is especially beneficial to the local economy since foreign tourists spend much more
per capita than native tourists, both for living expenses and for purchases.
Finally, cruise tourists, one-day visitors to the island, increased by 710 per
cent during the same decade.[4]

A detailed breakdown of Rhodian tourism by nationality reveals some
striking changes between 1955 and 1962 (Table 27). While Americans accounted
for forty per cent of all tourists in 1955, in 1962 they constituted only fourteen per cent of the total despite a doubling of their numbers. The rapid growth
of European tourism, especially that of Swedes and Germans, has eclipsed the
former American dominance. Swedes alone now account for more than one out of

---

[1]Great Britain, Naval Intelligence Division, op. cit., p. 23.

[2]National Tourist Organization.

[3]Ibid.

[4]Ibid.

123

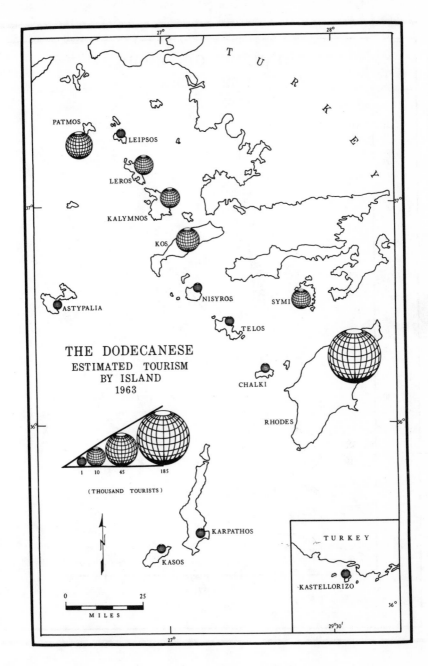

Figure 28.—Estimated tourism in the Dodecanese Islands in 1963.

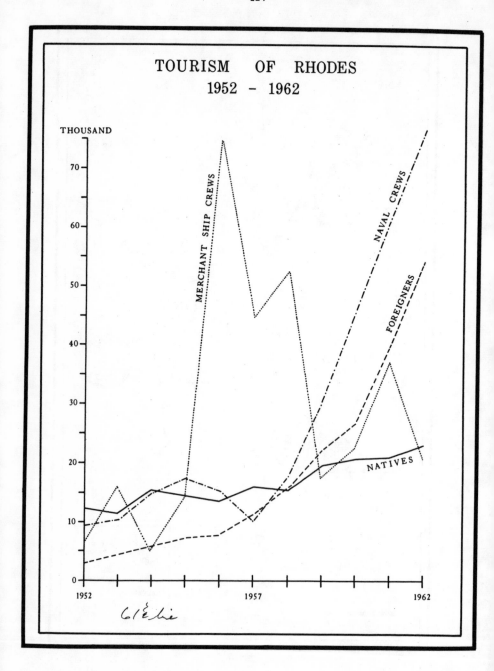

Figure 29.—Tourism of Rhodes, 1952-1962.

TABLE 27

OVERNIGHT TOURISM OF RHODES, BY NATIONALITY OF TOURIST,
1955 - 1962[a]

Nationality	Year								Per cent of total for 1962	Absolute total 1955-62	Per Cent of total 1955-62
	1955	1956	1957	1958	1959	1960	1961	1962			
American	2,948	3,051	3,077	3,339	4,881	6,943	7,200	7,527	13.86	38,966	20.96
German	775	996	2,375	5,743	5,587	6,454	8,646	9,286	17.10	39,862	21.44
Swedish	149	108	141	1,319	2,408	1,502	7,545	14,745	27.16	27,917	15.02
Swiss	223	602	1,714	1,709	2,373	1,777	2,626	3,138	5.78	14,162	7.62
English	744	305	421	819	1,489	2,640	3,546	4,552	8.38	14,516	7.81
French	426	526	1,064	723	1,183	1,389	2,074	2,368	4.36	9,753	5.25
Italian	229	180	296	262	706	808	767	1,102	2.03	4,350	2.34
Austrian	163	38	131	309	562	602	1,157	1,313	2.41	4,275	2.30
Greeks	484	479	498	246	310	305	324	211	.56	2,857	1.54
Belgians	122	130	224	188	208	749	552	722	1.33	2,895	1.56
Canadian	91	89	119	87	194	255	253	367	.68	1,455	.78
Dutch	55	85	118	166	213	328	452	509	.94	1,926	1.04
Turkish	80	123	139	154	212	204	233	176	.32	1,321	.71
Other	886	1,217	964	865	1,941	2,783	4,745	8,268	15.09	20,509	11.63
Total	7,355	7,929	11,281	15,927	22,267	26,739	40,120	54,284	100.00	185,904	100.00

[a]Source: Tourist Police of Rhodes

every four tourists. American tourism remains, however, of disproportionate economic influence because of a higher rate of per capita expenditure.

Duration of Stay

Stratification of tourism by both nationality and duration of stay also indicates some interesting comparisons (Table 28). The relative proportion of each nationality remained very similar in 1963 as in 1962. Yet, the high proportion of Swedish tourists staying overnight in hotels gives this group still greater significance than the Americans, English, Swiss, Israeli, and French tourists who are predominantly one-day visitors from cruises. The Israeli tourist epitomizes the cruise tourist par excellence with only four per cent of the total staying overnight in hotels.

TABLE 28

TOURISM OF RHODES STRATIFIED BY NATIONALITY AND TYPE, 1963[a]

Nationality	Stayed in Hotels		One-day Visitor (Cruises)	
	Numbers	Per Cent	Numbers	Per Cent
Swedish	18,567	27.4	1,711	1.5
German	10,360	15.3	13,134	11.5
American	8,367	12.3	22,202	19.4
English	5,423	8.0	15,050	13.2
Swiss	3,439	5.0	9,088	8.0
French	2,724	4.0	11,367	9.9
Danish	2,018	2.9	1,244	1.1
Austrian	1,580	2.3	1,605	1.4
Italian	1,445	2.1	2,279	2.0
Norwegian	1,043	1.5	203	0.2
Belgian	695	1.0	1,907	1.7
Greek (with passport)	225	.3	10,398	9.1
Yugoslavian	3	.0	6,155	5.4
Turkish	294	.4	1,879	1.6
Dutch	620	.9	1,513	1.3
Canadian	429	.6	995	0.9
Australian	262	.4	250	0.2
Israeli	341	.5	8,494	7.4
Other	9,705	15.1	4,798	4.2
Total	67,640	100.00	114,272	100.00

[a]Source: Tourist Police of Rhodes

On the whole, the increase in tourists staying more than one day on Rhodes is encouraging. Between 1957 and 1963, the increase was fully 232 per cent (Table 29). Of equal significance is the fact that, over the same period, the total number of nights stayed increased by 346 per cent. This lengthening duration of stay is of great economic importance to the Rhodian tertiary industry.

TABLE 29
OVERNIGHT VISITS TO RHODES,
1957-1963[a]

Year	Number of Tourists	Total Nights Stayed	Average Length of Visit (in days)
1957	27,399	137,107	4.89
1958	31,344	189,438	6.05
1959	41,979	245,720	5.85
1960	47,458	283,682	5.97
1961	61,148	405,562	6.63
1962	77,409	534,853	6.89
1963	90,661	611,859	6.77

[a]Source: Tourist Police of Rhodes

Seasonal Distribution

The distribution of tourism in Rhodes by category and by month (Table 30) illustrates a general problem of the industry.[1] Regardless of tourist category, there is a heavy concentration in the summer months. Fully 92 per cent of all tourists come in the April to October summer season. Consequently, a large proportion of tourist facilities and shops are forced to close during the winter season, and seasonal unemployment is widespread. The cultivation of Swedish tourism again assumes additional importance since Swedes make up the bulk of the foreign winter tourists. Attempts now under way to stretch the tourist season into November have met with little success thus far.

Organization and Problems of the Tourist Industry

Organization

Within the last five years, tourism has become a much more highly organized industry at the local level. In Rhodes, more than three tourist agencies now conduct tours to the various attractions on the island. A sound and lights program, modelled after its renowned predecessor in Athens, relates the turbulent history of the Knights in Rhodes.

At the national level, the over-all growth of tourism in Greece has inevitably benefited the Dodecanese. The profusion of tourist agencies in Athens nearly always include Rhodes, and often Kos and Patmos as well, in their Aegean

---

[1]This problem is analyzed at length in Miltiados I. Logothetis, 'Ο Τουρισμὸς τῆς Ρόδου (Athens: National Bank of Greece, 1961), pp. 41-45.

TABLE 30

SOURCES OF TOURISTS ENTERING RHODES,
1962 and 1963[a]

| Month | Residing in Hotels | | | | Not Residing in Hotels | | | | | | Totals | | | |
| | Greek Tourists | | Foreign Tourists | | Cruise Tourists | | Yacht Tourists | | Ships' Crews | | Total Tourists | | Total Days Spent | |
	1962	1963	1962	1963	1962	1963	1962	1963	1962	1963	1962	1963	1962	1963
January	821	895	290	439	1,031	623	----	----	----	----	2,142	1,957	5,082	5,927
February	716	744	469	546	1,308	855	----	----	----	----	2,493	2,145	5,698	5,283
March	966	724	2,490	2,032	2,529	3,418	69	----	5,500	180	11,584	6,354	14,250	14,335
April	1,265	1,821	6,097	7,295	9,653	10,761	76	84	2,600	4,700	19,621	24,661	47,916	59,706
May	2,861	2,123	6,759	8,539	7,451	11,750	261	119	----	1,380	17,332	23,961	62,533	73,672
June	2,298	2,234	5,928	10,020	8,280	9,068	87	134	----	20,332	16,593	41,788	54,273	71,315
July	3,566	3,448	6,715	9,170	11,944	19,723	148	191	580	----	22,953	32,532	79,962	91,588
August	4,797	3,974	8,884	10,605	15,080	25,730	90	250	320	300	29,171	40,854	98,015	165,904
September	2,591	3,064	8,857	10,147	9,945	15,289	40	91	4,060	600	25,493	29,191	87,141	101,614
October	1,598	1,542	6,312	7,345	7,966	12,466	51	140	7,350	----	23,277	21,493	61,591	63,677
November	826	1,218	1,052	1,036	697	3,647	4	----	195	120	2,774	6,021	12,435	11,264
December	820	1,234	501	466	1,842	942	----	----	200	----	3,363	2,642	5,957	8,173
Total	23,125	23,021	54,284	67,640	77,756	114,272	826	1,059	20,805	27,612	176,796	233,604	534,853	611,859

[a]Source: Tourist Police of Rhodes

cruises. In some cases, tourist organization at the country of origin has proven instrumental in the increase of tourism in the Dodecanese. Swedish tourism, for example, is very highly organized at its source.[1] The tourist pays a blanket price in Sweden which covers all expenses except for the purchase of gifts. Hotel charges, meals, tours, and tips—all are included in a flat fee. Special Swedish tour guides, speaking correct Greek but with characteristic Swedish intonations, accompany the tourist group from its beginning in Sweden to the end of its stay. In fact, organization at the source has been a major explanation for the striking increase in Swedish tourism.

The Role of the Government.

Undoubtedly, the single most important contribution of government to touristic development has been the creation of the National Tourist Organization. This organization has established rules and procedures designed to prevent exploitation of the tourist and also formulated a consistent, nationally-observed classification of hotels. Meanwhile, a newly-created tourist police enforces the measures designed to protect tourists and caters to their special needs. These steps have set new standards and revolutionized the quality of service in the tourist industry—an industry in which low standards of service were formerly a major obstacle to touristic development.

The Greek government has also assumed an active role in capital investments in the tourist industry. Under its five-year program for economic development, the State had, by 1964, invested over $3.5 million in the tourist facilities of Rhodes alone.[2] Even the smaller and more isolated Dodecanese islands are now the sites for new, small hotels. Under the influence of government investment, Dodecanese tourist facilities are expanding very rapidly.

Tourist Facilities.

Like the tourist industry itself, active hotel construction began during the Italian occupation with the erection of the renowned Grand Hotel. Since that time, Rhodian hotel facilities have progressed to the point where they now offer a wide diversity of accommodations in all classes (Table 31).[3] This rapid rate of construction stems from both the increasing investment of private capital and the public expenditures of the national government.

Besides Rhodes, only Kos shows diversified strength in tourist accommodations. Even here, the Ξενια (Xenia), a Class B hotel, is only recently

---

[1]For a detailed discussion of Swedish tourism in the Dodecanese, see "Οἱ Σουηδοὶ Τουρίσται Κατέκλυσαν τὴν Ρόδον," Ροδιακὴ, October 30, 1963.

[2]Konsola, op. cit., p. 85.

[3]See Logothetis, op. cit., pp. 51-57; Miltiados Logothetis, Τουρστικαι Μελεται (Athens: 1963), pp. 39-44.

completed. Nevertheless, a start is being made even on Kastellorizo, where a new hotel stands (as it has stood for several years) near completion, and even the inhabitants from smaller islands, envious of the success of Rhodes, anticipate their economic salvation in tourism.

TABLE 31

HOTEL FACILITIES OF RHODES, 1963[a]

Class	Numbers	Beds
Hotels	40	3,322
Deluxe	3	822
A	5	719
B	7	789
C	16	750
D	7	208
E	2	34
Inns	6	76
Rooms in Houses	--	1,122
Hostels	2	99
Total	48	4,619

[a]Source: Tourist Police of Rhodes

Restaurants are a problem throughout the islands and in Greece as a whole. The characteristic Greek belief in the "rightness" of Greek cooking and the resultant unwillingness to incorporate other "foreign" dishes produces a remarkably limited cuisine. In addition, the wide use of olive oil commonly produces a mild dysentery in the unaccustomed traveler. Consequently, both the lack of restaurants and the character of the cuisine are drawbacks to greater touristic expansion.

Problems of Touristic Development

Despite the rapid growth of tourists entering the Dodecanese and the substantial progress in the organization of the tourist industry and provision of facilities, a number of problems continue to plague a greater realization of the islands' potential. First, outside of the city of Rhodes, and perhaps Kos, tourist facilities are either primitive or non-existent. Even where hotels are now being constructed, they are usually only barely adequate at best in their provision of basic services. Luxuries, such as heating and air-conditioning, are still largely unknown. Even hot water is hard to come by in some instances. Restaurants, as indicated above, present a still greater problem. Finally, entertainment and recreational facilities are badly needed as ancillary functions. The Government presently has the provision of badly-needed accommodations as its major policy goal. The development of associated facilities must, for the time being, await the fulfillment of this basic objective.

A second problem involves transportation.[1] Only the ports of major
Aegean islands now have adequate communications, and then not always during the
winter season. Since approximately seventy-four per cent of all tourists entering Rhodes still come by ship and only twenty-six per cent by air, rough winter
seas are still a major problem. Moreover, only Rhodes at present has a commercial airport, though plans are under way for establishing airports at Kos and
Karpathos. Transportation among islands by the small island steamer, the
"Πανωρμητις" (Panormites), can be hazardous as well as uncomfortable. The general sea problem is also compounded by the dearth of adequate, deep-water harbors. Even on Rhodes, large cruise liners must anchor offshore and ferry tourists ashore by small boats.[2] In rough seas, island ships are frequently forced
to seek alternate ports because of the exposure of the Rhodian harbors.

In the hinterland of ports, transportation services are equally rudimentary. Modern tour buses and rental cars and scooters are available only on
Rhodes. Otherwise, the carriers are either rudimentary, incredibly crowded
buses, or mules. Provision of improved facilities would do much to overcome the
spatial restriction of tourism to a few major port cities.

A final problem, discussed above, is the need to lengthen the tourist
season. The imbalance of summer and winter tourism poses difficulties both for
owners and employees. A successful development of winter tourism would undoubtedly contribute significantly to greater stability in the Dodecanese economy and
a reduction in seasonal unemployment.

The Impact of Tourism

The Economic Impact.

Although tourism is a relatively new source of economic strength, its
impact has been only slightly less than that of remittances. In 1959, touristic
exchange produced over $1.6 million in the Dodecanese, or thirty per cent of all
invisible sources of income (Table 32). Furthermore, Konsola estimates that by
1962, touristic income in the Dodecanese had grown to over eight million dollars.
Given the rapid growth of tourism since 1959, this estimate would not appear to
be exaggerated. Finally, although statistics are unavailable, the overwhelming
proportion of this income is unquestionably concentrated in the city of Rhodes.

The impact of this large and rapidly increasing touristic income is
clearly evident in the tourist centers. The ports of Rhodes, Kos, and Patmos

---

[1]For a lengthy treatment of this problem, see Logothetis, 'Ο Τουρισμὸς
της Ρόδου, pp. 46-51.

[2]This problem has been the subject of widespread discussion in the local
Rhodian press. See especially the comprehensive analysis by Spyros S. Tepaldos,
"Τουρισμὸς καὶ Πλοῖον," Ροδιακὴ, January 10 and 11, 1964.

have experienced a major growth in service and retail industries. By 1962, Konsola estimates that there were 2,500 people employed in occupations directly related to tourism in Rhodes.[1] Ultimately, of course, a greater number of inhabitants benefit through the multiplier effect of the tourist industry.

TABLE 32

INVISIBLE SOURCES OF DODECANESE INCOME,
1954 - 1960[a]
(in 1,000 dollars)

Year	Total Invisible Income	Touristic Exchange
1954	2,085	1,557
1955	2,873	625
1956	3,344	821
1957	4,272	1,003
1958	5,193	1,261
1959	5,464	1,639
1960	9,810	b

[a]Source: National Statistical Service of Greece and Branch Offices of the Commercial Banks of Greece.
[b]Figures unavailable.

The general geographical effect of tourism has been to contrast sharply the economic status of inhabitants of the cities of Rhodes and Kos with those of other areas in the Dodecanese. Other Dodecanesians scarcely share at all in the prosperity tourism has brought to Rhodes, yet, regardless of this potential for development, see tourism as their chief hope for economic betterment.

The Social and Political Impact

The general rise in the standard of living of inhabitants in tourist centers has obvious social implications. As with remittances, touristic income has demonstrated the relatively poorer position of those still engaged in traditional occupations. Quite naturally, the upshot has been a widespread desire to capitalize on this new, lucrative source of income. This effort to share in the bounty takes myriad forms—posing in native costumes for fees, opening up a room for tourists, weaving rough fabrics for "tourist" clothing, or acting as guides. Increasingly, islanders look to a bright millennium when both tourists and "δολλάρια" will be plentiful on even the smaller islands.

Since tourism is one of the chief contacts the Dodecanesian has with the outside world, it also influences his view of other peoples and cultures. For perhaps the first time, many islanders have been exposed to differences in language, physical appearance, dress, and dietary preferences. Slowly, a limited amount of change is taking place and some of the more extreme forms of

---

[1]Konsola, op. cit., p. 87.

parochialism are disappearing. It is now generally realized that a foreigner may not speak Greek and still be literate and that women who wear slacks and shorts are not necessarily prostitutes.

Nevertheless, perhaps the more noteworthy aspect of the contact between islander and tourist is how little communication and exchange really takes place. Withdrawn from centuries of foreign rule into a shell of cultural protection, there is a deep suspicion, not unaccompanied by amusement, toward anything alien. In addition, since only a minute proportion of Dodecanesians speak any foreign language (except perhaps for Italian), both the quantity and quality of inter-action is necessarily severely restricted. Therefore, there is little genuine understanding or sympathy for alien values and behavior. By and large, the per-ceived ludicrous behavior of tourists tends to confirm the belief in the inher-ent superiority of Greek culture.

The characteristics of tourism have also contributed to the images that the islanders hold of particular nationalities. The Swedes, largely from middle-class families, are viewed as quiet, reserved, careful with their money, and pleasant. Americans, by contrast, are pictured as a people heavily prone to drunkenness and wild spending. Largely derived from the many American sailors stopping at Rhodes and from the "ugly Americans" of the "jet set," this view substantiates the image previously formed by second-rate American films. Also, the presence of a Coast Guard contingent the "Courier," the relay ship of the "Voice of America," has contributed to the problem. All tourists, however, have suffered of late from the increasing influx of "beggar tourists."[1]

Tourism, because of both its actual and perceived value to the local economy, has emerged as a controversial political issue, centered primarily upon the question of governmental allocations. Throughout the Dodecanese, islanders complain that the Greek government—by endowing Rhodes with an impressive array of tourist facilities and attractions, while neglecting the considerable poten-tion of other islands—has merely followed in the footsteps of Mussolini since reunification. This grievance is shared, not only by the inhabitants of other islands, but also by the villagers in other areas of Rhodes.

Finally, tourism as a total experience has had a number of political ramifications. The growing reliance upon yet another source of income from the outside world has reinforced attitudes, derived elsewhere, toward social change. Government is looked upon as but another of these external influences. Tourism has also affected attitudes toward human relationships. Living from the gratu-ities and spendings of other peoples seemingly generates modes of behavior

---

[1]Largely from the more affluent countries of Western Europe, these tour-ists sleep in the open and obtain funds for travel and food by begging in the streets. Greeks especially resent these individuals because they place an addi-tional strain on the already hard-pressed finances of Greece.

earlier Dodecanesians would have found shameful. Every outsider is viewed as
someone to be tricked out of his money. Among Dodecanesians, Americans are iden-
tified by the phrase "Εἶναι γιὰ κωροῖδο?" (Is he for making a fool out of?). A
Koan farmer embodied this general attitude by remarking, after the researcher
had expressed his gratitude for the farmer's generous hospitality:

> It is to our honor to philoxenize people—they will come and spend
> money and leave it here, and, who knows, we may be lucky enough to
> get some. Or maybe later, we may chance to see someone again and
> they may give us money to help us.[1]

The Role of Tourism in Island Contrasts

The variable impact of tourism in the Dodecanese inevitably plays a major role in spatial differentiation. Yet, the quantitative effect is perhaps
more readily apparent than the qualitative. Three case studies have been selected to illustrate both of these parameters of tourism. In Rhodes, tourism is
large in number and diverse in origin, but with a strong preponderance of foreign
tourists. In Kos, tourists come chiefly from other areas of Greece. Tourism in
Patmos, the religious capital of the Dodecanese, is composed nearly exclusively
of one-day visitors from cruise liners. Finally, these three islands also form
the major centers of Dodecanese tourism at the present time.

Rhodes

In his original development of the island, Mussolini was determined to
make Rhodes the touristic showplace of the eastern Mediterranean. Accordingly,
the Italians built hotels, restored ruins, excavated archeological sites, and
established gardens and parks. Since this early beginning, much has been accom-
plished in providing the city with a wide range of tourist facilities, and it is,
at present, the one Dodecanese port fully equipped to service international
tourism.

The rapid growth of tourism in Rhodes is indicated above. Of the total,
Greeks probably compose only between twenty to thirty per cent of the total.
Among cruise tourists, the proportion is significantly less (slightly over ten
per cent). Moreover, the impact of the Greek tourist upon Rhodes is less than
numbers indicate because of a lower per-capita expenditure, especially for meals
and lodging.[2]

Spatially, only relatively few points on the island benefit from the influx of tourists. The city of Rhodes is certainly the principal beneficiary.
Nearly all tourists who do visit other points of interest on the island do so on
one-day trips. Since only the city has the housing, comforts, and entertainments

---

[1] Personal interview, Kos, November 26, 1963.

[2] Logothetis, 'Ο Τουρισμὸς τῆς Ρόδου, p. 19.

which most visitors demand, they seldom stay overnight in these outlying places. The one village which benefits in any substantial way is Lindos, site of the famous breathtaking acropolis. Although there are other important archeological and scenic attractions, none is associated with a village which has profited from proximity. Sample interviews with village officials indicate that other Rhodian villages receive an annual maximum of 200 to 250 tourists, and most of them just passing through, although occasionally one may rent a room or even a deserted house.

The net result of tourism, then, has been to enrich the city of Rhodes and to hasten the rural-to-urban migration already in progress. Meanwhile, Rhodes has become, more and more, an international city, more cosmopolitan in most respects than Athens itself. The villagers and other islanders, in the meantime, have been the joyless spectators of Rhodian prosperity.

Kos

Many travelers refer to Kos as a "poor man's Rhodes." It seems to possess most of the tourist attractions of Rhodes, but in diminutive, less polished form. The archeological sites are less extensive and spectacular. The walls and fortifications of the Knights have not been fully restored and are far less impressive than those of Rhodes. Italian legacies, although ever-present in gardens and wide avenues, lack the majesty and serenity of the larger sister island. Finally, Kos cannot begin to compete with the luxury and first-class hotels or the Palace of the Grand Master in Rhodes.

The result of this comparative situation is that foreign tourists shun the island. In conversation with tourists of diverse origin, a surprisingly large number distastefully characterized the island as "seedy," "boring," or "decadent." Consequently, Kos has evolved a special function—serving, in actuality, as a "poor man's Rhodes" for Greek civil servants and merchants on their annual vacations. It is well-adapted for this role since prices are substantially lower than those in Rhodes.

The structure of tourism in Kos is shown in Table 33. Although tourism is increasing at a pace similar to that of Rhodes and although the relative proportion of foreign tourists is also increasing, Greek natives (72.5 per cent) continue to dominate. Many stay for the entire duration of their vacation period.

TABLE 33
TOURISM IN KOS, 1959-1962[a]

Nationality	1959	1960	1961	1962
Natives	11,000	17,177	18,477	20,000
Foreigners	9,000	11,122	10,631	14,500

[a]Source: National Tourist Organization

This preponderance of Greek nationals has implications for the island's tourist industry. Generally, Greek tourists do not support the wide range of ancillary tourist services found on Rhodes. Large numbers stay in the homes of relatives and friends, while others seek out the more inexpensive hotels. It is not surprising then that a relatively large number of Class D hotels have arisen in Kos—a fact, in itself, not conducive to foreign tourism. Moreover, in an effort to keep prices low so as to solidify their appeal to Greek tourists, officials have created a difficult problem for Koan farmers.[1] Since restaurant prices are lower than in Rhodes, Koan agriculturalists receive less for their produce, especially meat. Consequently, farm income is artificially kept in a depressed state on the island.

Tourism in Kos is more spatially restricted than on Rhodes. Whereas Rhodes has major attractions located at diverse points on the island, nearly all tourists attractions in Kos are in, or are immediately adjacent to, the city. In addition, transportation to the other four villages of the island is infrequent—one-day trips are virtually impossible and extremely rudimentary. Since tourists rarely travel outside the city, then, the impact of tourism is nearly exclusively limited to the city of Kos.

Patmos

The religious significance of Patmos gives it a special base for touristic development. The Apostle John took sanctuary on this island and allegedly wrote the Apocalypse between the years 81-96 A.D. In addition, the famous medieval monastery, founded in 1088 A.D. by St. Christodoulos, contains valuable manuscripts, tapestries, art treasures, and the bones of over 100 saints. Finally, including the chapels in the monastery, Patmos boasts a total of 364 churches, many erected in honor of particular saints or deceased members of the family.

Because of this religious importance, Patmos is a popular stop for Aegean cruises and tours. Consequently, tourism, on this island, is nearly exclusively composed of one-day or brief duration visitors. Only recently was a hotel constructed to serve overnight tourism. In 1963, Patmos had an estimated 29,000 tourists, of which approximately 22,000 came from cruises alone.[2] Despite this large number of tourists, greater than that of Kos, tourism has had a smaller impact than on either Rhodes or Kos. The major benefit of tourism is restricted to the transportation of tourists up the steep slopes to the monastery and the cave of the Apocalypse. This employs a total of four taxis. Other than that,

---

[1]Personal interview with K. Nikolopoulos, Agricultural Service of Kos, November 26, 1963.

[2]Local Tourist Organization of Kos.

two small hotels, three restaurants, and several gift shops comprise the tertiary services. As one islander put it, "Tourism is just enough to blunt emigration, which is not as serious a problem here as in other islands."[1] Of course, much of the population is associated directly with the monastery. The total effect on the Patmian is certainly diminutive compared to the impact in the cities of Rhodes and Kos.

Other Dodecanese Islands

None of the other Dodecanese has an extensive tourist industry at the present time.[2] Only Leros and Kalymnos receive more than 1,000 tourists a year, and most of these are emigrants or Greek natives. Leros has long functioned as a summer resort island for wealthy Lerians in Egypt and the United States. Kalymnos has a unique tourist attraction in its sponge industry and other basic components of hotels, movie theaters, restaurants, and thermal baths. Yet, the total array and quality of tourist enticements is still substantially less than Rhodes, Kos, and Patmos.

Among the other Dodecanese, anticipation runs far in advance of present achievements. Karpathos now has a new hotel of thirty rooms and a potentially attractive sand beach. Yet, Karpathians complain that the lack of good transportation and needed tourist facilities cause only a handful of foreign tourists to come each year. Kasos rarely has tourists except for Kassians returning for the summer. Kastellorizians anxiously, but skeptically, await the completion of their small hotel and look to a time when they might transport visitors on guided tours to Anatolia across the way. Nisyrians indicate only a very few annual tourists—chiefly Nisyrians returning for the summer and sick Greek nationals who wish to use the mineral springs. Telos has a new hotel, largely financed by remittances, but it stands nearly empty even during the summer period.

Conclusions

The present state of tourism in the Dodecanese reveals that the industry is still in its incipient stages. Nevertheless, nearly all Dodecanesians see tourism as their chief hope for economic progress. In islands where even a few tourists could add substantially to the island economy, people inevitably dream of the good fortunes of Rhodes.

---

[1] Personal interview, December 13, 1963.

[2] For a discussion of the role and problems of the smaller Dodecanese islands in tourism see Logothetis, "Ἡ Τουριστικὴ ἀξιοποίησις τῶν μικρὸν νησὸν τῆς Δωδεκανήσου," Τουριστικαὶ Μελέται, pp. 13-18. The special situation of Nisyros is described in Miltiados I. Logothetis, Τουρισμὸς καὶ Οἰκονομία τῆς Νησοῦ Νισύρου (Rhodes: 1963).

In the few centers of touristic concentration, tourism has fundamentally altered both the economic bases and related social characteristics. Contacts with tourists have helped to cause a spatial reorientation to social change and to shape the perception of other peoples and cultures. Finally, the impact of tourism has led to further spatial differentiation. Although potential touristic resources are available on nearly all islands, only the richest have been tapped. Tourism has, thus, further diversified the islands and contributed to inter-island conflicts over government-financed development allocations.

CHAPTER VII

THE IMPRINT OF POLITICAL SOVEREIGNTY

The State is the good ship that holds our fortunes all;
Farewell to friendship, if she suffers wreck.[1]

The history of the Dodecanese is, above all, a history of foreign occupations, some of brief duration, others of long centuries of stubborn rule, but
all forcibly against the will of the island's inhabitants. Since political sovereignty entails wide latitudes of control and organization over people's lives,
the experience of a succession of foreign occupations has shaped the economic
and social history of the Dodecanese. An illumination of the role of sovereignty, then, should enrich our understanding of the evolving human geography of the
islands. At best, it may also provide some clues as to what life was like in a
particular place during a particular period of political control.

An integral component of such an analysis is the function of sovereignty
as a vehicle for landscape change. Derwent S. Whittlesey described the impress
of central authority upon the landscape in 1935 when he observed:

Political activities leave their impress upon the landscape, just
as economic pursuits do. Many acts of government become apparent in the
landscape only as phenomena of economic geography; others express themselves directly. Deep and widely ramified impress upon the landscape is
stamped by the functioning of effective central authority[1]

Because the relations between man and the landscape are so delicate, changes in
the political order have left a lingering imprint upon patterns of land use,
architecture, and resource exploitation in the Dodecanese. Insofar as evidence
is available, the interaction between politics and landscape will be noted.

It is noteworthy that the evidence upon which to base such an inquiry is
highly unevenly distributed through time. More detailed discussion is possible
for the most recent centuries for foreign rule than for earlier occupations. In
addition, analysis is restricted to the pre-World War II era; changes since reunification are described in other portions of the study.

The Ancient Era

The pre-Roman era is perhaps the most complex period of political-geo-
graphical organization in Dodecanese history. The kaleidoscopic shifts of power

---

[1]Sophocles, Antigone, trans. F. Storr (New York: Macmillan Co., 1912),
p. 329.

[2]Derwent S. Whittlesey, "The Impress of Effective Central Authority upon
the Landscape," Annals of the Association of American Geographers, Vol. XXV
(June, 1935), pp. 85-97.

among a mosaic of city—states created a continual fluctuation of political fortunes and stability. Throughout this period, both regional and external organization contributed to economic and political changes.

Regional Political·Organization

Following the original settlement of the Dodecanese prior to the twelfth
century B.C., the islands soon became major maritime centers, actively trading
with Africa, Spain, Italy, and the Levant. Rhodes, especially, gained rapidly
in population and wealth, and soon established colonies in Karpathos, Chalki,
Symi, Nisyros, Karia, Lycia, and eventually in the more distant areas of Egypt,
Sicily, Italy, Spain, France, and the Black Sea.[1] From the coinage of the period,
it is clear that each of the three principal cities of Rhodes—Ialysos, Kamiros,
and Lindos—was independent of the others and had its own territorial sphere of
influence, both inside and outside the island. Apparently, similar territorial
divisions also prevailed on Kos, Karpathos, and the "Kalydnian" islands.[2] This
highly-decentralized political pattern soon changed, however, in the quest for
larger regional groupings.

The first major attempt at a federal political structure occurred with
the formation of the Doric Hexapolis. Composed of Kos, the three renowned cities
of Rhodes, and the coastal Anatolian cities of Knidos and Halicarnassos, the
League initially met for religious purposes, to hold games in honor of the Tri-
opian Apollo, and to discuss subjects of mutual concern. Later, Greek towns of
lesser importance probably participated in the League as associate members of
satellites of the original six cities. Adjacent to Knidos, for example, ruins
of the old town of Myndos (Gumushlu) indicate that it was fortified at this
time.[3]

The League soon expanded its activities from those of a strictly religious and social character to mutual military and political protection in the
face of the aggressive overtures of the Asian tribes and to attempts at broaden-
ing their geographical influence. Thus, the Hexapolis founded Gela (a highly
successful Greek colony in Sicily), a western "Roda" in northeastern Spain, colonies on the east coast of Italy, Kastellorizo in the east, Phaselis on the Pam-
phylian gulf, and Soloi in western Cilicia.[4] The League also came to perform a

---

[1]Volonakis, op. cit., p. 85; Doxiades, op. cit., p. 44; Torr, op. cit.,
pp. 31-37.

[2]Volonakis, op. cit., p. 89.

[3]John L. Myres, Geographical History in Greek Lands (London: Oxford University Press, 1953), p. 310.

[4]Ibid., p. 311

valuable function in behalf of the Dodecanese Islands by providing an effective
mainland screen against the Persian advance.

External Political Relations

External political linkages were insufficient in maintaining Dodecanese,
and especially Rhodian, security and, in fact, such alliances were often responsible for the period of warfare and political instability which extended from
525 to 130 B.C. The advance of the Persians eventually resulted in their control over the Dodecanese islands. The Dodecanese joined the Athenian confederacy and emerged from the successful war still wealthy and heavily-populated.
During the Peloponnesian War, however, these external commitments involved the
Dodecanese in civil strife when the islands divided their allegiance between
Athens and Sparta, while the smaller islands of Leros, Chalki, and Symi honored
their commitments and became strategic bases for the Athenian fleet.

The security problem created by this Dodecanese-Athenian alliance caused
the inhabitants of the three Rhodian cities, previously united only by loose
ties of confederation, to pool their efforts and wealth in one common government.
While this new city served as the decision-making center for foreign policy and
general problems of social welfare, the older cities continued to exist and to
administer their own internal affairs. In fact, the senates of the three ancient
cities continued to function as late as the Roman Empire.[1]

The defeat of Sparta did not terminate Dodecanese involvement in mainland
politics. In the Second Athenian Confederacy, Rhodes and Kos joined with seven-
ty-three other cities to contest a resurgence of Spartan military power. Later,
however, Athens failed to come to the defense of Rhodes and Kos, and the Dodecanese fell under intermittent Karian hegemony until the advent of Alexander the
Great.

With the support of Alexander, the Rhodians reached the zenith of their
maritime power. To remain independent from foreign entanglements and to insure
their neutrality, they rejected alliance overtures from other major states and,
instead, joined in a closely-knit federation with other maritime and island
cities. This regional organization permitted the Rhodians to enjoy a period of
relative stability during which they solidified their strong maritime position.
Nevertheless, from 300 to 130 B.C., powers to the east periodically attacked and
besieged the Dodecanese, and eventually the islands fell under the hegemony of
Rome.

Population and Resources

The population and economy of the islands fluctuated with their widely-

---

[1]Torr, op. cit., p. 65.

varying political fortunes. At the height of political stability and maritime power, the Dodecanese capitalized on their geographical position between Africa, Anatolia, and the Black Sea to emerge as the major commercial center in the eastern Mediterranean. The islands competed successfully with such formidable rivals as the energetic Phoenicians. At Kamiros, archeological finds of a re-markable series of painted vases and other artifacts indicate that the city en-joyed great wealth from the seventh century B.C. onward.[1]

Population growth contributed to the establishment of colonies at widely-scattered points on the periphery of the Mediterranean Sea. This territorial expansion reached its apex during and after the accord with Alexander the Great when the Dodecanesians accumulated extensive landholdings on the adjacent Ana-tolian coast and outlying islands. This land base supplemented the Dodecanese maritime strength by supplying the islands with corn, cattle, and timber. The newly-founded cities of Rhodes and Kos and numerous archeological remains attest to the sizeable population and enormous prosperity of the islands. The city of Rhodes was widely acclaimed for its excellent location, numerous harbors and fortifications, city morphology, arts and industries. In Kos, meanwhile, the Asklepion attracted from afar ill persons who were assured of the safety of the seas. Though not an effective rival to Rhodes, Kos also became very prosperous and produced renowned poets, painters, and textile-workers.[2]

During intervening periods of instability, warfare, and foreign occupa-tions, population and economy suffered severe recessions. On several occasions, invaders devastated the Rhodian fleet and serious economic declines followed. In the midst of political instability, Rome expanded its control over the Dodec-anese islands.

The Roman Occupation

Roman domination of the Dodecanese produced major political and economic shifts. Roman patronage of Delos diverted commerce away from Rhodes, and Delos became the great port of the Aegean. In addition, Roman indifference to mari-time security allowed piracy and slave-trading to run rampant. Piracy eventu-ally assumed such dimensions that it paralyzed commerce and destroyed the basis for Dodecanese prosperity. Within the Dodecanese, the location of the Roman regional naval base on Astypalia detracted further from the historical primacy of Rhodes.

On the positive side, the Rhodian tourist industry had its inception

---

[1]Ibid., p. 309.

[2]See Dēmētrios Hadjiamallos, ʽΗ Κῶς,τὸ νηδι τοῦ Ἱπποκράτους (Athens: N.D.),pp. 25-35; Christophoros N. Andriotakēs, Kos, The Motherland of Hippo-crates (Athens: 1961), pp. 10-19.

under Roman auspices. Large numbers of foreigners visited the island to experience firsthand the elegance of Rhodian culture and art, to study rhetoric, and to enjoy the amenities of her climate and scenery. Leading Roman statesmen and noblemen such as Mark Antony, Julius Caesar, Cicero, Cassius, and Brutus, were included in this pilgrimage to the "island of Apollo."[1]

As soon as Rhodes began to recover her former economic prosperity and naval preeminence, however, Rome launched a preventive attack upon the island and her fleet. The subsequent sack of the city and the shipment of its vast wealth to Rome left the inhabitants destitute. This devastation was especially harmful to the financial class of the island, as was a second blow which, following the battle of Philippi, included the seizure and burning of the entire rebuilt Rhodian merchant fleet.

Later, the rule of Mark Antony guaranteed the islanders freedom from such predatory attacks. At the same time, the restoration of the Rhodian dominion over the Cyclades, Andros, Naxos, and Tenos strengthened the commercial position of the island. Augustus confirmed the status of Rhodes as a "free and allied city," while Vespasian designated Rhodes as the capital of a new "province of the islands." Within the framework of such political stability, the Dodecanese steadily revived their seafaring and commercial activity. Rhodes again emerged a renowned center of commerce, artistic achievement, fine educational establishments, and efficient administration. In addition, the recently-established tourist trade again flourished and provided the island with a valuable source of income.

During the late period of Roman rule, especially in times of greater autonomy from centralized control, Rhodes dominated the other Dodecanese both politically and economically. Rome provided enough protection to ensure continued maritime affluence and enough internal freedom for self-government and self-expression in institutions and the arts. These advantages, however, were not to be continued during the Byzantine period.

The Byzantine Period

For the first few centuries, Byzantine rule imposed few major alterations on the lives of Dodecanesians. Administratively, the division of the islands was at first ecclesiastical and Rhodes continued as the capital of the island group. From the time of Justinian (527-565 A.D.), the old governmental system of the Roman underwent modification as administration was centralized under a unified military and political head. After the seventh century, further modification created large administrative areas (themata) under the jurisdiction of a

---

[1]Volonakis, op. cit., p. 201.

military figure. In all, there were some thirty themata in Europe and Asia within the Byzantine Empire. The Dodecanese were divided as follows: Rhodes and Symi were in the Theme of Kibyrraiotus, Kos and its adjacent islands in the Theme of Samos, Astypalia and the other Cyclades in the Theme of the Aegean, while Karpathos and Kasos were in the Theme of Krete.[1] In short, the islands were divided among four of the major naval themes of the Byzantine state.

Despite the progressive centralization of administration, the major effects of Byzantine sovereignty arose from its weakness rather than its strength. The Byzantine centuries were periods of repetitive and destructive pirate raids. The first attack occurred in 470 A.D. when the Isaurians attacked the city of Rhodes and rained widespread destruction upon its inhabitants. In 620, the Persians captured the city and were not expelled until two years later. Saracen attacks upon the Byzantine Empire followed shortly thereafter, and the Dodecanese, like Cyprus and Krete, suffered from the ravages. The Saracens soon became masters of the sea and the Dodecanese quickly felt their wrath. Kos was attacked, captured, and pillaged, and similar raids ensued on the other island. After Rhodes succumbed in 654, she did not regain her freedom until 659 when civil war broke out among the Saracens. Equally destructive raids followed in 717 and 807.

In view of this continual death and destruction, the demographic and economic collapse of the islands is not surprising. Forced to rely solely upon local agriculture and helpless before the onslaught of pirates, population shrank to low levels, and several islands were entirely depopulated. Settlements were abandoned as inhabitants sought refuge in the more protected, elevated, fortified towns. Maritime commerce, constantly harassed and plundered, declined to a fraction of its former level.

This instability continued until the dynasty of King Comnenus in the eleventh century. His control over the coves and harbors of Asia Minor and fortification of the larger islands brought maritime security to the Aegean Sea. The Dodecanese islands and fleet soon became a supply and provision center for the crusaders. In 1099, the Venetians passed the winter on Rhodes and remained to occupy the city. In 1125, when the Rhodians attempted to expel the intruders and refused to provide further food and supplies, the Venetians sacked the city.

The Crusader conquest of Constantinople in 1204 led to the dissolution of Byzantine control over the Dodecanese. The western states of Genoa and Venice then seized the islands. Leon Gabalas, self-styled "Lord of the Cyclades," ruled Rhodes, Karpathos, and other Dodecanese islands as an independent principality. Eventually, however, the Genoese captured Rhodes, but lost it to the

---

[1]Doxiades, op. cit., p. 51.

Greek emperor of Constantinople. Throughout, the Dodecanese continued to be a profitable prey for the Genoese and other corsairs. Effective stability did not reassert itself until the successful conquest of the islands by the Knights of the Hospital in 1310.

The Dodecanese under the Knights

Following their unsuccessful attacks upon Rhodes, the Knights quickly occupied the other islands of the Dodecanese. From all these islands, the Knights exacted a tribute (mortuary) of foods, materials, or money in the form of aspres or gold florins. In Symi, for example, the islanders paid an annual tribute of 500 aspres, and all monks forfeited their goods to the Knights at the time of their death.[1] In some cases, individuals paid to the Grand Master of Knights an annual consideration for lease of administration rights over certain islands—a situation which all too often led to the cruel exploitation of the local peasants. Such was the case, for example, of Chalki and Telos, which were leased to the Rhodian noble Barello Assanti in 1366 on the condition of an annual payment of 200 golden florins.[2] In 1391, Kalymnos and Leros were placed under the personal administration of the Governor of Kos.[3] Clearly, the taxes, duties, food requisitions, and labor recruitment levied upon the native islanders formed the foundation upon which the acclaimed military engineering feats and exploits of the Knights rested.

Initially, the political involvement of the Dodecanesians in the government of the Knights was negligible; after all, they had been forcefully subjugated. During the fifteenth century, however, the Knights found themselves under attack from the increasingly-powerful Ottomans to the east. To solidify their strength, the Knights found it advantageous to increase Greek participation in their regime. Thus, during the rule of the Grand Master Pierre Zacosta (1461-1467), local inhabitants began to perform minor functions in island administration.[4] Next, the Knights conducted a census of all Rhodians capable of bearing arms. Finally, Dodecanesians actually were invited to participate in the councils of war and in the military effort itself. During the successful resistance to the siege of 1480, the contribution of the loyal Rhodian soldiers caused the grateful Grand Master to reward them in a variety of ways.

The role of the islanders in the defense of Rhodes is more evident during

---

[1]Volonakis, op. cit., pp. 251-252.

[2]Ibid., p. 253.

[3]Ibid., p. 255

[4]Ibid., p. 260

the second siege when the defenders numbered only 600 Knights, 400 Kretans, and 500 of other nationalities, but more than 6,000 Dodecanesians.[1] Moreover, the food amassed by an intensive scouring of Dodecanese farmlands provided the supplies needed to withstand the siege. Inevitably, such activities left their imprint upon the islands.

The effects of the Knights upon the Dodecanese landscape were diverse and far-reaching. Perhaps most serious in the long run was the rapid depletion of local forests for ship-timber, for which the introduction of the European deer, the famed "Rhodian" deer of today, was scant compensation. In Rhodes and Kos, huge walls and massive fortifications, constructed all too frequently from the materials of archeological ruins, still dominate the landscapes of these island cities to the present time (Figure 30). On the smaller islands, observation posts and forts, whose remains can still be seen on Leros, Astypalia, Kalymnos, and Kos, provided protection against pirates and guaranteed forewarning against massive invasions. In the city of Rhodes, the enlargement of the Jewish section lingered on until the German occupation in World War II. Finally, the many churches and convents established by the Knights remain in lonely ruins throughout the islands.

The effects of the Knights upon the Dodecanese population and economy are equally noteworthy. During the early years of the occupation, the newly-established political stability and maritime security generated a rapid increase in commercial activity. Symi and Rhodes, in particular, again became wealthy entrepôts and prosperous centers of shipping. This economic resurgence led to a growth in population, both in numbers and distribution. In 1413, for example, the Grand Master Giovanni IV Quirini repopulated Astypalia, which had been depopulated during the centuries of pirate raids. Legend also has it that the Knights reintroduced the pottery industry to Rhodes by capturing a ship containing Persian and Damascene potters, enroute to Lebanon.[2] Since the sand in Lindos was especially suitable for glazing, the pottery industry allegedly became very successful and its products highly prized by Europeans.

In the latter part of the occupation, however, these impressive gains quickly dissipated in the wake of destructive Ottoman attacks. In 1455, the Turks successfully assaulted Kos and Symi, sacked the Rhodian village of Archangelos and ruined the surrounding farmlands, and raided the islands of Nisyros, Leros, and Kalymnos. Shortly after, the raids of Moslem pirates again depopulated

---

[1] Ibid., p. 276.

[2] See Paul P. Vouras, "The Development of the Resources of the Island, of Rhodes under Turkish Rule, 1522-1911," Balkan Studies, Vol. IV (1963), p. 44. Robert Liddell doubts the veracity of the legend. See Robert Liddell, Aegean Greece (London: Jonathan Cape, 1954), p. 197.

Figure 30.—The massive interior fortifications of the walled city of Rhodes. Constructed by the Knights for protection against the Turks during medieval times, the walls have been refortified numerous times. Huge cannon balls remain on the floor between the walls, while cemeteries ring the entire city. The two women in the right-center of the photograph indicate the scale of the fortifications.

Astypalia. During the eventual confrontation between the Turks and Knights, thousands of Dodecanesians lost their lives, 3,000 during the siege of Suleiman alone, while those remaining saw their homes and lands ravaged.

In summation, the rule of the Knights for over two centuries improved significantly the Dodecanesian's life for only a brief duration before bringing on widespread and catastrophic destruction. While the engineering works of the Knights were impressive and their churches and convents numerous, their failure to improve the agricultural and maritime economy, their lack of progress in education and the arts, the holocaust brought on by their military ventures are certainly the more remarkable and lasting features of the occupation. For the Greeks who contributed the money, labor, and arms for these ill-fated undertakings, the fruits of their efforts were bitter indeed.

The Turkish Occupation

The Privileged Islands

The terms under which the Dodecanese came under Turkish sovereignty bore significantly upon the political structure of the occupation, since the Turks distinguished between subjects of conquest and those of surrender. When the islanders surrendered to Suleiman, it was on the condition that their ancient privileges should be confirmed. Symi, in particular, ingratiated herself with the noted besieger by presenting him with gifts of bread and sponges.[1] Rhodes and Kos alone did not enjoy these privileges since they passed under Turkish control by conquest.

The privileges provided for the virtual autonomy of the Dodecanese under Turkish suzerainty. Exempt from all taxation except an annual tribute (maktou) of 800 piastres and a consignment of five sponges, the islanders were guaranteed complete freedom of trade, especially for timber imports from Anatolia, and special sponge-fishing rights. Turkish officials and admirals were prohibited from interfering in the language, customs, religion or local affairs of the inhabitants. Suleiman also granted the famed monastery at Patmos autonomy and permitted the islands to retain their armed fortresses for security against pirate raids. These privileges were confirmed in 1644, 1813, and 1956.

Administration

Throughout most of the occupation, the major impact of Turkish administration lay in the province of tax-collection. Collected once a year by a government functionary, the maktou itself was generally not oppressive, but the method of collection frequently was. In Rhodes, although the government

---

[1]Great Britain, Naval Intelligence Division, op. cit., p. 150.

was confined chiefly to tax-collection from each municipality, the arbitrary power of the Governor to fix the value of the lira in his district was ruinous both to the individual and the island economy.[1]

Moreover, the tax was not collected directly by the Governor. Instead, he sold the right of tax-collection to the highest bidder. The speculator, in turn, usually sold this right to others at a profit. This procedure resulted in a harsh exploitation of taxation, a comparatively small portion of which accrued to the state.[2] Farmers were especially heavily taxed because of their inability to conceal production, whereas shepherds and tradesmen were better able to evade onerous taxes.

During the early centuries of Turkish control, Dodecanese involvement in the Christian-Ottoman wars was another serious result of Turkish sovereignty. The frequent raids and battles ruined the islands economically and contributed heavily to their depopulation. In 1648, for example, the Venetians attacked Leros and destroyed the island fortress. Shortly thereafter, the Turks recaptured the island. In 1601, the Spanish ravaged the island of Kos, while in 1604 the Knights of Malta devastated its undefended villages.

Patmos perhaps best illustrates the repercussions of this pillaging.[3] In the seventeenth century, the island flourished commercially, its ships trading as far away as Holland, Africa, and the Black Sea. At this time, its hills and coasts were lined with the solid houses of its prosperous inhabitants. The town of Chora contained fully 800 houses—many of them three or four stories—at this time. By the eighteenth century, however, the island was bare, its forests and houses destroyed, only a handful of small boats remaining in the harbor, and its inhabitants few and poor.

Indifference of the Turkish Government to marauding pirates produced similar results on other islands. Symi, Telos, Kalymnos, Kasos, and Astypalia also suffered greatly from these periodic raids. The situation became so desperate in 1654 that Symi concluded a treaty with a Venetian admiral to protect the island's inhabitants and shipping against pirates. Despite this precaution, for which the Symians paid a generous annual sum, Savory records in 1798 in his Lettres sur la Grèce that Symi had fallen into pirate hands, all its ships and most of its resources destroyed, and its inhabitants plunged into "misery, sadness, and poverty."[4]

---

[1] Vouras, op. cit., p. 37.

[2] Ibid., pp. 37-38.

[3] The following is chiefly based upon William Edgar Geil, The Isle That Is Called Patmos (London: Marshall Bros., 1904), pp. 121-124.

[4] Quoted in Volonakis, op. cit., p. 304

Dodecanese participation in the Greek War of Independence inevitably produced Turkish reprisals when the islands could not be included in the new Greek state. In 1824, in retaliation for the active role her daring sailors played in the war, Turks sacked the island of Kasos, murdered most of the able-bodied men, and abducted 2,000 women and children for the slave market.[1] Eventually, however, intervention by the Great Powers led the Sultan to call a halt to the widespread reprisals against the Dodecanesians.

The nineteenth century, on the whole, was a period of marked liberality on the part of the Turkish administration and the islanders enjoyed a wide degree of autonomy. During this period, the Dodecanesians enjoyed a level of prosperity and a growth of population unparalleled since ancient times. Toward the end of the century, however, with the tensions produced by the Kretan rebellion, the pendulum of administrative control began to swing in the other direction.[2] Beginning in 1866, the Turks initiated a systematic reduction of the privileges of the islands. In 1867, the Government sent a battleship to Symi and installed local Turkish authority. Two years later, the Turkish fleet again blockaded the island and seized her public buildings. Kalymnians, with characteristic defiance, resisted all encroachments on their local autonomy and resisted the siege for a month. In 1871, Turkish tribunals replaced the local Greek courts, and in 1874 Turkish customs were established. In quick succession, Turkish harbor controls and police authority, passport payments, and new taxes on salt, spirits, and sponges followed. In 1885, Symian resistance to these measures produced an 18-day blockade of the island and the total abrogation of her ancient privileges.

The Young Turk revolution of 1908 produced widespread hopes throughout the Dodecanese that the new Turkish government would reverse the policy of local interference. In 1909, however, the Turks cancelled all special privileges, and shortly thereafter, they instituted new taxes and proclaimed Turkish the official language of all correspondence and tribunals. Moreover, the government required each community to submit a list of young men for compulsory military service. After prolonged negotiation, the Turks reinstated the status quo, but not before these measures ignited large-scale emigration from the islands.

Local Government.

A local council (demogerontia), composed of twelve members-at-large, a treasurer, and a president, governed the affairs of each island.[3] Elected

---

[1] A lengthy account of this period is available in Tryphonas Evangelidas and M. Michailidis-Nouaros, Ιστορία τῆς νήσου Κάσου (Athens: 1936).

[2] For the following, see Great Britain, Naval Intelligence Division, op. cit., p. 37; Volonakis, op. cit., pp. 316-318.

[3] The best account of local government at this time is in Volonakis, op. cit., pp. 298-299.

annually by the people of the island, the demogerontia had full administrative, judicial and financial power. In addition, a popular general assembly, called by the council president, met in the open to fix taxes and to discuss important issues.

A head tax paid by everyone except the elderly and the poor financed the various activities of the local government. These revenues were expended chiefly for education, medical services and supplies, and the salaries of administrators. The annual budget for the island of Symi in 1910 is shown below as an example:

TABLE 34

ANNUAL BUDGET FOR THE ISLAND OF SYMI, 1910[a]

Revenues

1.	Quota from Customs	23	0
2.	Revenue from sponges (this year's estimates)	1,110	0
3.	Import duties on goods	1,074	0
4.	Flour	259	0
5.	Spirits	110	0
6.	Contributions	117	0
7.	Rents	120	0
8.	Sheep and goats	88	0
9.	Harbour dues	66	0
10.	Documentary fees	56	0
11.	"Contributions" (which, owing to this year's numerous emigration of the inhabitants, are estimated at, only)	500	0
	Total	3,523	0

Expenditures

1.	To duty (Maktou) to the Imperial Government	488	75
2.	To medicines (reduced on account of the present economic difficulty)	546	0
3.	To doctors (limited to three on account of crisis)	445	0
4.	To salaries to the personnel of the communal apothecary	166	50
5.	To schools for boys and girls (retrenched this year owing to the crisis)	900	0
6.	To salaries—2 notables, 1 cashier, first secretary, 2 clerks, 1 chief messenger, 2 messengers, 2 collectors, 2 rural keepers, 10 road cleaners, 4 night watchmen	420	0
7.	To interest on loans	445	0
8.	To lighting expenses for the town	80	0
9.	To alms to the indigent	30	0
		3,521	25
	Surplus	2	55
		3,523	80

[a]Source: Volonakis, op. cit., p. 300.

Wealthy inhabitants of the island contributed to the support of the poor, gave them work, and were expected to make contributions for the general improvement

of the island and the promotion of education. In a sense, the local governments also conducted foreign relations, for they employed envoys to other countries and maintained resident agents in Constantinople. The islanders thus
safeguarded their local privileges. On the whole, the system of local government was highly democratic when measured in terms of elections, administration,
or the financial structure of governmental activities. In terms of its spatial
characteristics, the system was highly decentralized, reinforcing the economic
and social divisions among islands.

Land Tenure

Patterned after the Turkish mainland system, land tenure in the Dodecanese included three major categories of landholding.[1] Vakouf was property administered for the benefit of religious institutions. Mulk comprised property
held in full ownership over which the owner exercised certain rights well-
protected by law. He could, for example, sell the property, while either re-
taining or transferring sovereignty to someone else. Finally, the emiri class
was property officially the domain of the Sultan or Porte, but which, in prac-
tice belonged to the person who cultivated it. The Porte or Sultan could, however, claim the land if it remained uncultivated for a period of ten years. A
portion of this land was always assigned to the offices controlled by the
viziers.

Through the introduction of this system of land tenure, Turkish sovereignty produced a significant impact upon the rural landscape and upon agricultural organization. The Turkish system of land tenure encouraged the emergence
of a few large landowners who exploited their tenant labor. Supplemented by
inheritance laws dividing lands equally among descendants at the time of the
owner's death, the system contributed to a continual fragmentation of native
landholdings. Coupled with the Greek dowry system, there emerged a pattern of
very small landholdings (approximately three acres per farmer) which were divided into a number of fragmented parcels scattered about the village. The effects
of the system are still all too visible in the present patterns of land distribution and in current agricultural problems.

Agriculture.

The organization of Dodecanese agriculture under the Turkish regime re-
volved about the large estates (beylik) of absentee-owners who operated by wide
use of tenant labor. The relationship between the two was generally as follows:
the landlord provided the tenant farmer with a stable, donkey, seed, and land,
in return for which the tenant either paid a fixed rent (usually about two bush-
els of wheat to the acre) or divided the crop equally with the landowner.

---

[1]Vouras, op. cit., pp. 39-40.

The problem with this system is that it produced gross inefficiencies in agriculture. Obviously, landlords could dismiss tenants only at considerable economic loss, and tenants—fully aware that the proprietor had to continue to support them—grew disinterested and lethargic. Moreover, the landlord lacked sufficient control over the way in which lands were actually cultivated. More enterprising farmers often suffered from the competition of cheap grains from foreign areas. Consequently, the younger and more aggressive farmers emigrated to Asia Minor, where land was more plentiful and more fertile, or to Egypt. Agricultural production, then, remained at low levels throughout the occupation, despite the prosperity of other sectors of the Dodecanese economy.

The occupation also affected significantly the division of effort in the production of major crops. The large quantities of wheat imported regularly from the mainland reduced the role of wheat as the dominant component in the subsistence crop complex. At the same time, the role of viticulture and olive-growing became more important. In 1838 the Turks introduced the Sultana vine to the islands and, following an attack of phylloxera in European vineyards, the viticulture industry spread rapidly throughout the islands.[1] The industry contributed to an increased prosperity in Dodecanese agriculture until the 1890's when the disease was brought under control in European vineyards. This agricultural crisis coincided with a more general economic depression in the eastern Mediterranean following the Greek-Turkish War of 1897 to produce widespread suffering among Dodecanesians.

Another result of the Turkish occupation was an increased role for olive production. Olive-growing was especially well-suited to the turbulent political instability of the latter part of Turkish rule, since, if a peasant were forced to flee from his village, he could be assured that the means of his family's subsistence would remain available and he could easily resume olive-cultivation on his return. Consequently, olive production became an important source of security, especially in the more unstable regions of northern Rhodes and Kos.

Maritime Activities

Perhaps no effect of Turkish sovereignty was of greater importance than the re-establishment of active trade relations with Asia Minor, the natural hinterland of the Dodecanese. With strong financial assistance from Rhodian emigres in Egypt and liberal credit from La Credit Lyonnais, La Banque de Salonique, the Anglo-Egyptian Bank, and Die Deutsche Orient Bank, shipping and merchant activities flourished throughout the nineteenth century.[2] Patmos especially

---

[1] Ibid., p. 42.

[2] Ibid., p. 45.

owned merchant ships which traded as far away as the Black Sea, and Leros later gained maritime importance with the development of steamship trade. The entrepôt function of the islands was particularly pronounced during the portion of the occupation dominated by sail-propelled vessels, since they stopped en route from the ports of the Levant to Greece, mainland Turkey, or the Black Sea. The coming of steamers toward the end of the nineteenth century, however, decreased this entrepôt function, for reprovisioning was no longer necessary.

The Dodecanese economy prospered in other ways from the liberal (indifferent) Turkish administration. The sponge-fishing industry, described above, reached its zenith during this period. The opening of the mainland permitted many Dodecanesians to migrate to Turkish cities in search of alternative or supplementary income. Smyrna and Constantinople, in particular were major destinations for urban workers and shopkeepers, while many other islanders purchased farms in the vicinity of towns and cities.[1]

Industry

Since the Dodecanese economy was chiefly agrarian and maritime, most industrial activity centered about these primary occupations. Under the maritime resurgence of the islands, shipbuilding flourished until the middle of the nineteenth century. The principal demand was for the naval vessels of the Porte and sponge-fishing boats for the Kalymnians, Chalkians, and Symians. The precipitous depletion of local forests, however, especially during the frenetic shipbuilding of the Greek War of Independence, prompted a migration of the industry, and of the Dodecanese shipbuilders, to Turkish shipyards.

The pottery industry, allegedly reinitiated under the Knights, prospered significantly under Turkish administration. Mainland demand supplemented the European market and contributed to an expansion of the industry. The Turks were also responsible for shifting the industry to the city of Rhodes. The handicraft activities of the islanders provided another useful source of additional income. Concentrated in island cities, the making of brocades, silk, and linen apparel employed a sizeable number of workers. An embryonic textile industry enjoyed some success, especially in Rhodes, but declined when factory-produced materials became readily available to island inhabitants.

Settlement

The extensive economic changes of the Turkish occupation left an indelible mark upon the distribution of population in the islands. The effective elimination of piracy, the growth of maritime activities, and the beginnings of processing and fabrication gave rise to a shift of population from the protected settlements built around fortresses at the crests of hills to new ports

---

[1]Ibid., p. 46

immediately adjacent to the harbor. The growth of ports in Symi, Kalymnos, Patmos, and Karpathos illustrate this change quite effectively. Moreover, a strong rural to urban migration beginning in this period accelerated during the twentieth century.

Political Diversity and Unity

The Turkish occupation altered the traditional patterns of economic and political dominance in the Dodecanese islands. From the seventeenth to the nineteenth centuries, Rhodes lost the hegemony it exercised over the other islands during ancient and Frankish times. In the seventeenth century, Patmos, with its monastery, school, and maritime activities stood out from the other islands as a center of commercial and cultural activity. During the nineteenth century, by contrast, Symi and Kalymnos emerged as the islands of highest commercial development, based chiefly upon their shipping and sponge-fishing industries. Rhodes, with its predominantly agricultural economy, lagged behind. Since the Turks did not center any major economic activities on Rhodes, it did not enjoy a favored position among the islands.

The Dodecanese also betrayed a similar pattern of decentralization in social and political prominence. Throughout the eighteenth and nineteenth centuries, the leading Greek schools in the Aegean were located at Patmos and Symi, to which scholars traveled from throughout Greece and the Levant.[1] Symi, in particular, functioned as the cultural center of the Dodecanese and produced renowned scholars, poets and artists and hosted several major intellectual organizations. This rich history led one present-day Symian to recall wistfully, "We were an island of leading men, with teachers, schools, merchants in Athens, theatres, and writers, while the Rhodians still did nothing but farm their land. Look at us now!"[2] Of equal significance is the fact that Symi and Kalymnos served as the political vanguards for the Dodecanese—the hotbeds for Greek nationalism and the spearheads for Greek resistance to Turkish rule.

In short, the Turkish occupation witnessed a diminution of Rhodian dominance, economically, culturally, and politically. This transformation contrasts markedly with the overwhelmingly dominant position of Rhodes under the Knights. Italian rule was soon, however, to re-establish Rhodes as "the mistress of the Aegean."

---

[1] Volonakis, op. cit., pp. 301-303.

[2] Personal interview, Symi, December 30, 1963.

The Italian Occupation

Character of the Occupation

The Italian occupation may be divided into two major periods: the pre-
Fascist period (1912-1922) and the Fascist period (1922-1943). The former was
generally a time of political indecisiveness during which Italy refrained from
undertaking positive economic rehabilitations. Awaiting a resolution of the
future political status of the islands, Italian authorities placed a rigid clamp
on Greek economic and political freedom. For "military reasons" in 1916 they
prohibited Dodecanesians from engaging in sponge-fishing and from selling their
fishing boats. Shortly thereafter, they strictly rationed foodstuffs and expro-
priated livestock. Visiting the Dodecanese at this time, Myres records the view
of a Kalymnian woman who said that she no longer taught her children the traditional island folk songs and dances: "No, we do not do that now. We cannot
sing to them any more, for there is no hope left."[1] Another islander characterized this early period of Italian administration by observing: "The Turks had
a bad system, but it did not work, and we got on fairly well. The Italians have
taken the Turkish system and made it work."[2]

The renunciation of the Tittoni-Venizelos agreement in 1922 initiated
the Fascist period of Italian administration. Assured of continued control over
the islands, the Italian Government embarked on an extensive program to estab-
lish the Dodecanese as a model of modern colonialism. In distinction to the
pre-Fascist years, large-scale economic assistance and the introduction of a
long-range program for economic development characterized this period.

Unfortunately, a policy of accelerating "assimilation" to Italian culture and polity went hand-in-hand with this economic commitment.[3] In 1926,
municipal and endowed schools were brought under Italian educational control.
"Naturally, like all conquerors, they struck at education. Education is what
such people fear—they fear classical learning which makes men—free men!"[4] The
present illiteracy problem in the Dodecanese results chiefly from the refusal of
islanders to attend such schools. In 1930, judicial changes enlarged the power

---

[1]Myres, op. cit., p. 335.

[2]Ibid., pp. 335-336.

[3]See the discussion in Great Britain, Naval Intelligence Division, op.
cit., pp. 39-42. For a contemporary Greek view, see the Dodecanese League of
America, The Dodecanese are not Enemy Aliens (N.Y.: Dodecanese League of America,
1942); N.G. Mavris, Sforza vs. Sforza (N.Y.: Dodecanese League of America, 1943).
A contemporary Italian view is available in Giuseppe Gianni, Le isole italiane
dell'Egeo (Florence, Italy: Istituto geografica militaire, 1928).

[4]Personal interview, Symi, December 29, 1963.

of Italian civil courts at the expense of the Greek ecclesiastical courts. In 1931, Italian authorities deprived the municipal school managers of all control over the teachers they employed. Similarly, in 1936, they forbade the use of Orthodox rites in Greek weddings and funerals. These interferences finally reached their climax in 1937 when Governor del Vecchio arrived "to institute Fascism in the Dodecanese."

Changing Spatial Relations

Free and secure movement of maritime commerce and the open hinterland of Anatolia have always been the two pillars of Dodecanese prosperity. Italian sovereignty destroyed both of these bases and in doing so reoriented the external relations of the islands. The "closing of the doors" to the Anatolian hinterland, more than any other single factor, precipitated a loss in trade, agricultural land, and alternative employment opportunities. Italian rule also introduced numerous restrictions on inter-island intercourse and travel to the mainland. Even fishing by small boat to supply local demand was severely restricted. The Italian monopoly over the Libyan grounds also sharply curtailed the Dodecanese sponge-fishing industry. Finally, the Italians established competing state-aided agencies which vied for the transportation and marketing of island production.

In place of these traditional economic linkages, Italy developed close commercial ties with the islands. In 1929, some twenty per cent of all exports went to Italy; in 1938 this figure had risen to 58.8 per cent. Over the same period, Dodecanese exports to Turkey and Greece decreased sharply (Table 35). The trend of imports revealed a similar pattern—the Italian portion growing from twenty-seven per cent in 1929 to seventy-two per cent in 1937 (Table 36). The results of this spatial reorientation were not, on the whole, beneficial to the islanders and gave rise to their widespread emigration.

Land Tenure

Italian sovereignty produced several modifications on the Ottoman landholding system.[1] Five major classes of landholding were recognized: Mulk comprised all forms of freehold. Land in this class could be worked by the owner or leased to a tenant. All mulk land descended from father to sons while houses belonged to women and passed from mother to daughters. Most of the highly-cultivated Turkish fruit-farms and market-gardens adjacent to the city of Rhodes were in this category. Miri was the domain of the State, usually leased for cultivation with provision for inheritance or conversion into mulk by the

---

[1]For a complete analysis of the impact of the Italian occupation upon agriculture in Rhodes, see Roger E. Kasperson and Paul Vouras, "The Development of Agriculture on the Island of Rhodes under Italian Rule, 1912-1943," Balkan Studies (forthcoming).

TABLE 35

DODECANESE EXPORTS, 1929-1937[a]
(in 1,000 lire)

Principal Classes	1929	1930	1931	1932	1933	1934	1935	1936	1937
Spirits, wine oil	1,348	3,000	1,445	3,848	5,036	5,212	7,465	3,586	3,526
Tobacco, drugs, etc.	4,431	3,100	884	682	1,283	388	1,065	1,231	2,693
Chemicals, medicines	59	9	19	19	18	8	16	24	54
Colours, dyes	35	7	21	16	27	20	6	56	10
Jute, manilla, etc.	58	7	45	28	15	28	22	168	274
Cotton, flax, hemp	204	1,000	70	22	27	8	2	3	---
Wool	1,081	2,942	667	159	394	203	355	443	816
Silk	33	241	2	1	---	---	---	---	1
Wood, straw	84	120	194	227	183	248	323	298	250
Paper	540	750	417	240	245	42	36	70	97
Leather, shoes	254	180	54	116	82	40	27	66	121
Metal goods	81	40	444	644	890	5,776	169	148	1,170
Vehicles	106	326	44	2	62	40	12	225	125
Stone, clay, glass, etc.	109	89	90	70	90	43	52	40	82
Rubber, etc.	2	1	17	153	12	17	21	4	19
Cereals	1,490	1,450	835	607	554	526	301	2,066	1,786
Animal products	3,146	260	6,399	4,880	4,279	3,551	3,444	2,005	6,854
Total, all classes	16,240	15,916	12,488	12,713	14,892	17,714	15,154	13,093	19,705
Exports to Italy	3,265	5,752	3,690	6,402	9,281	12,975	8,730	10,113	11,605
Greece	1,424	191	1,060	486	402	374	1,284	111	135
Turkey	887	1,341	545	136	61	30	32	264	6
Elsewhere, including Egypt	8,194	8,632	7,183	5,689	5,148	4,356	5,108	2,605	7,959

[a]Source: Great Britain, Naval Intelligence Division, op. cit., p. 65.

159

TABLE 36

DODECANESE IMPORTS, 1929-1937[a]

(in 1,000 lire)

Principal Classes	1929	1930	1931	1932	1933	1934	1935	1936	1937
Spirits, wine, oil	8,537	15,607	6,588	7,377	6,809	8,564	13,105	9,274	13,044
Tobacco, drugs, etc.	4,919	6,729	4,238	3,294	2,834	2,073	2,543	3,065	4,326
Chemicals, medicines	1,720	3,320	1,851	1,317	1,140	1,287	2,123	1,735	2,683
Colours, dyes	830	350	341	230	213	340	408	266	614
Jute, manilla, etc.	208	240	148	97	23	57	55	68	127
Cotton, flax, hemp	6,264	9,024	6,293	3,841	3,376	3,744	4,624	3,789	6,862
Wool	2,565	3,300	3,427	2,173	1,377	1,536	1,717	1,404	3,344
Silk	1,028	1,130	1,790	916	612	716	1,394	965	1,821
Wood, straw	2,817	3,220	2,155	2,400	1,575	2,122	1,739	224	4,449
Paper	1,421	1,966	1,577	1,066	936	908	1,672	1,087	3,227
Leather, shoes	1,367	1,528	1,390	1,019	753	601	934	680	1,683
Metal goods	4,441	4,219	7,910	4,734	4,225	10,929	24,251	7,555	24,881
Vehicles	1,734	4,130	1,351	907	610	896	2,979	1,326	2,660
Stone, clay, glass, etc.	4,077	6,320	2,994	2,209	454	1,949	5,871	4,228	8,077
Rubber, etc.	577	3,446	658	470	530	318	346	483	755
Cereals	20,324	9,617	12,774	11,130	8,035	7,086	15,363	12,091	24,262
Animal products	9,505	10,050	15,321	10,980	7,845	8,786	10,938	8,054	13,870
Total, all classes	75,200	89,621	75,964	56,350	48,427	56,217	111,030	62,113	122,374
Imports from Italy	20,972	23,554	18,083	16,714	21,015	16,099	78,216	24,128	88,439
Greece	4,786	4,797	7,092	5,615	5,174	6,035	1,193	2,884	822
Turkey	9,382	13,576	10,392	9,858	7,868	7,545	3,872	9,147	4,698
Egypt	3,132	6,567	3,874	2,797	2,424	3,646	2,206	244	1,331
Elsewhere	36,948	41,127	22,823	21,366	18,716	14,102	25,543	22,430	25,543

[a]Source: Great Britain, Naval Intelligence Division, op. cit., p. 64.

leaseholder. If the land were neglected, however, the State could resume ownership. Mevkoufi was land held in trust for religious or charitable uses and usually leased for cultivation. Metroukhi included land in communal ownership,
chiefly for pasture. Individuals could acquire grazing rights, however, and
municipal authorities administered the land. Finally, mevat was waste land.

While these modifications did not represent major changes over the Ottoman system, they did, when combined with Italian agricultural policy, provide
ample opportunity for the implementation of Italian political and economic objectives. In this respect land tenure acted as a catalyst for Italian political
economy.

Italian Agricultural Policy and Accomplishments

Italian agricultural policy coincided with several political objectives.
One important goal was to alter the ethnological structure of the Dodecanese by
encouraging the Greek portion of the population to emigrate or relocate on other
islands. In the place of departed Greeks, the Italian government hoped to relocate large numbers of its own nationals. A second aim was the allocation of
resources to public projects espoused by the occupational regime.

In accordance with these goals, land expropriation occurred in the islands whenever fields remained uncultivated for three years or longer. Land in
the miri class was especially susceptible to such actions. Since Italian authorities frequently prohibited Greek farmers from sowing crops wherever trees
or bushes were present, large tracts of land passed to direct Italian control.
Encouraged to work on public projects at attractive wages, many Greeks vacated
farmlands for possible Italian settlement and supplied cheap labor for construction.

On the positive side, Italian authorities conducted extensive work in
reclamation and agricultural education.[1] By 1938, in Rhodes alone, they re-
claimed fully 2,404 acres of land and established four agricultural settlements
and three agricultural experimental stations.[2] Located in close proximity to
tourist sites, these model settlements served Italian propaganda purposes by
presenting a visible and striking contrast with the traditional Greek agricultural communities. The Italian governor also established agricultural exhibits
in Dodecanese villages, while technicians demonstrated the use of the iron plow,
the value of tree-pruning, the proper planting of fruit trees, and the need for
improving livestock.

Despite the extensive activities of the Italian administration,

---

[1] For a summary of these activities, see Gianni, op. cit., pp. 38-45.
[2] Ibid.

the over-all results showed relatively little improvement in the traditional situation of the Dodecanese farmer. The Italian regime did not solve effectively such fundamental economic problems as the general lack of agricultural credit for fertilizer and machinery, rudimentary transportation, backward cultivation, and inefficient, outmoded marketing methods. Low crop yields and market prices forced many farmers to abandon their land and to migrate to the city of Rhodes in search of employment as construction or factory workers. The more fortunate managed to emigrate to Egypt and the United States, where the small remittances they sent back permitted many relatives to continue to eke out their bare existence.

The progress recorded since reunification with Greece (Table 37) suggests the possibilities for agricultural development in Rhodes. With a fuller utilization of available manpower through increased capital investment and improved farm management, Italy could have substantially ameliorated Rhodian agricultural problems. The problems of increasing the output of manpower and improving farm methods remained unsolved, however, largely because the government could not enlist the participation and cooperation of the native Greek farmers. To a great extent, then, the rural Greek peasantry shares the responsibility for the depressed state of agriculture during the Italian occupation. Rooted in the social and political estrangement between ruler and ruled, the lack of agricultural progress cast a chain about the neck of Italian economic efforts.

Greek nationalism and cultural identity prevented Dodecanesian farmers from wholehearted support of the Italian-sponsored agricultural reforms. Since the Dodecanesian held a fatalistic view of man's place in the world, a natural skepticism of progress also militated against cooperation. Finally, Dodecanesians and other Greeks would have regarded any participation in the Italian agricultural program as a symbol of acquiescence to a bitterly-resented foreign occupation.

The Development of Tourism

Although the effects of Italian policy on maritime and agricultural industries were generally unimpressive, substantial progress was recorded in the development of an important tourist industry. Included in Mussolini's "showplace" plans for the Dodecanese was the dream of Rhodes as the tourist Mecca of the eastern Mediterranean. The activities undertaken by Italian authorities during the occupation unquestionably laid the foundation for the present tourist industry.

The contributions of Italian policy were lasting and diverse. In 1923, Governor Senatore Mario Lago instituted a program for the intensive development of Rhodes as a commercial center and health resort. Prior to Italian control, there had been no systematic exposition and restoration of archeological sites

TABLE 37

PRODUCTION OF SELECTED AGRICULTURAL CROPS UNDER
ITALIAN AND GREEK ADMINISTRATIONS
(in kilograms)

Crop	Total Production, 1935-1940	Total Production, 1950-1955	Per Cent Change
Wheat	16,804,900	41,721,888	148.3
Barley	12,049,600	30,454,676	152.7
Oats	3,484,400	9,737,088	179.4
Lentils	156,300	705,395	351.3
Cotton	76,800	243,820	217.5
Sesame	190,100	2,494,848	1212.4
Tobacco	1,892,100	1,699,710	-11.8
Maize	54,100	1,294,092	2292.0
Cabbages	881,600	8,456,192	359.2
Apricots	607,967	1,795,527	195.3
Peaches	542,400	661,951	22.0
Pears	607,100	2,336,556	284.9
Almonds	610,800	2,849,951	366.6
Walnuts	59,300	466,188	686.2
Fresh figs	3,083,300	3,808,895	23.5
Dry figs	3,121,100	5,484,269	75.7
Oranges	2,708,000	8,812,560	225.4
Tangerines	3,998,800	11,816,744	195.5
Lemons	1,479,800	3,764,144	153.7
Melons	10,835,900	65,602,688	505.4
Tomatoes	4,148,600	92,676,736	2133.9
Cucumbers	3,738,700	10,338,560	176.5
Potatoes	4,000,000	55,442,816	1286.1
Olive Oil	5,056,600	6,921,036	36.9
Eating Olives	2,305,710	1,959,750	-15.0
Grapes	32,749,200	23,199,164	-29.2
Onions and garlic	2,585,400	43,068,224	1565.8

Source: Soterios Agapetides, The Dodecanese Islands, their Economy during the
Italian Occupation and under the Greek Administration (Athens: Greek Productivity Center, 1958), pp. 8-9.

on the islands and the Italians devoted great expenditures for these activities. In the island ports, cleaning, material improvements, and road building enhanced touristic appeal. In the cities of Rhodes and Kos, the Italians established wide avenues and impressive gardens and parks. Perhaps the construction of a number of large and impressive hotels in the city of Rhodes and the forested health resort at Apollona was of still greater significance.

This extensive touristic development, especially of Rhodes, attracted a rapidly-increasing number of tourists. In 1922, Rhodes attracted only 700 tourists, but twelve years later the annual figure had skyrocketed to 60,000 and it remained stable throughout the 1930's.

The Legacy of Military Activity

Italian military authorities took various steps to insure the strategic value of the islands. They stationed a battalion of infantry at Rhodes and Kos, a naval establishment at Rhodes, and airfields at Rhodes, Karpathos, Leros, and Astypalia. None of these, however, had a lasting impact upon the islands or their inhabitants, although the major naval base at Leros did result in lasting changes.

During the 1930's, Leros became the second most powerful Italian naval base in the Mediterranean. By 1940, the island population numbered 9,000 Italians to only 4,500 Greeks. The extensive construction of fortifications and buildings induced most Lerians, and many Dodecanesians from nearby islands, to work as laborers. The massive military construction program produced a period of unrivalled prosperity on the island, as compared to the general economic depression that prevailed on other Dodecanese islands.

The special economic situation in Leros produced among the local inhabitants unique attitudes toward the Italian occupation. Lerians frequently assured the author that the Italians were a "good people" and that times were "παράδεισος" ("paradise") when they were on the island. "You should have seen the harbor then—bzz-bzz, a beehive!" While other Dodecanesians recalled with pride how they fought the Italians with nothing but their hands and stones, Lerians complacently explained that the other islanders had troubles with the Italians only because they were foolish enough to oppose the occupation. An elderly Lerian farmer fondly recalled Italian rule by observing that

> The Italians were good people, we will never forget them. We loved them and they loved us. Now many times they come back in the summer. When Lerians go to Italy, they're so happy to see us that they lift us in the air.[1]

This attitude, bordering on heresy for other Dodecanesians, the Lerians carried over to the German occupation:

---

[1]Personal Interview, Leros, December 5, 1963.

The German is a good person as long as you don't bother him. He doesn't
want to be bothered. If you bother the Germans—kill one—they will
take 200 to the square and kill them. We Lerians are a good peaceful
people. We never bothered the Germans and they didn't kill anyone on
this island.[1]

Other Dodecanesians view such attitudes with disdain, yet Lerians have
been ill-regarded since ancient times. The poet Phoclydes used the name of
Leros (Λέρος, i.e., "dirt") to throw mud at an enemy unlucky enough to be born
there.[2] Islanders frequently assured the present author that Lerians were unlike other Dodecanesians. A Kalymnian sponge-fisher taciturnly characterized
the island as follows: "Rhodes is nice, Kastellorizo now small and poor, Kalymnos the best, Leros is different!"[3] Durrell's description exemplifies the
common view:

> It is a beastly island without any character, despite its rather noble
> Frankish castle and picturesque village. There is, however, no pastoral
> or agricultural land worth the name. Simply gigantic port installations
> now crumpled with bombing, and rotting away in the damp—prodigious
> jumbles of copper, steel and brass. The harbour is choked with sunk
> craft, and the little town has been very badly bombed. A miasmic gloom
> hangs over everything. God help those born here, one mutters, those who
> live here, and those who come here to die. The water is brackish—like
> the wits of its inhabitants.[4]

While this description may be unnecessarily harsh, and indeed inaccurate in its
estimate of land value, it does capture the common characterization of Leros.
Somehow, most islanders deem it entirely appropriate that the chief economic
support of the island is presently mental asylums. One Kalymnian actually re-
ferred to Leros itself as a big "τρελλόσπιτι" (crazyhouse).

The Imprint on the Landscape

The Italian occupation produced several distinctive features in the
landscape of the Dodecanese islands. In rural areas, a dispersed form of settlement, exceptional save for summer houses, remains to the present time as a mark
of the occupation. When an earthquake leveled the city of Kos in 1933, Italian
authorities rebuilt many of the houses upon actual landholdings, rather than in
the city. Officials also created similar settlement patterns in areas of Italian agricultural settlement on Rhodes, while Italian settlers in Leros characteristically lived in dispersed farmsteads (Figure 31). In both rural and urban
areas, many houses remain a defiant blue and white, the national Greek colors.
In some isolated villages, the traveler may even still find a flag painted on a

---

[1] Personal interview, Aghia Marina, Leros, December 6, 1963.

[2] Durrell, op. cit., p. 62.

[3] Personal interview, Kalymnos, November 30, 1963.

[4] Durrell, op. cit., pp. 61-62.

Figure 31.—An example of dispersed settlement on the island of Leros. Houses are rarely found on actual land-holdings in the Dodecanese Islands. During the Italian occupation, however, officials induced numerous Italian farmers to settle in Leros by providing lands and farms. This action resulted in the settlement pattern shown above. The only other cause of dispersed settlement in the Dodecanese is the "summer" houses characteristic of parts of Leros, Kos, and Kalymnos.

Dodecanesian home (Figure 32).

Political Diversity and Unity

Italian sovereignty sharply reversed the pattern of decentralization characteristic of the Turkish occupation. Under the Ottomans, Rhodes lost its traditional dominance to the smaller, maritime islands. The closing of the Anatolian hinterland, Italian restrictions on commerce and sponge-fishing, and a purposeful policy of economic development, however, restored Rhodes to her traditional dominant position. The price of the Rhodian resurgence, however, was widespread emigration and economic destitution in the islands of Symi, Kalymnos, Kasos, and Kastellorizo. One Symian sadly characterized the results as follows: "We small islands fell as the Italians built up Rhodes. Rhodes became the capital—buildings, roads, gardens."[1] Gesturing to the barren hills and empty houses, he rhetorically inquired, "Where are their great works here?" Only Leros and the city of Rhodes profited substantially from the Italian occupation.

Conclusions

Centuries of successive foreign occupations have dominated the economic and political history of the Dodecanese islands. Foreign powers, through their control over the spatial relations of the islanders, the allocation of resources, the security of maritime commerce, and internal political stability, affected nearly all aspects of island life. Another legacy of changing political sovereignty, more intangible in nature, also merits consideration. Foreign control since ancient times inevitably has influenced attitudes toward social change and the political stance of Dodecanesians. An inability to alter their economic and social position via their political environment has produced a widespread alienation from the political environment and entrenched prevailing patterns of fatalism.

In addition, changing political sovereignty has altered the entire political decision-making framework of the individual. In most decisions, the Dodecanesian will choose that alternative which he believes will be to the maximum benefit to the family in the short-run. In such a society, community activity is tightly restricted since any type of concerted action must be justified by each individual. The Dodecanesian fears that his sacrifice might benefit others in the village more than his own family and thereby weaken his family position vis-a-vis the rest of the village. This political environment, undoubtedly in part a product of the succession of occupation by alien states, militates against community innovation and the development of effective local political leadership and institutions.

---

[1]Personal interview, Symi, December 30, 1963.

167

Figure 32.—A remnant of Greek defiance to the Italian occupation. The flag on this house in Pyli, Kos, was painted in the 1930's and remains today as a symbol of Dodecanesian resistance. The white cubic architecture is characteristic of the Aegean islands, the terracing is characteristic of Greece generally, while the clothing on the line exemplifies Dodecanesian reliance upon gifts from America.

168

CHAPTER VIII

CONCLUSIONS

In conclusion, it is appropriate to reconsider the entire study in the light of initial objectives. The central research problem has been "to explore the effects of selected economic, social, and political experiences upon political diversity and unity in the Dodecanese islands." In other words, what has been the process by which areas within the Dodecanese islands have become politically different from or similar to each other? The research involved also a secondary concern with "the interaction of man, land, and the political order." Given these problems, what conclusions can be drawn from the study? One might profitably divide these conclusions into the general relation of experience to political behavior and the effects of selected experiences and insularity upon political diversity and unity.

Experience and the Evolution of Patterns of Political Behavior

The Selection of Experiences

Since any interpretation of the evolution of patterns of political behavior inevitably requires selectivity in the analysis of causal factors, the process of selection looms as an important problem. The variety of man's existence precludes a comprehensive analysis of all experiences, so that some choice is mandatory. Moreover, since not all experiences are equally significant in the process of political differentiation, an unbiased selection would not be a desirable research methodology.

Rather, the selection of experiences should evolve out of hypotheses centered on the research problem and reflecting an intimate knowledge and empathy for the area. The experiences selected, then, reflect hypothetical explanations for the growth of self-awareness in a particular place. The experiences discussed above appear to have vitally affected not only the islanders' identifications with a particular place or area, but also patterns of political attitudes and behavior.

The Existential Character of Experience

It might be argued that geography is as fundamentally concerned with the question—what does it mean to be alive in one place rather than another?—as with explanations of particular distributions. Certainly both the quantity and quality of experience at different places are at the root of geographic inquiry. The study of common experiences among a particular people contributes to our understanding of these differences.

An example may better illustrate this approach to geography. The treatment of tourism as a "touristic" experience involves a widening of research horizons. Ultimately, the research is concerned not only with the effects of tourism upon per capita income, for example, but also with changes in attitudes and behavior arising not only from the economic change itself but from the full range of interaction between islander and tourist. If the political geographer is fundamentally concerned with the spatial differences as they exist in men's minds, then he might profitably examine such phenomena. With these goals in mind, then, how have the selected experiences affected political regionalism in the Dodecanese islands?

Selected Experiences and Political Behavior in the Dodecanese Islands

The Agricultural Experience

Agricultural activity within the Dodecanese islands has had an important impact upon political attitudes and behavior. The vulnerability of islanders to environmental problems has encouraged a fatalism which impedes improvements. This fatalism now extends into the social and political spheres and results in a lack of community initiative. It has also encouraged a drift of political functions and innovation from the local to the central government. In addition, a disdain for and an apathy toward agriculture as an occupation has helped to create a landscape which has reverted to "less cultivated forms." Whenever the opportunity arises, farmers quickly desert their lands for some other occupation.

The political order, in turn, has shaped the character of the agricultural experience. The Greek Government has made a profound impression upon the agricultural industry in the Dodecanese. Improvement works, the redistribution of Italian land, improvement in agricultural organization and education, and an increase in cheap, available credit have materially altered the industry. The concentration of effort on the larger islands of Rhodes and Kos has diversified further the islands from each other and has provided their inhabitants with very different experiences with agriculture since 1947. At the same time, however, inhabitants of smaller islands have complained that these larger islands were developed at their expense. Also, government aid and activity has reinforced the islander's attitude toward government as an institution to be exploited and relied upon for local innovation.

Finally, the agricultural experience has had other important ramifications for political attitudes and behavior. The Dodecanesian farmer tends to judge the quality of any government in terms of easily measurable improvements in his economic position. Disgruntled with his position in the economy, the agriculturalist felt moved to revolt against the Karamanlis regime. He held the Government strictly responsible for his situation and translated his grievances into an ideological position. He tends to apply a class basis to political parties and sees politics as a constant struggle between the left and the right. Moreover, the agricultural experience has colored the way local islanders see political issues and programs. These differing views are evident in the regional shifts, over time, of political support among the various agricultural zones of Rhodes and also among islands. In the last few elections, there has been a marked shift of support from the E.R.E. to the Center Union in the poorer agricultural areas.

The Sponge-Fishing Experience

The sponge-fishing experience has had equally significant economic and political implications. Historically, technological and economic changes led to a concentration of the industry upon the island of Kalymnos. Meanwhile, the other former sponge-fishing islands suffered economic declines and large-scale emigration. Another difference throughout recent history has been the contrasts between sponge-fishing and other Dodecanese islands. During the nineteenth century, for example, the sponge-fishing islands spearheaded the resistance to the Turkish occupation. Educational and cultural achievements, voluntary theaters and intellectual organizations, and local community government were most fully developed on the islands of Symi and Kalymnos. Symi in particular reversed the traditional pattern of Rhodian dominance and usurped her cultural and political leadership within the island group.

The sponge-islanders have an unusually intense loyalty to birthplace. Kalymnians and Astypalians almost all return to their island at some time. Their devotion to their island is widely recognized as a distinctive characteristic of these islanders. The sponge-fishing islanders now also have a greater knowledge of and interaction with the outside world. Priding themselves on greater vigor and initiative, they see themselves as markedly different from other islanders. In fact, Kalymnians refer to their island as the "navel of of the earth." These characteristics are translated into distinctive forms of political behavior. As an analysis of electoral behavior clearly indicates, the spirit of liberality and independence is nowhere in the Dodecanese more pronounced than on the sponge islands. As a group, the sponge-islanders voted consistently more for the Center than other Dodecanesians. In addition, they tend to see their political position in strong ideological terms, derived largely from their distinctive experiences under foreign rulers. Finally, the sponge islanders also reveal an unusual development of political activity at the local level—an experience which has given rise to effective political leadership and institutions in the community.

The Experience of Emigration and Depopulation

The major significance of this experience to political regionalism in the Dodecanese arises indirectly, through its effects upon the social and

economic structure of the islanders. Emigrant remittances, since they constitute a major source of per-capita income, serve as the chief vehicle of change.
Emigrants in foreign lands become exploitable sources of economic support for
the islanders; yet their generous contributions do not, on the whole, stimulate
the economic transformation of the island. Dodecanesians use these gifts chiefly as replacements for, not adjuncts to, island economic activities. Seldom do
individual or community improvements arise from these funds.

Remittances entail a wide range of effects, not restricted to economic
changes alone. The relationship between donor and receiver engenders to life a
parasitic quality which has important implications in the social and political
psychology of the islanders. Gifts from emigrants make Dodecanesians increasingly aware of their own inability to alter their existence through efforts at
the local level. Fatalism, already present, receives substantial reinforcement.

The social effects of emigration are equally noteworthy. Sex differentials among emigrants have created a problem of unmarried females throughout the
islands. The departure of large numbers of young men have created labor shortages in rural areas. In addition, the disruption of families has been a cause
of widespread grief throughout the Dodecanese.

Emigration and depopulation are in themselves a major political issue
in Greece generally and even more so in the Dodecanese. Emigration, which is
pronounced throughout the Aegean islands, is especially serious in the diminutive maritime islands of the Dodecanese. Dodecanesians tend to equate emigration with a loss of national vigor and vitality. The elections of 1963 and 1964
revealed emigration as a central issue in the political campaigns. Failure to
resolve this problem contributed to the downfall of the Karamanlis regime and
the related success of Papandreou and the Center Union.

Finally, remittances from emigrants have caused a spatial reorientation
in methods of acquiring wealth and improving both the personal and community
situation. In areas of heavy reliance upon remittances, such as Karpathos and
Nisyros, emigration has aided the retardation of more responsible and vigorous
local government and community organization. The geographical structure of
emigration and remittances, then, has contributed significantly to political
diversity within the Dodecanese.

The Touristic Experience

Tourism has been an experience particularly instrumental in spatial differentiation. The ports of Rhodes, Kos, and Patmos have been the unquestioned
beneficiaries of tourism, whereas their hinterlands and other islands have
scarcely profited at all. In these tourist centers, tourism has extensively
altered the economic base and political characteristics of the islanders. The
result has been to further diversify patterns of political behavior in the

Dodecanese.

Inevitably, the rich fruits of tourism have reinforced a desire in all other Dodecanese islands to capitalize on this newly-acquired wealth. This "geography of expectation" has influenced local government spending, rural-to-urban migration, and private economic decisions. In addition, the wealth derived from tourism at these ports has indicated again the ineffectiveness of traditional occupations. Inevitably, tourism has accelerated the depopulation of small islands and more isolated villages.

Contacts with foreign tourists have been instrumental in shaping knowledge and modes of perception of the outside world. Within tourist centers, while the quantity of interaction has been high, the quality of interaction has been sharply limited. Language and cultural differences have been particularly effective in restricting greater communication. Nevertheless, the limited contact has precipitated characteristic views of foreign nationalities.

Finally, tourism has contributed to inter-island conflicts, particularly over the question of government allocations. Other islanders and many Rhodian villagers complain that Rhodes has been touristically developed at their expense. Tourism has also reinforced attitudes toward social change and contributed much toward a spatial reorientation of methods of innovation. All islanders tend to see their economic salvation in a future utopia abounding with tourists and dollars. There is, then, little motivation for self-induced social and economic change.

The Experience of Changing Political Sovereignty

Changing political sovereignty has left a strong imprint upon both political regionalism and the landscape of the Dodecanese islands. Inevitably political sovereignty, because of its wide political and economic control, extensively alters and shapes the quality of life in any area. In the Dodecanese, the chief effects have arisen through the implications of political sovereignty upon political stability, administrative and military organization, patterns of land use and resource exploitation, and spatial interaction.

Historically, the presence or absence of political stability has often been the key to economic progress. Disruptions in political stability have led frequently to the economic decline of islanders and, in many cases, to the complete depopulation of islands. Political stability has played a special, crucial role in its effects upon maritime commerce, one of the major economic bases of the islands. The sack of islands and their subsequent slow demographic and economic resurgence is a recurring theme in Dodecanese history.

Administrative and military organization has been closely related to political regionalism within the island group. To cite two examples, Roman sponsorship of Delos as the political and economic capital of the Aegean and

Astypalia as its major naval base precipitated the decline of Rhodes. The military activities of the Knights concentrated population and wealth upon Rhodes and, to a lesser extent, Kos. Turkish administration and "privileges" encouraged the evolution of Symi and Kalymnos as the cultural and political centers of the Dodecanese. Finally, the purposeful Italian development of Rhodes reversed this pattern, while also establishing Leros as the major military base on the eastern Mediterranean.

The historical stamp of political sovereignty upon the landscape and patterns of resource exploitation in the Dodecanese has been equally great. Although the Turkish occupation produced a land-tenure system which prevented a fuller development of land resources, it is noteworthy that maritime activities reached their zenith during this same period. Italian sovereignty, by contrast, made agricultural policy an integral part of Italy's political objectives. Italian administration caused extensive changes in the traditional exploitation of land and maritime resources. Throughout the centuries of foreign occupations, the political estrangement between ruler and the ruled has impeded economic progress in the Dodecanese.

The effects of political sovereignty upon patterns of spatial interaction have directly influenced political behavior. The entire structure of political and economic geography within the Dodecanese has been related intimately to the "open door" to Anatolia and unrestricted maritime activities. Changes in either of these two factors, which have been numerous in Dodecanese political history, have influenced greatly the entire human geography of the islands. The effects of Italian sovereignty upon spatial interaction between 1912 and 1943 illustrate how severe these repercussions can be.

Changing political sovereignty has modified the ethical framework of political decision-making in the Dodecanese. Most individuals tend to choose that alternative which they believe will be of maximum benefit to their families in the short-run. Particularly, the islander seeks to obtain the best social position possible of his family vis-a-vis other families in the village. Sacrifices to the community or to the "public interest" are unusual and consequently innovation seldom occurs at the local level.

Insularity and Political Diversity

Several final observations may be noted as to the role that insularity plays in prevailing patterns of political attitudes and behavior. Table 38 presents a summary of these patterns stratified by islands. Although this table represents only a general inventory of characteristic modes of attitude and behavior, it does provide some insight into the cumulative effects of the experiences examined in the study and into the specific relevance of insularity. There can be little doubt that islands form the essential spatial framework for

174

TABLE 38
SUMMARY CHARACTERISTICS OF POLITICAL ATTITUDES AND BEHAVIOR

Island	Local Political Institutions and Activity	Knowledge of and Interaction with Outside World	Attitudes to Social and Political Change	Voting Behavior
Rhodes	Well-developed in city & nearby villages; underdeveloped in distant villages	High in city; variably moderate in villages	Dynamic and receptive in city and suburbs; more passive in other villages	Evenly divided between ERE and the Center, but with growing support for Center
Kos	Moderate centralization in city; underdeveloped in villages	High in city, low in villages	Receptive in the city; passive in the villages	Evenly-divided 1956-1961; Strongly Center 1963-1964
Kalymnos	Strong innovation and dynamic developments at local level. Highly centralized	High	Very dynamic and with much innovation. Inner-oriented	Consistently strongly Center
Symi	Moderate development	Moderate	Generally receptive	Evenly balanced 1956-1961; Strongly Center 1963-1964
Leros	Local political institutions underdeveloped and parisitic	Moderate	Passive and strongly externally oriented	Variable between the ERE and the Center
Karpathos	Local political institutions Underdeveloped and passive	Moderate	Passive and externally oriented	Strongly favoring ERE 1956-1961; strongly Center 1963-1964.
Nisyros	Decentralized and weak political activity	Low	Generally passive	Consistently Center
Patmos	Moderate development	Moderate	Passive, taking lead from monastery	Slightly ERE 1956-1961; gravitating toward Center
Chalki	Generally weak	Very low	Passive and externally oriented	Consistently strongly Center
Kasos	Generally weak	Very low	Passive and externally oriented	Consistently strongly ERE
Telos	Weak and decentralized	Very low	Passive and externally oriented	Strongly ERE, 1956-1961; Strongly Center,1963-1964
Astypalia	Generally weak	Very low	Passive and externally oriented	Increasingly ERE,1956-1961; Strongly Center, 1963-1964
Kastellorizo	Underdeveloped and tied to national minister	Very low	Passive and externally oriented	Variable, 1956-1961; Strongly Center, 1963-1964
Leipsos	Strongly autocratic, with much control by merchants	Very low	Passive and externally oriented	Consistently strongly ERE

political differences within the Dodecanese. The role of islands in these geographical contrasts is closely related to questions of scale, technological levels, and patterns of circulation and communication.

Scale is important because, in smaller islands, the limits of major settlements and resource opportunity are coterminus with the territorial limits of the island. Territoriality and spatial diversity are essentially defined by the physical limits of the island. People within the island have all shared generally a set of common historical and economic experiences. Identification to birthplace and community coincides closely with loyalty to the island.

On the larger islands, however, this simple pattern of territoriality disintegrates. Settlement and resource diversity characterize the island. The village, not the island, defines territoriality. The sense of community thus arises from an awareness of the uniqueness of the village. To justify and assert their individuality, their raison d'être, villagers emphasize and even distort differences which distinguish them from others, much as the inhabitants of smaller islands do with respect to other islands. The inhabitants of larger islands, moreover, do not share a common set of historical and economic experiences. The result is that on larger islands political diversity is usually greater within than between islands, while the reverse is usually true on smaller islands.

Finally, political diversity is closely related to levels of spatial interaction (Table 39). Since political diversity is closely linked to the differences from place to place in men's minds, barriers to social communication are of prime importance in the political geography of the islands. In the Dodecanese, these interruptions are, among the smaller islands, most pronounced between islands; on larger islands, between port and hinterland and between rural villages. Technological level, however, bears heavily on these patterns. Greater communication is presently eradicating spatial differences in attitudes, knowledge, and political behavior. A greater sharing of common experiences is emerging and is extirpating the roots of political diversity. Yet, perhaps most remarkable, is the Dodecanesian's overwhelming sense of identity and self-awareness which continues to resist the inroads of modern technology.

TABLE 39

SUMMARY CHARACTERISTICS OF CIRCULATION AND COMMUNICATION, 1964

Island	Radios	Telephones	Newspaper Circulation	Personal Travel	Movie Theaters	Touristic Development
Rhodes	Nearly universal in city & villages	In city, officials, merchants & private homes. Villages, official use.	High in city, low to moderate in villages	City dwellers to Athens for business and visits. Villagers—shop.& Doctor.	Many in city, villages lack	High in city, low in village
Kos	Nearly universal city; perhaps 30% of families in villages.	In city, official use and some stores. In villages official use only.	Moderate in city, low in villages	City dweller to Rhodes for business. Others only for medical.	1 permanent + 3 summer in city; villages lack	High in city; low in villages
Kalymnos	Nearly universal	Officials, merchants & private homes	590 daily	To Kos and Rhodes for shopping and amusements. Athens for business & visits	2 permanent + 2 summer in city	Moderate
Symi	Nearly universal	Official use only	119 daily	Regular shopping and amusement in Rhodes	1 permanent	Moderate
Leros	Nearly universal	Official use, some stores, and three homes	90 daily	To Athens for medical trips	1 summer	Moderate
Karpathos	Nearly universal	Official use and several stores	205 daily	To Krete and Rhodes for medical reasons and specialized shopping	Traveling cinema	Low
Nisyros	Perhaps 50% of families	Official use, doctor, and one house	80 daily	To Rhodes and Kos for medical trips	Traveling cinema	Low
Patmos	Nearly universal	Official use only	85 daily	To Rhodes, Athens & Kos for medical trips & business	None	High
Chalki	50-75% of families	Official use only	60 daily	To Rhodes for medical trips and shopping	None	Low
Kasos	Nearly universal	Official use only	85 daily	To Karpathos for visits; Rhodes for medical trips	None	Low
Telos	Nearly universal	Official use only	50 daily	To Kos and Rhodes for business or medical trips	None	Low
Astypalia	Nearly universal	Official use only	30 daily	To Athens for visits and medical trips	None	Low
Kastellorizo	Nearly universal	Official use only	30 daily	To Rhodes for medical trips	None	Low
Leipsos	50-75% of families	Official use only	15 daily	To Kalymnos and Leros for medical trips	None	Low

SELECTED BIBLIOGRAPHY

Books

Agapētidēs, Sōtērios I. Ἡ Δωδεκάνησος εἰς τὴν συνθήκην τῆς εἰρήνης. Athens: 1947.

_____. Ἡ Θέας τὸ μέλλον τῆς Δωδεκάνησιακὴ σπογγαλιείας. Athens: 1946.

_____. Ἡ ἐργασία εἰς τὴν σπογγαλιείαν. Athens: 1938.

_____. Ἡ κατάστασις εἰς τὴν Δωδεκάνησον. Athens: Central Dodecanese Commission, 1946.

_____. Ὁ πληθυσμὸς τῆς Δωδεκανήσου. Athens: 1948.

_____. Ἡ Σύμη ἀπὸ δημοσιονομικῆς καὶ δημογραφικῆς ἀπόψεως. Athens: 1930.

Andriotakēs, Christophoros N. Κῶς, ἡ πατρὶς τοῦ Ἱπποκράτους. Athens: 1962.

_____. The Motherland of Hippocrates. Athens: 1961.

Banfield, Edward. The Moral Basis of a Backward Society. Glencoe: Free Press, 1958.

Benson, Jack Leonard. Ancient Leros. Durham, North Carolina: Duke University, Greek, Roman, and Byzantine Monographs No. 3, 1963.

Betoulēs, Elias. Οἰκονομικὴ ἀνάπτυξις τῆς Δωδεκάνησου ἀπὸ προσαρτήσεως αὐτῆς εἰς Ἑλλάδα καὶ ἐντεῦθεν. Athens: National Printing Office, 1958.

Booth, Clarence D. and Booth, Isabelle. Italy's Aegean Possessions. London: Arrowsmith, 1928.

Bradford, Ernle. The Companion Guide to the Greek Islands. London: Collins, 1963.

Brunetti, E. and Mochi, A. Les eaux de Callithea. Le Caire: 1933.

Buchanan, William and Cantril, Hadley. How Nations See Each Other. Urbana: University of Illinois Press, 1953.

Buckle, Henry Thomas. History of Civilization in England. New York: Hearst's International Library, 1913.

Campbell, Angus et al. The American Voter. New York: John Wiley and Sons, 1964.

Casavis, Jack Nicholas. Δωδεκανησιακαὶ ἐνέργειαι. New York: 1951.

_____. The Dodecanesian Greeks. New York: 1944.

_____. Οἱ Δωδεκανήσιοι. New York: 1950.

_____. Τὰ Ἑλληνικὰ Δωδεκάνησα. N.Y.: The National Herald, 1941.

_____. Τά Ἰταλοκρατηθέντα Δωδεκάνησα, 1912-1943. New York: 1953.

_____. La tragedia del Dodecaneso, 1912-1943. New York: 1953.

Cawkell, M.B.R., Maling, D.H. and Cawkell, E.M. The Falkland Islands. London: Macmillan and Co., 1960.

177

Center of Planning and Economic Research, National Statistical Service of Greece, and Social Sciences Centre, Athens. Economic and Social Atlas of Greece. Athens: 1964.

Chaviaras, Dēmosthenēs. Περί σπόγγων καί σπογγαλιεία. Athens: 1916.

Collingwood, R. G. The Idea of History. New York: Oxford University Press, 1956.

Coutsoumaris, George. The Location Pattern of Greek Industry. Athens: Center of Economic Research Lecture Series No. 4, 1962.

_____. The Morphology of Greek Industry. Athens: Center of Economic Research, Research Monograph Series No. 6, 1963.

Cresswell, Ernest J. Sponges: their Nature, History, Modes of Fishing, Varieties, Cultivation. N.P.: 1930.

Cumberland, Kenneth B. Southwest Pacific. New York: McGraw-Hill, 1956.

Doxiadēs, Kōnstantinos A. Δωδεκάνησος; τετράτομος μελέτη τοῦ Υπουργείου Ανοικοδομήσεως καί συνεργάτων τοῦ ὑπό την διεύθηνσιν. Athens: 1947.

Drakidos, Gerasimos. Ροδιακὰ. Athens: Bitsikounakis Press, 1937.

Duijker, H. C. and Frijda, N. H. National Character and National Stereotypes. Amsterdam: North Holland Publishing Co., 1960.

Durrell, Lawrence. Reflections on a Marine Venus. London: Faber and Faber, 1963.

Evangelidos, Tryphonos E. and Michaelides-Nouaros, M. ῾Ιστορία της νησου Κάσου. Athens: A. P. Chalkiopoulos, 1936.

Febvre, Lucien. A Geographical Introduction to History. New York: Alfred A. Knopf, 1925.

Field, Henry M. The Greek Islands and Turkey After the War. New York: Charles Scribner's Sons, 1886.

Firey, Walter. Land Use in Central Boston. Cambridge: Harvard University Press, 1947.

_____. Man, Mind and Land. Glencoe: Free Press, 1960.

Fischer, John L. The Eastern Carolines. New Haven: Pacific Science Board and the Human Relations Area File, 1957.

Forbes, W. Cameron. The Philippine Islands. Cambridge: Harvard University Press, 1945.

Fox, James W. and Cumberland, Kenneth B. Western Samoa: Land, Life and Agriculture in Tropical Polynesia. Christchurch, New Zealand: Whitcombe and Tombs, 1962.

Fraser, P. M. and Bean, G. E. The Rhodian Peraea and Islands. London: Oxford University Press, 1954.

Friedl, Ernestine. Vasilika: A Village in Modern Greece. New York: Holt, Rinehart, and Winston, 1962.

Gardner, Ernest A. Greece and the Aegean. London: George G. Harrap, 1938.

Geil, William Edgar. The Isle that is Called Patmos. London: Marshall Bros., 1904.

Geōrgiou, Geōrgios M. Καρπαθιακὰ. Piraeus: 1958.

Gianni, Giuseppe. Le isole italiane dell' Egeo. Firenze: Istituto geografica militaire, 1928.

Grant, Bruce. Indonesia. Parkville, Australia: Melbourne University Press,1964.

Great Britain, Naval Intelligence Division. Dodecanese. London: Her Majesty's Stationery Office, 1943.

Gregoropoulos, Michalis S. ʽΗ νῆσος Σύμη. Athens: 1878.

Guerin, Victor. Etude sur l'île de Rhodes. Paris: A. Durand, 1856.

Hadjiamallos, Dēmētrios. ʽΗ Κῶς.ʽΙστορία καὶ ἀρχαιότητες. Athens: 1962.

Jacobs, Philip E. and Toscano, James V. (eds.). The Integration of Political Communities. Philadelphia and New York: J. B. Lippincott Co., 1964.

Jeancard, Paul. L'Anatolie; Smyrne, Sparte, Bourdour, Hiérapolis, le Dodécanèse. Paris: Librairie française, 1919.

Jones, Horace Leonard (trans.). The Geography of Strabo. Vols. I-VIII. New York: G. P. Putnam's Sons, 1929.

Kates, Robert W. Hazard and Choice Perception in Flood Plain Management. Chicago: University of Chicago, Department of Geography Research Papers No. 78, 1962.

Konsola, Nicholas I. ʽΗ στατικὴ καὶ δυναμικὴ ἐποπτεία τοῦ οἰκονομικοῦ χώρου τῆς Δωδεκανήσου. Athens: Ekdoseis "Kyklos," 1964.

Lambiri, Ioanna. Social Change in a Greek Country Town. Athens: Center of Planning and Economic Research, Research Monograph Series No. 13, 1965.

Leotsakos, Spyros. Ροδος — Τὸ σμαράγδενιο νησί. Athens: The Author, 1949.

Levi, Carlo. Christ Stopped at Eboli. New York: Farrar, Straus and Co., 1947.

Liddell, Robert. Aegean Greece. London: Jonathan Cape, 1954.

Lindzey, G. (ed.). Handbook of Social Psychology. Cambridge: Addison-Wesley Publishing Co., 1954.

Livi, Livio. Storia demografica di Rodi e delle isole dipendenti. Firenze: 1944.

Logothetis, Miltiados I. Τουρισμὸς καὶ οἰκονομία τῆς νησοῦ Νισύρου. Athens: Society for Nisyrian Studies, 1963.

_____. ʽΟ τουρισμὸς τῆς Ρόδου. Athens: National Bank of Greece, 1961.

_____. Τουριστικαὶ μελέται. Athens: 1963.

Long, Andrew, et al. (trans.). The Complete Works of Homer: The Iliad. New York: Modern Library, 1950.

Lowenthal, David. The West Indies Federation: Perspectives on a New Nation. New York: Columbia University Press, 1961.

Lynch, Kevin. The Image of the City. Cambridge: Massachusetts Institute of Technology Press, 1960.

Lynch, Kevin, and Appleyard, Donald. The View from the Road. Cambridge: Joint Center for Urban Studies, 1964.

Martinis, Georgios. Ρόδος. Piraeus: 1962.

_____. Στὸ Αἰγαῖο, κάποτε. Rhodes: Dodecanesian Library, 1962.

Maull, Otto. Griechisches Mittelmeergebiet. Breslau: F. Hirt, 1922.

McCorkle, Chester O. Fruit and Vegetable Marketing in the Economic Development of Greece. Athens: Center of Economic Research, Research Monograph Series No. 3, 1962.

McVey, Ruth T. (ed.). Indonesia. New Haven: Human Relations Area File, 1963.

Mears, Eliot G. Greece Today. Stanford: Stanford University Press, 1929.

Megas, T. A. ʽΗ λαϊκὴ κατοικία τῆς Δωδεκανήσου. Athens: 1949.

Michalarias-Botiatzis, Maria. Ροδοπέταλα. Rhodes: 1962.

Michaēlidēs-Nouaros, Michalis. Γιὰ νὰ γνωρίσουμε τῆ Δωδεκάνησο. Athens: 1946.

_____. Ἱστορία (1821-1947) τῆς νήσου Καρπάθου. Athens: I. Serdinis, 1950.

_____. Χρονικὸν τῆς νήσου Καρπάθον. Pittsburgh: 1951.

Montesquieu, Baron Charles Louis. The Spirit of the Laws. New York: Hafner, 1949.

Moskovis, Erinis. Σύμη ἀγαπημένη. Athens: 1963.

Myres, John L. Geographical History in Greek Lands. Oxford: Clarendon Press, 1953.

Nestoridos, Aristotelos. Ἡ σπογγαλιεία ἐν Χάλκη. Athens: 1930.

Oliver, Douglas L. The Pacific Islands. Cambridge: Harvard University Press, 1951.

Phina, Kypriakou I. Ἡ ἀγροτικὴ ἐκπαίδευσις εἰς τὴν Δωδεκάνησον. Rhodes: 1963.

_____. Ἡ γεωργία τῆς Δωδεκανήσου καὶ αἱ προϋποθέσεις ἀναπτύξεως αὐτῆς. Rhodes: 1961.

_____. Τὰ ὀπωροκηπευτικὰ εἰς τὰ πλαίσια τῆς Δωδεκανησιακῆς οἰκονομίας. Rhodes: 1961.

Phrankopoulos, Hippokratēs. Ἡ Δωδεκάνησός ὑπό Ἰταχοκρατίαν. Athens: 1958.

Pizanias, N. Ἡ θέσις καὶ τὸ μέλλον τῆς Δωδεκανησιακῆς σπογγαλιείας. Athens: 1946.

_____. Διὰ τὴν ἀνασυγκρότησιν τῆς σπογγαλιείας τῆς Δωδεκανήσου. Rhodes: 1950.

Sanders, Irwin T. Rainbow in the Rock: The People of Rural Greece. Cambridge: Harvard University Press, 1962.

Sertoli Salis, Rinzo. Le isole italiane dell 'Egeo dall' occupazione alla souranita. Roma: Vittoriano, 1939.

Serbētis, Christos. Ἡ σπογγαλιευτικὴ ἐπιχείρησις. Athens: 1944.

Sprout, Harold and Margaret. The Ecological Perspective on Human Affairs. Princeton: Princeton University Press, 1965.

Tarsoulē, Athēna N. Δωδεκάνησα. Vols. I-III. Athens: I. M. Skazikis, 1947.

Thompson, Kenneth. Farm Fragmentation in Greece. Athens: Center of Economic Research, Research Monograph Series No. 5, 1963.

Torr, Cecil. Rhodes in Ancient Times. Cambridge: Cambridge University Press, 1885.

_____. Rhodes: In Ancient Times. Cambridge, England: University Press, 1885.

Tsakalakis, Antoine. Le Dodécanèse; étude de droit international. Alexandria: Cassimatis and Jonas, 1928.

Volonakes, Michael D. The Island of Roses and her Eleven Sisters. London: Macmillan, 1922.

Ward, Benjamin. Greek Regional Development. Athens: Center of Economic Research, Research Monograph Series No. 4, 1963.

Whittlesey, Derwent S. The Earth and the State. New York: Henry Holt, 1939.

Zervos, Skēnos G. The Dodecanese; the History of the Dodecanese through the Ages — Its Services to Mankind and its Rights. London: A. Page, 1919.

Articles

Anthem, Thomas. "Communism in Greece," Contemporary Review, CCVI (May, 1965), 234-238.

_____. "The Greek Crisis," Contemporary Review, CCVII (September, 1965), 119-126.

Armstrong, H. F. "Unredeemed Isles of Greece," Foreign Affairs, IV (October, 1925), 154-157.

Baxevanis, Jean. "Population, Internal Migration and Urbanization in Greece," Balkan Studies, VI (1965), 83-98.

Broek, Jan. "Diversity and Unity in Southeast Asia," Geographical Review, XXXIV (April, 1944), 175-195.

Burghardt, Andrew F. "The Bases of Support for Political Parties in Burgenland" Annals of the Association of American Geographers, LIV (September, 1964) 372-390.

Burton, Ian and Kates, Robert W. "The Perception of Natural Hazards in Resource Management," Natural Resources Journal, III (January, 1964), 412-441.

Damaskenides, A. N. "Problems of the Greek Rural Economy," Balkan Studies, VI (1965), 21-34.

Gottman, Jean. "Geography and International Relations," World Politics, III (January, 1951), 153-173.

_____. "The Political Partitioning of Our World: An Attempt at Analysis," World Politics, IV (July, 1952), 512-519.

Hartshorne, Richard. "The Functional Approach in Political Geography," Annals of the Association of American Geographers, XL (June, 1950), 95-103.

Jones, Stephen B. "A Unified Field Theory of Political Geography," Annals of the Association of American Geographers, XLIV (June, 1954), 113-123.

Kasperson, Roger E. "Toward a Geography of Urban Politics: Chicago, A Case Study," Economic Geography, XLI (April, 1965), 95-107.

_____ and Vouras, Paul. "The Development of Agriculture on the Island of Rhodes under Italian Rule, 1912-1943," Balkan Studies, forthcoming.

Lowenthal, David. "The West Indies Chooses a Capital," Geographical Review, XLVIII (July, 1958), 336-364.

_____. "Geography, Experience, and Imagination: Towards a Geographical Epistemology," Annals of the Association of American Geographers, LI (September, 1961), 241-260.

_____. "Not Every Prospect Pleases — What is our Criterion for Scenic Beauty?" Landscape, XII (Winter, 1962-1963), 19-23.

_____. "English Landscape Tastes," Geographical Review, LV (April, 1965), 186-222.

_____ and Price, Hugh C. "The English Landscape," Geographical Review, LIV (July, 1964), 309-346.

Manus, Willard. "Kalymnos and its Sponge Divers," Greek Heritage, I (1964), 52-63.

Mavris, Nicholas G. "Certain Misconceptions in Relation to the Eastern Mediterranean and Greece," Social Science, XXI (January, 1946), 22-30.

Modiano, Mario S. "Greek Political Troubles," World Today, XXI (January, 1965), 33-42.

Moore, Henry. "The Commercial Sponges and the Sponge Fisheries," Bulletin of the Bureau of Fisheries, XXVIII (1908), Part I.

Myres, John L. "The Position of Greece in the Eastern Mediterranean," Geography, XXVI (1941), 101-109.

Papandréou, Andréas. "A New Economic Policy for Greece," Greek Heritage, II (1965), 75-80.

Sebald, Hans. "Studying National Character through Comparative Content Analysis," Social Forces, XL (May, 1962), 318-322.

Spate, O. H. K. "Toynbee and Huntington: A Study in Determinism," Geographical Journal, CXVIII (December, 1952).

Spoehr, Alexander. "Cultural Differences in the Interpretation of Natural Resources," Man's Role in Changing the Face of the Earth, William L. Thomas (ed.). Chicago: University of Chicago Press, 1956, 93-102.

Vouras, Paul P. "The Development of Resources of the Island of Rhodes under Turkish Rule, 1522-1911," Balkan Studies, IV (1963), 37-46.

Whittlesey, Derwent S. "The Impress of Central Authority upon the Landscape," Annals of the Association of American Geographers, XXV (June, 1935), 85-97.

Documents and Reports

Commercial Bank of Greece. Report of the Chairman of the Board of Directors for 1962. Athens: Commercial Bank of Greece, 1963.

Gouvernat général du Dodécanèse. Le premier congrès panhellenique des armateurs d'eponges. Rapports et procès-verbaux. Rhodes: National Printing Office, 1951.

Greece. Ministry of Reconstruction. ῾Η ἀνοικοδόμησις τῆς Δωδεκάνησος. Athens: 1948.

National Statistical Service of Greece. Agricultural Statistics of Greece, Year 1961. Vols. I-II. Athens: 1962.

_____. Résultats du recensement de la population effectivé le 7 avril, 1951. Vols. I-III. Athens: 1958-1961.

_____. Results of the Annual Industrial Survey. Vols. I-IV. Athens: 1962.

_____. Results of the Population and Housing Census of 19 March, 1961. Vols. I-V. Athens: 1962-1963.

_____. Statistical Yearbook of Greece. Annuals for 1961-1964.

Wallace, A. F. C. "The Modal Personality Structure of the Tuscarora Indians as Revealed by the Rorschach Test," Smithsonian Institution, Bureau of American Ethnology, Bulletin 150.

Pamphlets

Casavis, Jack Nicholas. Nissyros. New York: 1947.

_____. Italy and the Unredeemed Isles of Greece. New York: Dodecanesian League of America, 1935.

Délégation du Dodécanèse à la conférence de la paix. Le Dodécanèse ensanglanté demande sa liberté. Paris: F. A. Tourbier, 1919.

Dodecanesian League of America. The Dodecanesians Are Not Enemy Aliens; a Memorandum Submitted to the U.S. Dept. of Justice by the National Committee for the Restoration of Greece. New York: The League, 1942.

Dodecanesian National Council. The Dodecanese Islands: Two Articles by American Experts. New York: The Dodecanesian National Council, 1943.

Dodecanesian Union of Alexandria. Memorandum on the Dodecanesian Question and Especially on the Recent Decree Concerning Public Instruction. Alexandria, Egypt: Dodecanese Union of Alexandria, N.d.

Doxiades, Constantinos A. Ταξίδι στα Δωδεκάνησια. Athens: 1948.

Martinis, Georgios. Κάλυμνος; τὸ νησὶ τῶν σφουγγαράδων. Rhodes: Dodecanesian Library, 1962.

_____. Τῆλος, τὸ νησὶ μὲ τῆς ἀμυγδαλιές. Rhodes: Dodecanesian Library, 1962.

Mavris, Nicholas G. The Dodecanesians Are Not Enemy Aliens. New York: The Dodecanesian League of America, 1942.

_____ (ed.). The Greek Dodecanese: a Symposium by Prominent Americans. New York: Dodecanese National Council, 1944.

_____. Sforza vs. Sforza. New York: The Dodecanesian League of America, 1943.

National Radical Union. Πῶς μᾶς βλέπουν οἱ ξένοι. Athens: 1961.

Papandreou, Soterios. The Dodecanese Islands: Their Economy During the Italian Occupation and under the Greek Administration. Athens: Greek Productivity Center, 1958.

_____. Ἡ οἰκονομία τῆς Δωδεκανήσου ἐπὶ Ἰταλικῆς κατοχῆς καὶ Ἑλληνικῆς διοικήσεως. Athens: Greek Productivity Center, 1957.

Paris. Peace Conference, 1919. Islands of the Aegean. Le Dodécanèse ensanglanté demande sa liberté; mémoires, résolutions, rapports, télégrammes, lettres documents soumis à la conférence de la paix du 27 mai au octobre 1919. Paris: F. A. Tourbier, 1919.

Robinson, David Moore. The Great Glory and Glamor of the Dodecanese. New York: The Dodecanesian National Council, 1944.

Royal Institute of International Affairs. Information Department. The Italian Colonial Empire, with Chapters on the Dodecanese and Albania. London: Royal Institute of International Affairs, 1940.

Volonakes, Michaël D. Le Dodecanese; ses aspirations, ses efforts. Paris: 1919.

Zervos, Skēnos G. The Dodecanese and the British Press, 4th December, 1918 - January 27, 1919. London: A. Page, 1919.

_____ (ed.). La question du Dodecanese et ses documents diplomatiques. 2nd. ed. Athènes: P. D. Sakellarios, 1926.

_____ and Roussas, Pâris. The Dodecanese: Resolutions and Documents Concerning the Dodecanese, 1912-1919. New York: A. Page, n.d.

Newspapers

Ἐλευθερία, June 14, 1963.

Ροδιακη, October 30, 1963; January 10-11, 1964.

Unpublished Materials

Kasperson, Roger E. "The Know-Nothing Movement in Massachusetts, 1853-1857. A Study in Historical-Political Geography." Unpublished M.A. thesis, Department of Geography, University of Chicago, 1961.

Photiadis, John D. "The Coffee House and its Role in Stavroupolis, Greece," Unpublished M.A. thesis, Cornell University, 1956.